MEMOIRS
OF THE
LIFE AND WRITINGS
OF
EDWARD GIBBON

MEMOIRS
OF THE
LIFE AND WRITINGS
OF
EDWARD GIBBON

EDITED, WITH INTRODUCTION AND NOTES

BY

OLIVER FARRAR EMERSON, A.M., PH.D.

GYAN

Published by

Gyan Publishing House
5, Ansari Road
Daryaganj, New Delhi-110002
Phone: 011-47034999, 9811692060
E-mail: books@gyanbooks.com

Distribution Network
gyanbooks.com
India, USA, Canada, UK, Australia, France

ISBN: 978-81-212-7757-0 (PB)
First Published, 1898

2nd Impression 2023

Printed at: Gyan Press, Delhi.

MEMOIRS OF THE LIFE AND WRITINGS OF EDWARD GIBBON
Author: EDWARD GIBBON, Editor: OLIVER FARRAR EMERSON

THE ATHENÆUM PRESS SERIES

G. L. KITTREDGE AND C. T. WINCHESTER

GENERAL EDITORS

Athenæum Press Series

MEMOIRS

OF THE

LIFE AND WRITINGS

OF

EDWARD GIBBON

EDITED, WITH INTRODUCTION AND NOTES

BY

OLIVER FARRAR EMERSON, A.M., PH.D.

PROFESSOR OF RHETORIC AND ENGLISH PHILOLOGY IN
WESTERN RESERVE UNIVERSITY

BOSTON, U.S.A., AND LONDON
GINN & COMPANY, PUBLISHERS
The Athenæum Press.
1898

PREFACE.

THIS book was begun some years ago to supply the lack of an accurate and adequately annotated edition of Gibbon's well-known autobiography. Not long after it was commenced, a reprint of the Gibbon manuscripts, which had been kept from the public for a century, was announced, and the editor gladly waited for the new light which they might throw on various problems. When *The Autobiographies of Edward Gibbon* appeared, it became evident that no former edition of the *Memoirs* could longer be regarded as even a fairly accurate presentation of what Gibbon wrote. It was equally clear that the reprint of the manuscripts, invaluable as it will always be, made no attempt at uniting parts of the overlapping accounts into such a connected story of the historian's life as the student and the general reader will always require. Besides, there was not then, as there had never been, a critical examination of the various manuscript memoirs and their relations to each other. The field seemed clear, therefore, for a critical edition, and this the present editor has modestly attempted. Whatever may be the defects of the work, there is presented, for the first time, as accurate and complete an account of Gibbon's life as can be made from the several sketches left by the historian. For the first time, also, a critical introduction to the *Memoirs* has been written, and the annotation of them has been made fairly complete. Such a statement may seem to savor of self-praise, but the conditions which make it possible will be clear, I think, from those parts of the introduction which relate to the manuscripts and to the manner in which they have been edited in the past.

In preparing the book, the editor has not hesitated to ask assistance of several friends. They will not think mention of their names necessary, perhaps, and the omission will relieve them from any responsibility for errors made in following their suggestions, or otherwise. I desire, however, to make public, as I have made private recognition of their helpfulness. Special thanks of a more public character are due and gladly tendered to Mr. John Murray of London, editor and publisher of *The Autobiographies of Edward Gibbon*, for gracious permission to use such parts of the recently reprinted manuscripts as had not been published before. To him every reader as well as every editor of Gibbon's *Memoirs* will long be grateful.

O. F. E.

CLEVELAND, September 24, 1898.

TABLE OF CONTENTS.

INTRODUCTION.

I. THE CONTENTS OF THE MEMOIRS.

Gibbon's *Memoirs* have received the unanimous praise of critics and have interested and inspired countless readers in the century since they were first published.[1] Yet Gibbon's autobiography is not like many of its class. Instead of being filled with anecdotes of others, with history of the times in which he lived, with descriptions of places and characters of persons, it keeps remarkably close to the uneventful life of a scholar and man of letters. Living in a momentous period for both Europe and America, he gives only a glance here and there at the memorable events happening in the outside world. The struggle with George III for constitutionalism in England, the conflict between England and France in India and America, the American revolt from the mother country, the French Revolution and the tottering of continental thrones, scarcely receive a passing notice from the scholar whose eyes remained riveted upon the revolutions in the ancient Roman world. Nor can we suppose Gibbon intended anything else. Even if he had completed the *Memoirs* to his satisfaction, there is good reason to believe he would have made them little different. At one time he

[1] *Miscellaneous Works of Edward Gibbon, Esq., with Memoirs of his Life and Writings, Composed by Himself, Illustrated from his Letters, with Occasional Notes and Narrative, by John Lord Sheffield.* London, 1796.

expressed his purpose in the words, "I now propose to employ some moments of my leisure in reviewing the simple transactions of a private and literary life."[1] At another he says,

> "It would most assuredly be in my power to amuse the reader with a gallery of portraits and a collection of anecdotes; but I have always condemned the practice of transforming a private memorial into a vehicle of satire or praise."[2]

Such a close record of a literary career has seldom been written. Most autobiographies are the accounts of lives passed in public activities. Even Gibbon might have given us many a view of public life in the eighteenth century, for he was not only a member of parliament, but was also known in the best literary and social circles of London. He was a member of the Literary Club with Johnson, Burke, Goldsmith, Garrick, Sir Joshua Reynolds, and the others. After Goldsmith's death in 1774, Gibbon was Sir Joshua's regular attendant to the theater, masquerades, and social events. He was also a member of Brooks's, Boodle's, White's, and Almack's Clubs, which were frequented by statesmen and gentlemen of leisure. He was entertained at the best houses in London, and could gossip in his letters of all that was happening from the court to the last masquerade, and from parliament to Grub Street. All this, too, would have been intensely interesting, but to Gibbon it was not of great importance, compared with the aim he had in mind. He proposed from the first to limit himself to a record of his mind and intellectual conquests.

But if the limitation which Gibbon put upon himself has made the *Memoirs* less extensive, it has correspondingly increased their intensity in the more circumscribed field.

[1] See p. li. [2] See note to 164, 11.

They are preëminently the record of a literary life. The accounts of his reading and study in youth and mature manhood are given in detail, while the nine years during which Gibbon sat in parliament — a period in which a modern historian takes the greatest interest — are passed over in a few paragraphs. The manner in which the self-taught youth soon learned to put aside the merely popular and superficial historical writers for the originals upon which all history is based, shows the keenness and penetration of Gibbon's mind. The devotion to his subject, the application early and late to systematic study at a time when other young men were giving themselves up to society and pleasure, shows the singleness and disinterestedness of his purpose.[1] All this, however, adds to the clearness with which we see the growth of the historian's mind, his manner of acquiring the vast knowledge needed for his life work, and the painstaking way in which he composed his famous *History*.

Gibbon's intellectual development, too, was in every respect exceptional. It is much that he owed his mental progress mainly to himself. From his early school training he evidently received little. The fourteen months at Oxford were "the most idle and unprofitable" of his whole life.[2] Even the beneficial guidance of pastor Pavilliard, at Lausanne, was soon unnecessary and valueless.[3] But not only was Gibbon a self-made scholar, he had also overcome the narrowness particularly common among self-made men, and what is far more remarkable, the insular conditions and prejudices so general in his time among Englishmen. In this, too, lies his real intellectual greatness. His residence at Lausanne had helped to make him cosmopolitan. The studies which he there began, the correspondence with

1 See notes to *Memoirs*, 55, 20 and 99, 8.

2 *Memoirs*, p. 47.

3 *Ibid.*, p. 76.

famous French and German writers[1] which, as a boy, he delighted to carry on, burst forever the narrow bounds of English scholarship, and made his range unusually wide and free. Owing to this, and this alone, Gibbon's *History* far surpassed those of his contemporaries, Hume and Robertson, and has retained to the present much of its pristine value. Owing to this, he may well be ranked with Bentley and Porson in the triumvirate of eighteenth century scholars who gained for themselves a name in every learned nation.

In another respect the *Memoirs* at once make a marked impression on the reader. They are undeviatingly sincere. As a rule, what men say of themselves may be taken with some grains of allowance. This is due, not so much to any intentional misinterpretation of acts or motives, as to the difficulty in objectifying our characters, and seeing ourselves in the uncolored light in which others see us. But there are few passages in Gibbon's *Memoirs* about which the sincerity of his statements has ever been questioned, and these, which will be discussed in another place, are capable of favorable as well as unfavorable interpretation. In the main, in passages which reflect credit, as well as in those which are more or less discreditable, the writer of the *Memoirs* appears profoundly candid and undisguised. Perhaps in no part is this sincerity more strikingly seen than in the account of the violent attacks made upon his *History* when the first volume was published.[2] The storm of opprobrious criticism which burst upon the unsuspecting historian forms one of the curious chapters in the history of eighteenth century thought. Gibbon was assailed, not with the critical acumen of the scholar, but with the rancor of impassioned fanaticism, which, in defending religion, often forgot its spirit and commands. Yet the

[1] *Memoirs*, p. 83, and for the letters of his foreign correspondents, *Miscellaneous Works*, I, 433 *ff*.

[2] *Memoirs*, pp. 169, 170.

historian received the outburst against him with silent dignity, only once deigning to reply, and then not because his accuracy, but his good faith, was attacked.[1] Even in this *Vindication*, Gibbon not only treated his opponents with unwonted temperance for the time, but the impression is unusually strong of a sincere purpose to make clear his own innocence, rather than to demolish a foe who certainly merited severe treatment.

But if this impression of sincerity has usually been made by the *Memoirs*, in the mutilated state in which they were first printed, it is even more striking in the autobiography as now restored to us. Lord Sheffield, the first editor, with a desire to shield his friend, had omitted many passages which he thought might lead to criticism.[2] These relate sometimes to Gibbon's opinions, sometimes to his personal character. The restoration of the omitted passages shows in a striking way how thoroughly frank Gibbon intended his *Memoirs* to be, not only in respect to every greater and more important part of his life, but also in regard to such follies as he was sometimes led into, in an age when grosser pleasures were far more common than to-day. He does not tell us everything, it is true. There is no account of the gambling scrape at Lausanne,[3] and of his attempt to leave Switzerland, in order to raise money in London for his gambling debts. But he refers to this in such a way as to show there is clearly no intention of shielding his character.[4]

Mention has already been made of certain passages in the *Memoirs*, about which there has been more or less dis-

[1] *Memoirs*, p. 169. [2] See p. xlviii.

[3] *Private Letters of Edward Gibbon, with an Introduction by the Earl of Sheffield.* Edited by Rowland E. Prothero. London, 1896, I, 2.

[4] *Memoirs*, p. 72.

cussion in the past. The first of these relates to Gibbon's engagement with Mdlle. Susanne Curchod, afterwards Mme. Necker. The account of this affair by the historian is too well known to need repeating.[1] Yet some new light has been thrown on the romantic episode by a recent biographer of Mme. Necker,[2] and by the publication of additional letters of Gibbon.[3] It thus seems that Gibbon has not told the whole story of his early love, though it may be questioned whether he has not referred to it in a wise and dignified manner.[4]

It was in the month of June, at one of the reunions of the *Printemps*, as the young ladies of Lausanne called their Society, that Gibbon, a youth of twenty, first saw Susanne Curchod. They were of the same age. She was handsome, witty, and of unusual education for a girl of her time and country. The young people saw each other freely and frequently, for the young ladies of the Pays de Vaud were under no such restrictions as were usual in continental society. At Mdlle. Curchod's suggestion, the young gentlemen became cavaliers of the *Acadèmie des Eaux ou de la Poudrière*,[5] of which "the pretty Miss Curchod" was president. According to the regulations of the *Acadèmie*, the cavaliers wore the colors of the ladies they liked best, and in other respects followed the customs of romantic lovers in medieval times. Under these circumstances, it

[1] *Memoirs*, p. 87.

[2] *The Salon of Madame Necker, by Viscomte d'Haussonville.* Translated from the French by Henry M. Trollope. London, 1882.

[3] *Letters*, edited by Prothero.

[4] It is said, on the authority of an unpublished letter of Maria Holroyd, "that this passage was privately shown to Madame Necker, just before her death (May, 1794)." *Proceedings of the Gibbon Commemoration*, p 30.

[5] Named from a spring in a valley near Lausanne, where the *Acadèmie* generally held its meetings.

is not strange that the young Gibbon became infatuated, though it is a little difficult to picture the future historian of the Roman Empire "stopping the country people near Lausanne, and demanding, at the point of a dagger, whether a more adorable creature existed than Susanne Curchod."[1] In the next few months Gibbon paid Mdlle. Curchod marked attention. He visited her at her home in Crassy, at Geneva, at Rolle, and again for a week at Crassy.[2] He avowed his love and received assurances that his affection was returned. It was the understanding between them that, on his return to England, Gibbon should try to obtain his father's permission to marry and live in Switzerland, for such was the pledge which Mdlle. Curchod had required in consenting to an engagement.[3] Yet the latter had disclaimed beforehand[4] a marriage of which Gibbon's father should not fully approve, and Gibbon had himself intimated to his betrothed the shock which he knew that his father must feel at the thought of again losing his son. There are hints also of lovers' quarrels or misunderstandings,[5] before Gibbon left Lausanne in April, 1758, less than a year after first seeing Mdlle. Curchod.

It is upon the conduct of Gibbon from this time that the biographer of Mme. Necker is particularly severe.[6] He complains that in four years following his return to England, Gibbon gave his betrothed "no sign that he was alive, beyond sending to her his *Essay on the Study of Literature*, with a dedicatory letter (June, 1761)." It is not easy to get a clear idea of what passed in those years. Yet d'Haussonville's charge cannot be reconciled with the letters which he himself prints in his pages. Gibbon

[1] *Julie von Bondeli*, by Eduard Bodemann, Hannover, 1874, p. 217.

[2] See note to *Memoirs*, 88, 10.

[3] *d'Haussonville*, I, 47.

[4] *Ibid.*, I, 49.

[5] *Ibid.*, I, 47.

[6] *Ibid.*, I, 50.

wrote twice[1] during the two weeks of his journey to England, and once from London. According to Mdlle. Curchod's last letter also, in which she recites the history of these years, he had written of his father's refusing his consent to their marriage, and letters had been exchanged by the lovers.[2] Gibbon had meanwhile received a "faithful report," probably from his friend Deyverdun, "of the tranquillity and cheerfulness of the lady herself," and he seems to have believed the report.[3] He also knew that other offers of marriage had been made Mdlle. Curchod, and she herself had tried to relieve his mind of anxiety on her account.[4]

The real difficulty is to explain the long interval between these letters of 1758, and that of Gibbon finally breaking the engagement in 1762. The latter[5] shows that Gibbon had not heard of the death of Mdlle. Curchod's father, in January, 1760, so that if he did not write to his betrothed, he also received no letter from her. It is known, too, that Gibbon proposed a foreign trip in 1760, and that this was prevented by his enlistment in the militia.[6] From her own somewhat confused account of these years,[7] it may be gathered that Mdlle. Curchod was ill for some time before her father's death, that she wrote to Gibbon, and received an answer in which she thought she saw stronger proofs of his delicacy, in not

[1] *d'Haussonville*, I, 52.

[2] *Ibid.*, I, 65. Prothero (*Letters of Gibbon*, I, 40, note 3) says, "when Gibbon left Lausanne, in 1758, she wrote to him once; then all correspondence between them seems to have ceased, though Gibbon says that he wrote to her twice on his journey, and once on his return to England." Part of a letter from Mdlle. Curchod, dated Nov. 5, 1758, is given in the *Gibbon Commemoration* (p. 40), but it has never been printed in full.

[3] See *Memoirs*, p. 88, and note; also *Letters*, I, 40, note 3.

[4] *d'Haussonville*, I, 65.

[5] *Ibid.*, I, 52.

[6] *Letters*, I, 22.

[7] *d'Haussonville*, I, 63.

asking her to reject other offers of marriage, and wait until he should be free at his father's death. Finally, when her father died, and there was apparently no hope of Gibbon, she seems to have accepted some offer of marriage, only to withdraw at the last moment and take up the work of teaching. This was done, she afterwards said, with a lingering hope that time might bring the wished-for union with her English lover. About July, 1761, Gibbon sent Mdlle. Curchod a copy of his *Essay on the Study of Literature*, with a dedicatory letter,[1] and Aug. 24, 1762, he wrote definitely breaking the engagement. To neither of these did Mdlle. Curchod respond, so far as appears.[2]

On his visit to the continent after leaving the militia, Gibbon arrived at Lausanne May 25, 1763; on the thirtieth Mdlle. Curchod wrote from Geneva,[3] begging him to make a frank avowal of his indifference, and thus relieve her mind forever. How Gibbon answered this letter is not known, but a few days later she wrote again, showing her realization of his true feeling, begging his friendship, and asking his advice about the position of lady's companion in England.[4] She also sent some notes on his *Essay*, and offered to procure for him, if he desired, a letter of introduction to Rousseau, then at Motiers. The latter offer, even her biographer allows, was not without a certain design. Pastor Moultou, a warm friend, had already acquainted Rousseau with Mdlle. Curchod's story, and the latter had agreed to use his influence in her behalf, in case Gibbon should visit him. Before this, as we learn from one of Moultou's letters to Mdlle. Curchod, she had

1 *d'Haussonville*, I, 51.

2 This may be inferred from her letter of June 4, 1763 (*d'Haussonville*, pp. 57, 58), in which she makes a reference to this part of her life.

3 *d'Haussonville*, I, 55.

4 *Ibid.*, I, 57. See also *Memoirs*, p. 89.

asked the latter to see Gibbon in her behalf, but he had declined, preferring to rely on the good offices of the philosopher. Gibbon did not visit Rousseau, and perhaps never knew to whom he owed the opinion of him, which the latter expresses in one of his letters.[1]

Meantime, though with his usual delay in correspondence, Gibbon answered Mdlle. Curchod's letter, accepting her friendship, replying to her questions, and thanking her for her note, but begging that correspondence should cease, as the wisest course for both of them. The correspondence did cease, except for one letter. In September, the lovers met by chance at Ferney — doubtless at one of Voltaire's dramatic performances[2] — and Gibbon's conduct was such as to grieve and anger the lady. The next day (Sept. 21, 1763), Mdlle. Curchod wrote a long letter, to which reference has before been made as recounting the history of their intimacy. She undertook to justify her conduct since their engagement, as if she had first learned of Gibbon's regarding her as inconstant, a charge which he seems to have heard from Deyverdun, and firmly believed, as shown by his journal.[3] The letter does not seem to leave much

[1] *Œuvres de Rousseau*, XXXIII, 88, 89; see note to *Memoirs*, 88, 29.

[2] *Memoirs*, p. 86.

[3] *Letters*, I, 40, note 3. In Gibbon's unpublished diary, he thus comments on the receipt of this letter, Sept. 22, 1763: "J'ai reçu une lettre des moins attendues. C'étoit de Mademoiselle C[urchod], fille dangereuse et artificielle! Elle fait une apologie de sa conduite depuis le premier moment qu'elle m'a connu, sa constance pour moi, son mépris pour M. de Montplaisir, et la fidélité délicate et soutenue qu'elle a cru voir dans la lettre où je lui annoncois qu'il n'y avoit plus d'espérance. Ses voyages à Lausanne, les adorateurs qu'elle y a eu, et la complaisance avec laquelle elle les a écouté formoient l'article le plus difficile à justifier. Ni Deyverdun (dit elle), ni personne n'ont effacé pendant un instant mon image de son cœur. Elle s'amusoit à Lausanne sans y attacher. Je le veux. Mais ces amusements la convainquent toujours de la dissimulation la plus odieuse et, si l'infidélité est

room for friendship, yet they met again at Lausanne, in February, 1764, apparently on friendly terms.[1]

Gibbon left Lausanne in April, 1764. Before the end of the year, Mdlle. Curchod had considered and rejected the proposals of a thriving barrister of Yverdun, and had met and married M. Necker. In the following year Gibbon was received with cordiality at the house of the Neckers in Paris, and Mme. Necker's feminine vanity prided itself in a complete triumph over her former lover.[2] If there was any resentment on account of the way the early romance ended, it does not appear from their conduct, or from their letters. The Neckers visited London in the spring of 1776, and Gibbon saw much of them.[3] On their invitation he made

quelquefois une foiblesse, la duplicité est toujours un vice. Cette affaire singulière dans toutes ses parties m'a été très utile; elle m'a ouvert les yeux sur le caractère des femmes, et elle me servira longtemps de préservatif contre les séductions de l'amour."

1 *Letters*, I, 40, note 3. Gibbon's *Journal* has the following entries: "Elle me badine sur mon ton de petit maître. Elle a du voir cent fois que tout étoit fini sans retour." . . . "Nous badinons très librement sur nôtre tendresse passée, et je lui fais comprendre tout clairement que je suis au fait de son inconstance."

2 *Lettres Diverses Recueillies en Suisse*, par le Comte Fédor Golovkin, Geneva, 1821, pp. 265, 266. In a letter to Madame de Brentés, Madame Necker says: "Je ne sais, madame, si je vous ai dit que j'ai vu Gibbon. J'ai été sensible à ce plaisir au-delà de toute expression, non qu'il me reste aucun sentiment pour un homme qui je vois n'en mérite guère; mais ma vanité féminine n'a jamais eu un triomphe plus complet et plus honnête. Il a resté deux semaines à Paris; je l'ai eu tous les jours chez moi; il étoit devenu doux, souple, humble, décent jusqu'à la pudeur; témoin perpétuel de la tendresse de mon mari, de son esprit et son enjouement, admirateur zélé de l'opulence, il me fit remarquer pour la première fois celle qui m'entoure, ou du moins jusqu' alors elle n'avoit fait sur moi qu'une sensation désagréable."

3 *Letters*, I, 282. Gibbon wrote to his friend Holroyd: "At present I am very busy with the Neckers. I live with her just as I used to do twenty years ago, laugh at her Paris varnish, and oblige her to become

his second visit to Paris in May, 1777, and was entertained by them in the handsomest manner.[1] Again, when Gibbon had settled at Lausanne, and the Neckers were at Coppet, they visited each other on the friendliest terms, at a time when sorrow made friendship helpful to both. Mme. Necker grieved with her husband at his abandonment by the country that he had served so well, and Gibbon had just lost Deyverdun, the friend of his youth, with whom he had lived so pleasantly at Lausanne. In all this time the freedom with which the former lovers recalled their early attachment, is sufficient proof that the two friends, each happy in the life fortune had allotted, remembered with pleasure rather than with regret or disappointment the tender attachment of their youth. In sending Mme. Necker the second and third volumes of his *History*, Gibbon wrote in apology for long silence:

"Forgetfulness or indifference? I utter these words with sorrow, but I am sufficiently punished by the thought that my conduct may have laid me open to a reproach which my heart alone can contradict. No, madame, no, I shall never forget the sweetest moments of my youth, and to these pure and indelible recollections is now joined the truest and most unalterable friendship. After a long separation, I had the happiness of being able to spend six months in your company. The feelings of respect and of gratitude which I owed to you grew stronger every day, and I left Paris with the strong but idle resolution always to keep up a correspondence which alone could repay me for what I had lost."[2]

After one of Gibbon's visits, Mme. Necker wrote her old lover:

a simple, reasonable Suissesse. The man who might read English husbands lessons of proper and dutiful behavior is a simple and good-natured creature."

[1] *Letters*, I, 312.
[2] *d'Haussonville*, I, 72.

"We think often, monsieur, of the days so full of charm which we passed with you at Geneva. I felt during that time a sentiment new to me, and perhaps to most people. By a rare favor of Providence, I was uniting in the same place one of the sweet and pure affections of my youth with that which is my lot on earth and which makes it so worthy of envy. This singular circumstance, joined to the pleasure of unrivaled conversation, produced in me a kind of enchantment; and the connection between past and present made my days seem like a dream sent through the gate of ivory to console mortals. Will you not help us to prolong it?"[1]

If such were the sentiments of the former lovers, it is needless that we, a century after their death, should waste ourselves in regrets or criminations.

Apart from the romance of Gibbon's life, the period to which the critic will naturally turn is that in which the historian sat in parliament. Yet the consideration of Gibbon's political career is not flattering. In early life, when his father proposed to procure for his son a seat in the Commons, Gibbon closed his reasons against the idea with the words, "My genius (if you will allow me any) is better qualified for the deliberate compositions of the closet, than for the extemporary discourses of the parliament."[2] He was then eager for foreign travel and study, which he felt necessary to his proper development. It is unfortunate, perhaps, that he did not remember his early reasons against the parliamentary seat when he came into possession of his estate and was still more free to choose. He entered parliament in 1774 and finally resigned in 1783. The period was one of greatest moment, one in which England never more needed good sense rather

[1] *Miscellaneous Works of Gibbon* (1814), II, 450.
[2] *Letters*, I, 23.

than passion, and statesmanlike judgment rather than party subserviency. Yet during this whole time Gibbon never made a speech, regularly voted with the North and Fox-North ministries, and seemed to care more for his salary as member of the Board of Trade than for his political duties. When he lost his sinecure, and found that hope of another was vain, it was a misfortune to remain a member of the House of Commons, and he was ready to quit parliament forever.

Such conduct on the part of the great historian is not pleasant to contemplate. Besides, little can be said in extenuation of his apathy and indifference. It is of course true that Gibbon's conduct was no worse and no better than that of many of his countrymen. To be a member of parliament in the eighteenth century was too often regarded as simply a pleasant addition to one's honors, entailing neither obligations nor serious duties. To vote with one's party without actually engaging in the struggles of debate, then less sharp and important than to-day, was at the time far from discreditable, even in a man of Gibbon's ability. Moreover, until the passage of Burke's *Bill for Economical Reform*,[1] which abolished the Board of Trade among other useless and costly offices, sinecures were regarded as the legitimate spoil of the party in power. Like many of his colleagues, Gibbon looked on his seat in parliament wholly from the personal standpoint. The position was scarcely more than a means of bringing himself into pleasant social relations with the prominent men of the nation, and, if a lucrative and slightly laborious position could be obtained without the sacrifice of honor, so much the better.

If any part of Gibbon's parliamentary conduct need be cited as furnishing indisputable proof of his lack of

[1] The bill was passed in 1782.

insight or disregard of duty, it is his attitude toward American affairs during the Revolution. It is clear from the outcome that most politicians seriously misunderstood the grave situation in the colonies. Many treated the matter lightly, and among these one regrets to find the historian. The famous speeches of Burke and Chatham, both of whom foreshadowed the true outcome of the struggle, are scarcely mentioned in Gibbon's letters, and, remarkable as they are, had certainly made little impression upon him. At the beginning of the difficulties, he wrote: "I am more and more convinced that with firmness all may go well. Yet I sometimes doubt Lord N[orth]."[1] Again he indicates the indifferent temper of the House of Commons: "The House tired and languid. In this season and on America, the archangel Gabriel would not be heard."[2] The battle of Lexington, which so encouraged the colonists, is thus apologetically described:

"It cannot fairly be called a defeat of the king's troops, since they marched to Concord, destroyed or brought away the stores, and then returned back. They were so much fatigued with their day's work (they had marched above thirty miles) that they encamped in the evening at some distance from Boston without being attacked in the night. It can hardly be called an engagement; there never was any large body of provincials. Our troops during the march and retreat were chiefly harassed by flying parties from behind the stone walls along the road, and by many shots from the windows as they passed through the villages. It was then they were guilty of setting fire to some of those hostile houses. Ensign Gould had been sent with only twelve men to repair a wooden bridge for the retreat; he was attacked by the saints with a minister at their head, who killed two men and took the Ensign with the others prisoners. The next day the country rose."[3]

[1] *Letters*, I, 250. [2] *Ibid.*, I, 256. [3] *Ibid.*, I, 257, 258.

Gibbon also referred with evident pleasure to the questionable methods of warfare with which Great Britain sullied her name in this contest. At one time the use of Indians and mercenary troops is thus mentioned:

"Something will be done this year. But in the spring the force of the country will be exerted to the utmost. Scotch Highlanders, Irish Papists, Hanoverians, Canadians, Indians, and so forth, will all in various shapes be employed." [1]

At another time he says:

"We have great hopes of getting a body of these barbarians [the Russians]. In consequence of some very plain advances, George with his own hand wrote a very polite epistle to sister Kitty [the Empress Catherine] requesting her friendly assistance. Full powers and instructions were sent at the same time to Gunning to agree for any force between five and twenty-five thousand men, *carte blanche* for the terms; on condition, however, that they should serve not as auxiliaries but as mercenaries, and that the Russian general should be absolutely under the command of the British. They daily and hourly expect a messenger and hope to hear that the business is concluded. The worst of it is that the Baltic will be soon froze up, and that it must be late next year before they can get to America." [2]

Again he writes:

"Lord G[eorge] G[ermain], with whom I had a long conversation last night, was in high spirits, and hopes to reconquer Germany and America. On the side of Canada he only fears Carleton's slowness, but entertains great expectations that the light troops and Indians under Sir William Johnson, who are sent from Oswego down the Mohawk River to Albany, will oblige the provincials to give up the defense of the lakes for fear of being cut off." [3]

[1] *Letters*, I, 265. [2] *Ibid.*, I, 270. [3] *Ibid.*, I, 290.

How incorrectly the colonists themselves were judged may be seen from his remark, "They show little courage or conduct, but the ground is incredibly strong, and it seems running into a war of posts";[1] and again:

"Things go on very prosperously in America. Howe is himself in New Jersey, and will push at least as far as the Delaware River. The Continental, perhaps now the rebel, army is in a great measure dispersed, and Washington, who wishes to cover Philadelphia, has not more than six or seven thousand men with him. Clinton designs to conquer Rhode Island on his way home."[2]

It is true that Gibbon began to appreciate the difficulties. In August, 1776, the war is "a tough business indeed. You see by their declaration that they have now crossed the Rubicon and rendered the work of a treaty infinitely more difficult. You will perhaps say so much the better, but I do assure you that the thinking friends of the government are by no means sanguine."[3] A year later he wrote:

"What a wretched piece of work do we seem to be making of it in America! The greatest force which any European power ever ventured to transport into that continent is not strong enough even to attack the enemy. The naval strength of Great Britain is not sufficient to prevent the Americans (they have almost lost the appellation of rebels) from receiving every assistance they want; and in the meantime you are obliged to call out the militia to defend your own coasts against their privateers."[4]

In December of the same year he chronicles:

"Dreadful news indeed. You will see them partially in the papers, and we have not yet any particulars. An English army of nearly ten thousand men laid down their arms and surrendered prisoners of war, on condition of being sent to England and of

[1] *Letters*, I, 298.
[2] *Ibid.*, I, 300.
[3] *Ibid.*, I, 287.
[4] *Ibid.*, I, 316.

never serving against America. They had fought bravely and were three days without eating. Burgoyne is said to have received three wounds. General Frazer has two thousand men killed; Colonel Ackland likewise killed; a general cry for peace."[1]

Even to the last, Gibbon seems to have had more fear of the fall of Lord North's ministry, and consequent trouble for himself, than of the loss of America. In November, 1781, he writes: "We all tremble on the edge of a precipice, and whatever may be the event, the American war now seems to be reduced to a very small compass both of time and place."[2] The end had already come. In October Cornwallis had surrendered at Yorktown, and Great Britain had lost her most important colonies.

But if his parliamentary life does not reflect credit upon him, it must be remembered that through most of these years Gibbon was diligently employed in his real life work, the great *History*. The resolution to begin such an undertaking goes back to his Italian tour in 1764.[3] For nearly ten years thereafter, he was engaged in collecting and digesting the materials before he began to put pen to paper. During all this period there is no mention of the work in any of his published letters, and, from his fear as to precipitancy in the forthcoming venture, it would seem that his friend Holroyd, afterwards Lord Sheffield, knew nothing of his progress.[4] In reality, he began to write in 1773,[5] and for more than two years was steadily employed on the first volume. Not until June, 1775, does he first mention

[1] *Letters*, I, 324. [2] *Ibid.*, II, 9. [3] *Memoirs*, p. 144.

[4] *Letters*, I, 264. "Your apprehensions of a precipitate work, etc., are perfectly groundless. I should be much more addicted to a contrary extreme. The head is now printing? True, but it was wrote last year, and the year before. The first chapter has been composed *de nouveau* three times, the second twice, and all the others have undergone reviews, corrections, etc."

[5] *Memoirs*, p. 164.

the work, and then by the title which it has since borne. In writing to his stepmother he says: "I am just at present engaged in a great historical work, no less than a *History of the Decline and Fall of the Roman Empire*, with the first volume of which I may very possibly oppress the public next winter."[1] Before the end of the month the printing began, and in February, 1776, the first volume was given to the world.

The success of the first volume of the *Decline and Fall* is well known. It obtained a rapid sale, and, for the time and character of the book, a remarkable one. But, above all, Gibbon's monumental work has had a lasting value. It was repeatedly issued in his lifetime, and it has been edited many times since his death by men who were themselves great scholars. One part of it was long used in German universities as a handbook for students, and translations of the whole are found in most European languages. It is still read and studied as one of the most notable contributions to the knowledge of an important epoch.

The explanation of Gibbon's success is not far to seek. Some idea of his intellectual breadth, and the reason therefor, have already been indicated. In mind, Gibbon may be considered a product, not so much of English conditions in his time, as of that intellectual revival in France, which produced Voltaire and Rousseau in literature, and a long array of men engaged in more serious writing and research. But to the same stimulus which produced the *Encyclopédists* in France, Gibbon added a lifelong devotion to his subject, a devotion that is the more remarkable since so many opportunities were open to him. The six volumes of the *Decline and Fall* occupied nearly twenty years of his life, to say nothing of almost another decade in which he

[1] *Letters*, I, 259.

was acquiring that general view of the field which was so necessary in itself. To this masterly and long-continued devotion, rather than to any stroke of genius, was due the work which gave to Gibbon sudden and lasting fame.

The unfortunate incompleteness of Gibbon's autobiography is most noticeable in connection with his life work, the *History of the Decline and Fall of the Roman Empire.* Memoir E, the only authority for Gibbon's later life, must be taken up at the time of his moving to London in 1772, two years after his father's death. It is at best a series of annals, much less complete than any other part of the *Memoirs* as usually printed, and clearly but provisional. Yet it gives the only story of the last twenty years of the historian's life, and especially of the fifteen years (1773–1788) during which he was composing his great work. To the latter important years scarcely more than as many pages are given. To be sure, there are in the extant *Memoirs* many interesting details concerning Gibbon's method of work. Yet how much more entertaining might the story have been, had the historian written with anything like the completeness with which the earlier years are treated. The vast reading, the laborious collection of materials, the minutely careful sifting and arranging of historical and archæological facts, the making and remaking of many plans — all these must have occurred in those years, and the story of them, at the hands of the historian, could not fail of being happy and instructive.

There is but one partial compensation for this incompleteness in the account of the great *History*. That compensation is the large space given to the period in which Gibbon was laying the foundation for his scholarly and immortal work. Though the historian did not begin the composition of the *History* until 1773, nor the collection of materials until his second return from abroad in 1765, the foundation for his future fame had been laid in his earlier reading and study. The importance of this has been already mentioned, but it cannot be overestimated. Nor can any estimate fail to emphasize the significant part which the native and almost unaided genius of the youth had in the formation of England's greatest historian. It was at Rome in 1764, as Gibbon tells us in a most striking passage of the *Memoirs*,[1] that the thought of writing an account of the decadence of the Eternal City first came to him. But the preparation for that undertaking had really begun, when, as a boy of fourteen,[2] the first *Roman History* was eagerly devoured, and the keen instinct of genius led him to search all records then available in finding the basis for what had been written. This early and independent search for sources of history must be set down as the most indisputable mark of Gibbon's originality and scholarly penetration.

In another respect the incompleteness of Gibbon's *Memoirs* is now evident, though through no particular fault of the historian. The account of the historian's family which begins the book bears evidence of no little labor on the part of the writer. Yet, so far as it deals with his remoter ancestors, that account can now be shown to be inaccurate in important particulars. This Gibbon himself knew and admitted, as we shall see, though he learned of his mistake in tracing his ancestry too late to revise his narrative. Unfortunately, too, Gibbon's statement has usually been followed, and no previous edition of the *Memoirs*, or biography of the historian, has taken account of material which has long been at hand.[3]

[1] *Memoirs*, p. 144, and notes. [2] *Ibid.*, p. 42.

[3] The writer of the Gibbon article in the *Dictionary of National Biography*, without expressing any personal judgment, simply says:

Gibbon bases his sketch of his remoter ancestry upon the supposition that his great-grandfather Matthew was the brother of John Gibbon, an heraldic writer whose life extended over the years from 1629 to 1718. The only basis for this connection seems to have been that his great-grandfather had a brother John, and John Gibbon (Bluemantle) had a brother Matthew, as he learned from John Gibbon's *Introductio ad Latinam Blasoniam.*[1] He himself tells us that he was "totally ignorant" of his great-grandfather Matthew, except as to his being "a linen draper of Leadenhall Street, in the parish of St. Andrew's."[2]

In the *Gentleman's Magazine* for August, 1788,[3] there appeared a communication signed N. S., which incidentally, in a notice of records concerning the writer's ancestry, referred to the family of the historian. The writer showed conclusively that Matthew Gibbon, "the linen draper of Leadenhall Street" and the historian's great-grandfather, was a younger son of Thomas of Westcliffe, a more remote branch of the Rolvenden family of Gibbons. The historian, owing to his residence at Lausanne, did not see this communication until the beginning of the year 1792, when he happened upon it, and was at once struck with its importance for his *Memoirs*. He immediately wrote (Feb. 24, 1792) to the editor of the *Gentleman's Magazine*,[4] testifying to the

"An article in the *Gentleman's Magazine*, 1788, p. 698, by Sir Egerton Brydges, gives an account of the ancestry differing from that in Gibbon's autobiography."

1 *The Autobiographies of Edward Gibbon*. Edited by John Murray. London, 1896, p. 356.

2 *Memoirs*, 5, 10. In Memoir A, Gibbon says, "Of the life and character of Matthew Gibbon, the son of Robert, I am totally ignorant, and must be content to repeat, that he was a linen draper in Leadenhall Street."—Murray, p. 365.

3 *Gentleman's Magazine*, LVIII, 698; continued in LIX, 584.

4 *Ibid.*, LXIV, 5.

general accuracy of the account of the Gibbon family, and asking to be put in communication with the correspondent N. S. In this letter Gibbon explained his accidental discovery of the communication, and said, "He is only mistaken in one fact, in confounding my grandfather with my father." This confusion was not strange, as both Gibbon's father and grandfather bore the name of Edward, and N. S. had referred to them only incidentally.

For some reason Gibbon did not succeed in learning the identity and address of N. S., until he reached England in 1793, notwithstanding that he had written to J. Nichols,[1] to whom he had been referred in regard to the matter. When on his last visit to England, Gibbon discovered that the unknown correspondent of the *Gentleman's Magazine* was Egerton, afterwards Sir Egerton Brydges, and a distant relative. He immediately wrote to him from Sheffield Place, Aug. 7, 1793,[2] and made further inquiries of his distant kinsman. As a result, the correspondents planned to meet,[3] but Sir Egerton's delay in making an appointment, together with the ill health and unexpected death of Gibbon, put a stop to further inquiries, and, of course, to any possible alteration in the *Memoirs*.

After the publication of Gibbon's *Memoirs* in 1796, Sir Egerton Brydges again wrote to the *Gentleman's Magazine*[4] calling attention to the error in the account of the historian's family, and expressing the belief that Gibbon himself would have changed this "had he lived a little longer." With this belief no one can fail to agree, after a careful examination of the communications from Sir Egerton Brydges, and of the letters of Gibbon printed in the mag-

[1] *Gentleman's Magazine*, LXXIX, 459.
[2] *Ibid.*, LXVII, 916.
[3] *Autobiography of Sir Egerton Brydges*, I, 225.
[4] *Gentleman's Magazine*, LXVI, 71.

azine referred to. Unfortunately the latter, though easily accessible, were not included among those published by Lord Sheffield,[1] or by the more recent editor of the *Letters*.[2] On this account, perhaps, no former editor of Gibbon's *Memoirs* has made any reference to the correct ancestry of Gibbon.

The most important of these century-old facts in regard to the historian's family may be briefly given. According to Gibbon's own account, the male line from the Rolvenden family, to which he believed himself to belong, is as follows:

Robert of Rolvenden (died 1618).
|
Robert of London (died 1643).

John, the herald (1629–1718) ⋯ Matthew, the linen draper (no dates).
|
Edward (1666–1736).
|
Edward (1707–1770)
|
Edward, the historian (1737–1794).

It will be seen at once that the weak point in the line is in connection with Matthew Gibbon, the historian's great-grandfather, of whose birth and death he tells us he knew nothing. The connection of Matthew with John, the herald, so fully described in the *Memoirs*,[3] was merely a supposition.

[1] *Miscellaneous Works*, 1796, 1814.

[2] Edited by Prothero, London, 1896. The latter edition contains many letters never before printed, but it unfortunately omits many printed by Lord Sheffield in his first or second editions of the *Miscellaneous Works*, a few to be found in *The Salon of Madame Necker*, in the *Gentleman's Magazine*, and in *Notes and Queries*. Others are said to exist at Port Eliot, in Cornwall, the home of Gibbon's kinsman, Lord Eliot; see Sir Egerton Brydges's *Autobiography*, I, 225.

[3] *Memoirs*, p. 5 *ff*.

The Gibbon line, according to Sir Egerton Brydges, was as follows:[1]

Thomas, purchaser of Westcliffe (died 1596).
|
Philip, eldest son (died 1629).
|
Thomas, eldest son (1590–1691), married (1635) Alice Taylor, third wife.
|
Matthew, the linen draper (1642–1709), third son by third wife.[2]
|
Edward, eldest son (1666–1736).
|
Edward, eldest son (1707–1770).
|
Edward, the historian (1737–1794).

The ultimate connection of the Gibbons of Westcliffe with the Gibbons of Rolvenden is shown by their bearing the arms "Sable, a lion rampant gardant or, between three scallop shells argent"—a slight and easily explainable variant of the Rolvenden arms "Azure, a lion rampant, etc.,"[3] which the historian assumed. The former arms were also held by Thomas Gibbon, who purchased the manor of Frid, in Betherston, in the last of Elizabeth's reign. This Thomas is known to have belonged to a younger branch of the Rolvenden family, since Sir William Seager, mentioned in the *Memoirs*,[4] confirmed to him the sable variant of the Rolvenden arms.

II. HOW AND WHEN THE MEMOIRS WERE WRITTEN.

It has been known since the first edition of Gibbon's *Memoirs* (1796), that the historian left "six different

[1] Many other data confirming and supplementing these will be found in the elaborate communications of N. S., referred to above.

[2] The fifth son of Thomas and Alice Taylor was John (born 1644), a London merchant, confounded by Gibbon with John, the herald.

[3] *Memoirs*, p. 3. Gibbon omitted, perhaps inadvertantly, the word *or* after gardant.

[4] See p. 3.

sketches, all in his own handwriting."[1] None of these sketches is complete in itself, and all were unsatisfactory to the writer, as he tells us in a letter to Lord Sheffield, written Jan. 6, 1793: "Of the *Memoirs* little has been done, and with that little I am not satisfied. They must be postponed till a mature season, and I much doubt whether the book and the author can ever see the light at the same time.[2] Even then Gibbon was planning the journey from which he never returned to his Swiss home, and it is probable that, owing to his many engagements in England, the *Memoirs* were never touched after the date of the letter quoted. These various attempts remind one of the many

[1] See Lord Sheffield's advertisement to the first edition of *Miscellaneous Works*.

[2] *Letters*, II, 359. Only two other allusions to the work are found in the published letters of Gibbon. The first is in a letter to Lord Sheffield, Dec. 28, 1891, in which Gibbon says: "I have much revolved the plan of the *Memoirs* I once mentioned, and as you do not think it ridiculous, I believe I shall make the attempt. If I can please myself, I am confident of not displeasing; but let this be a profound secret between us. People must not be prepared to laugh, they must be taken by surprise." (*Letters*, II, 281, 282.) The other is quoted on p. xlvi of this introduction. As to publishing the *Memoirs* in his lifetime, Gibbon expressed the same view in the introduction to Memoir A (see p. lii). On the latter passage Lord Sheffield added a note as follows: "Mr. Gibbon, in his communications with me on the subject of his *Memoirs*, a subject which he had not mentioned to any other person, expressed a determination of publishing them in his lifetime, and never appears to have departed from that resolution, excepting in one of his letters annexed, in which he intimates a doubt, though rather carelessly, whether in his time, or at any time, they would meet the eye of the public. In a conversation, however, not long before his death, I suggested to him that, if he should make them a full image of his mind, he would not have nerves to publish them, and therefore that they should be posthumous. He answered rather eagerly that he was determined to publish them in his lifetime." (*Miscellaneous Works* I, 1, footnote.)

unsuccessful efforts at composing the *History* before he "could hit the middle tone between a dull chronicle and a rhetorical declamation."[1] The same was the method employed in writing his *Essay on the Study of Literature*, and it is significant that even after gaining an established reputation as a writer, Gibbon worked in the same pains-taking and laborious manner.

The first complete description of these sketches is found in *Proceedings of the Gibbon Commemoration* (Royal Historical Society, 1895), p. 36. Such parts of this description as are necessary read as follows:

1 A.[2] "The Memoirs of the Life of Edward Gibbon, with Various Observations and Excursions by Himself." Written in 1788–1789, but only giving particulars of his family.

2 B. "My Own Life." Written in 1789–1790, and ending in April, 1764, just before his tour in Italy.

3 C. "Memoirs of the Life and Writings of Edward Gibbon." Written in 1790, and brought down to October, 1772.

4 D. Memoirs without title. Written in 1790–1791, and brought down to October, 1772, when he "bid an everlasting fare-well to the country," and removed to London.

5 E. "My Own Life." Dated at the end "Lausanne, March 2, 1791," and ending with the death of his friend Deyverdun, in July, 1789, with notes added in 1792–1793.

6 F. Memoirs without title. Written in 1792–1793, but only brought down to the date of his leaving Oxford in June, 1753.

In the recent publication of these sketches in their entirety,[3] they are described as follows:

[1] *Memoirs*, p. 164.

[2] The lettering A, B, C, etc., is intended to indicate the order in which the various sketches were composed, and for convenience the manuscripts will be referred to by them as Memoir A, etc.

[3] *The Autobiographies of Edward Gibbon*. Edited by John Murray. London, 1896. Referred to hereafter as simply Murray.

A. The earliest sketch, written in 1788–1789. From the early records of the family down to the death of Mr. Wm. Law, in 1761. [Murray, pp. 353–390.]

B. From his birth till the eve of his journey into Italy in 1764. [Murray, pp. 104–210.]

C. Written about 1789. From his birth till 1772, when, two years after his father's death, he let the farm of Buriton, and removed to London. [Murray, pp. 211–292.]

D. From his birth to his father's death. Written 1790–1791; not hitherto published. [Murray, pp. 391–415.]

E. From the early history of the family to July, 1789. [Murray, pp. 293–352.]

F. The latest and most perfect. Written in 1792–1793, brought down to 1753. [Murray, pp. 1–95.]

Besides these six sketches, there is a short fragment of general and introductory character, and a memorandum of the important events connected with Gibbon's first residence at Lausanne.[1] The first, with other introductory matter from Memoirs A and B, has usually been printed at the beginning of the autobiography. The second is a mere outline, apparently for a continuation of Memoir F.

The several sketches, as said before, vary in length, and especially in completeness of treatment for different periods of Gibbon's life. Besides, they have certain relations to each other which deserve to be mentioned. Memoir A gives an account of Gibbon's ancestors and his own life to his father's retirement at Buriton, in December, 1747, after the death of his first wife.[2] Memoirs B and C have a close interrelation. They cover almost the same period of Gibbon's life, though B ends at the Italian tour in 1764, while C continues to Gibbon's establishment in London in

[1] Murray, p. 416 *ff*.

[2] Memoir A mentions Mr. Law's death in 1761, as Murray says above, but it is in no true sense an account of Gibbon's life up to that time.

1772. Memoir B, however, is relatively longer and much more detailed than C, so that, from both the dates assigned and from internal evidence, the latter is doubtless the earlier sketch, which was then rewritten and elaborated into B.[1] These two texts should therefore change places in the schemes given above, though for convenience the earlier sketch will still be called C, and the later B, as heretofore.

The close relation existing between B and C is paralleled by that between Memoirs D and E. The first is a brief sketch, which is most detailed for the period from Gibbon's exile in Switzerland to his father's death in 1770. The latter, which has much of similarity in expression to Memoir D, hastens over the earlier parts of Gibbon's life, but is particularly full for the years from his father's death to its close in March, 1791. The last Memoir to be written, that called F, is evidently the last attempt, and is the most nearly complete so far as it goes.[2]

When Gibbon wrote the different sketches which make up his *Memoirs* cannot be absolutely determined. Only one of them, Memoir E, was dated by Gibbon. This bears at the end the note, "Lausanne, March 2, 1791," the place and date of its completion. Moreover, most of the statements which have been made as to the dates of compo-

[1] The order of the sketches was first assigned in *Proceedings of the Gibbon Commemoration* (Royal Historical Society), London, 1895, p. 36. At this time the MSS. had not yet been printed or carefully examined. No date is assigned by Murray to Memoir B, but in the *Proceedings*, the date 1789–1790 is given. This is later than the date assigned by Murray to C.

[2] Some idea of the relative completeness of Memoir F may be gained from the fact that it devotes ninety-five pages to the ancestry and first sixteen years of Gibbon, while the completest of the other sketches, the B text, includes the ancestry and twenty-seven years of the historian's life in a hundred and six pages.

sition are mere approximations, some of which can easily be shown to be wrong. The dates assigned in the Gibbon memorial volume [1] certainly need revision. The reprint of the manuscript memoirs by Murray adds nothing of importance in this particular, though it omits a date for Memoir B. For these reasons an attempt will be made to bring together all the data, both internal and external, relating to the time and order of composition, so that some more definite conclusions may be reached as to how and when the *Memoirs* were composed.

The earliest indication of the time at which the autobiography was written occurs at the beginning of Memoir A. Gibbon there says: "In the fifty-second year of my age, after the completion of a toilsome and successful work, I now propose to employ some moments of my leisure in reviewing the simple transactions of a private and literary life." [2] This would indicate that Memoir A, which must be the first sketch, was begun between May 8, 1788, Gibbon's fifty-first birthday, and May 8, 1789, the beginning of his fifty-third year. The last volume of the *Decline and Fall* was issued on Gibbon's fifty-first birthday.[3] The historian remained in England until after the middle of July, 1788, and he reached Lausanne on the last day of that month.[4] According to his own account, on reaching Lausanne he immediately plunged into a course of classical reading for pleasure, and this was soon stopped by a "long interval of study," preceding and following the death of his friend Deyverdun, which occurred July 4, 1789.[5] That Gibbon could not have begun Memoir A before his departure from England is clear from a reference in it to his "last visit to England,"

[1] *Proceedings of Gibbon Commemoration*, p. 36.

[2] Murray, p. 353, and this *Introduction*, p. li.

[3] *Memoirs*, p. 182.

[4] *Letters*, II, 176.

[5] *Ibid.*, II, 194.

when he had been led to examine some memorials of his own family.[1] If we allow some months for his classical reading, the date of writing Memoir A must then be the last months of 1788, or the first of 1789.

The next in order of the sketches, Memoirs B and C, have the respective dates 1789–1790 and 1790 assigned them in the Gibbon memorial volume.[2] The date of Memoir B can be made somewhat more definite by a reference to Sir Stanier Porten as "barely alive."[3] The latter died June 7, 1789, and Gibbon mentions the fact in a letter of July 25, 1789.[4] Thus, Memoir B must have been begun in the spring of 1789. There are two further references in B which are of value in determining when the text was written. The first is to Miss Hester Gibbon, the historian's aunt, who is mentioned as still living "at the age of eighty-five."[5] Miss Gibbon died in the spring of 1790, at the age of eighty-six, so that the early part of B could not have been written in the latter year. This reference, therefore, confirms the former, and will also be of use hereafter. More accurate data from the reference to Miss Hester Gibbon cannot be given, since the date of her birth is not known, and was not to the historian himself, as he intimates in Memoir A.[6]

[1] Murray, p. 356. See also *Introduction*, p. liii.

[2] Murray says Memoir C was written in 1789, but gives no date to Memoir B.

[3] Murray, p. 111.

[4] *Letters*, II, 201.

[5] Murray, p. 110.

[6] *Ibid.*, p. 383: "I have mentioned my two aunts on the father's side. . . . Their names were Catherine and Hester, though I do not pretend to ascertain the order of their respective births." Hester was the elder, and was born in 1704 or 1705. As Gibbon's father, younger than both, was born in 1707, Catherine must have been born in 1705 or 1706. In the death notices of the *Gentleman's Magazine*, that of Gibbon's aunt is recorded under the somewhat indefinite "lately," after the record of June 30, but before that of July 1.

The second note of time in Memoir B is to the French minister Necker, who is mentioned as "the minister, perhaps the legislator of the French monarchy."[1] It will be remembered that Necker, who had been banished from Paris in 1787, was recalled and made director-general of finance in September, 1788. Almost immediately arrangements were made for calling together the States-General, which met May 5, 1789. But Necker was unable to cope with the new spirit of the deputies and resigned his office in June. He was again recalled after the fall of the Bastile in July, and again resigned in September, 1790. As the latter period could not have been in Gibbon's mind, this part of Memoir B must have been written between September, 1788, and May, 1789. The significant phrase, "perhaps the legislator," probably refers to the spring of 1789, when Necker's influence with the nation was at its height, and when all were looking forward to reforms which should be brought about by the National Assembly under his direction. It may be incidentally noted that one other circumstance, of negative rather than positive evidence, is in favor of assigning the composition of B to the early part of 1789. In January of that year died Baron d'Holbach, with whom Gibbon was on terms of intimacy when visiting Paris in 1765. Had news of this event reached Gibbon before he wrote Memoir B, he would probably have mentioned it in alluding to his friend.[2] On all accounts, therefore, Memoir B must have been begun and well under way in the spring of 1789.

Before there is any further consideration of the date of Memoir B, it is important to consider when Memoir C was composed. It has already been noted that Memoirs B and C have the closest interrelation. Naturally, therefore, some of the references which assist in dating Memoir B

[1] Murray, p. 152. [2] *Memoirs*, p. 134.

also occur in C. In Memoir C, as in B, Miss Hester Gibbon is referred to as "at the age of eighty-five." Memoir C must therefore have been begun before 1790. The same Memoir refers to Necker as "the first minister of the finances of France," but without the significant phrase of B, "perhaps the legislator of the French monarchy." There is also no mention in Memoir C of Sir Stanier Porten, and this must be regarded as significant. All things at least suggest that Memoir C was written about the same time as B, — that it could have been composed neither much earlier nor much later.

There is no certain proof from these allusions to time as to whether Memoir C was written before or after B. It is highly probable, however, that the reference to Necker as "perhaps the legislator of the French monarchy" refers to a later time than the reference to him in C, as simply "first minister of the finances of France." Far more likely is it that, if Memoir C were written after B, some allusion would have been made to the illness or death of Sir Stanier Porten. This is more than probable, because Gibbon took great interest in the family of Sir Stanier,[1] and eventually made the latter's children heirs to his estate. When, however, we turn to other internal data in the case of Memoirs B and C, the weight of evidence is overwhelmingly in favor of placing C before B in order of composition. The same expressions are used in both on page after page, yet B is much more detailed and complete than C, so far as it goes, just as F, the last Memoir written, is more detailed than B or C. The first editor perceived this, and used Memoir B for that part of Gibbon's life not recorded in F, and only then took up the briefer and less adequate Memoir C. Indeed, no one can closely compare the two without becoming convinced that Memoir B is an elaboration of C.

[1] *Letters*, II, 201; *Miscellaneous Works*, II, 426.

No special attempt has been made to prove that Memoirs B and C are later than A. The latter, as clearly shown already, may have been written in the last part of 1788, while the two former cannot have been composed before the beginning of 1789. Similarity of expression and similar ordering of material show that Memoir A could not have been written later than the two more elaborate sketches. The whole discussion also proves that the order of writing and the dates of each of the first three sketches must be set down as follows: Memoir A was prepared in the winter of 1788–1789; Memoir C in the early part of 1789; Memoir B before May or June of the same year.

There remain three sketches to be accounted for. Of these Memoir E is dated at the end "March 2, 1791." The time of writing is still further established by several references to external events. Gibbon mentions his inheritance from his aunt, Hester Gibbon, who died in the early part of 1790; Lord Sheffield's election to represent Bristol in parliament, first mentioned in a letter of congratulation, Aug. 7, 1790;[1] especially, also, the time since he had settled in Lausanne, as "more than seven years."[2] The latter reference clearly shows that Memoir *E* must have been written some time after Oct. 1, 1790, as Gibbon reached Lausanne Sept. 30, 1783.[3]

Before attempting a more accurate dating of Memoir E, it will be well to examine the date of Memoir D, which, as already noted, has special relation to the former. In the latter there are but three references to external events which are of material assistance in dating its composition. The most important of these is an allusion to his first arrival at Lausanne, June 30, 1753, as thirty-seven years

[1] *Letters*, II, 219.

[2] Murray, p. 328.

[3] *Letters*, II, 74.

ago.[1] This part of Memoir D must therefore have been written after July 1, 1790. Besides, Miss Hester Gibbon is referred to in such a way as to indicate that she was already dead,[2] and the mention of Mme. Necker[3] more clearly points to the time following Necker's second dismissal from office, September, 1790. On the other hand, internal evidence shows that Memoir E is an elaboration of Memoir D, as B is of C, so that D and E must have been written in the order named. This fact will be clear only from a close comparison of the Memoirs, but of the fact there can be no reasonable doubt. In all probability the winter of 1790–1791 must be assigned to the composition of Memoirs D and E.

It has been mentioned that a large body of Gibbon's notes belong to Memoir E. These, according to the Gibbon memorial volume,[4] were added in 1792–1793. The reason for these dates is not evident. It is more natural to suppose that the notes were written about the same time as the Memoir itself. An examination of every allusion which could assist in assigning a date tends to confirm this idea. There are several references which show that the notes must have been written after the year 1790.[5] On the other

[1] Murray, p. 396: "At the distance of thirty-seven years, I can still remember the melancholy impressions of my first arrival at Lausanne —at Lausanne, the beloved school of my youth, and the chosen retirement of my declining age."

[2] *Ibid.*, p. 392.

[3] *Ibid.*, p. 398: "I felt (and I am proud that I felt) the beauty and merit of a lady who has supported with equal propriety the scenes of fortune, from the daughter of a country clergyman to the wife of the first minister of the finances of France."

[4] *Gibbon Commemoration*, p. 37.

[5] Two or three of these will be conclusive. *The Monthly Review* of October, 1790, is once quoted. In another note Gibbon refers to his visit to the Neckers in October, 1790 (see note to *Memoirs* 178, 24; also Mme. Necker's invitation, dated at Coppet 13 Octobre, 1791, in *Miscel-*

hand, no allusion in them points to a later date than the early part of 1791. Especially in alluding to the works of Lord Sheffield, Gibbon makes no mention of the former's pamphlet on *Abolishing the Slave Trade*,[1] which he did not see until February, 1791.[2] Too much should not be made of this negative evidence, but it is certainly probable that the notes to Memoir E were written in the early part of 1791. Further, a comparison of the early notes to E with Memoir F shows that many of them were incorporated in the latter,[3] and the conclusion is inevitable that the former were written before Memoir F was begun.

The interval between the writing of Memoirs B and E may be easily accounted for. The historian himself tells us of the "long interval of study" after Deyverdun's death in July, 1789. The latter event required his making new arrangements in regard to his home. The death of Sir Stanier Porten about the same time suggested his adopting the latter's daughter Charlotte, and this was seriously considered. The delay occasioned by the sale of Buriton was, at the same time, making no end of trouble. Finally, nearer him the wonderful panorama of the French Revolution was being unrolled, and the historian, as we know from his letters, was a keen and close observer.

laneous Works, II, 441, and *Letters*, II, 236). He also alludes to Burke "On the Revolution in France" (see note to *Memoirs* 185, 22; Murray, p. 342); this is evidently the famous *Reflections on the Revolution in France*, which was not printed until November, 1790, and probably did not reach Lausanne before December or January, 1791. The first mention of the book in his letters is in one of January, 1791 (*Letters*, II, 237), and from one of Lord Sheffield's letters (*Ibid.*, II, 239), we learn that he had recently sent a copy to Gibbon on learning that the latter had not received one.

1 Published anonymously, 1790, with the author's name, 1791.

2 See *Letters*, II, 239, where Sheffield (Feb. 5, 1791) mentions having delivered it to Elmsley to send.

3 Murray, pp. 293–296.

Memoir F, the last attempt of the historian at his autobiography, is said to have been written in 1792–1793. This date, like most of the others, is mainly conjectural, and at any rate deserves careful verification. Fortunately there are a number of incidental allusions which assist in dating the text. Long before the publication of the manuscript memoirs, it had been pointed out that two passages in the part now known as Memoir F were probably written after Gibbon had seen Boswell's *Life of Johnson*, published in 1791.[1] By the publication of the manuscripts, with Gibbon's notes, this inference is made doubly sure. In notes Gibbon twice refers to Boswell's *Johnson*,[2] though on different passages from those hitherto thought to refer to that work. These clearly indicate that Memoir F was not written till after Gibbon had seen and read the famous *Life*, which appeared in May, 1791. Besides, as his friends, the Sheffields, were with him at Lausanne from the middle of July to October, 1791, and as he paid a visit to the Neckers at Coppet in the latter month,[3] it seems more probable that the autobiography was not taken up until late in that year, or at the beginning of the next. The latter would be even more likely, since in a letter to Lord Sheffield, Dec. 28, 1791, Gibbon says, "I have much revolved the plan of the *Memoirs* I once mentioned, and as you do not think it ridiculous, I believe I shall make an attempt."[4] It is not improbable that at this time Gibbon began Memoir F, which he no doubt expected to be the last account of his early life.

[1] These were first pointed out by G. Birkbeck Hill in his edition of Boswell's *Life*, II, 8, note and II, 448, note 2; see notes to this edition on lines 51, 3 and 55, 25.

[2] Murray, pp. 26, 39; see notes on 19, 16 and 28, 27.

[3] See Mme. Necker's invitation to Gibbon in *Miscellaneous Works*, II, 441.

[4] *Letters*, II, 280; see also note to p. xxxiv.

The time at which Memoir F, or the first part at least, was completed is fully established by another important fact. On Feb. 24, 1792, Gibbon wrote a letter to the *Gentleman's Magazine*[1] in regard to a communication relating to the Gibbon family which had appeared in that journal in August, 1788.[2] Gibbon explains that, owing to his distance from London, he had just seen the communication and earnestly desired to be put in correspondence with the author. As the account of Gibbon's ancestry in the *Gentleman's Magazine* differs decidedly from that in Memoir F, and as Gibbon later accepted the former, though without changing the latter, the first part of Memoir F must certainly have been written before Feb. 24, 1792, the date of his letter of inquiry. Gibbon spent the month of March, 1792, with the Neckers, and he purposed to visit England in the summer. Besides, as he had been stopped in February by seeing the communication in the *Gentleman's Magazine*, and as he did not find the correspondent until his last visit to England, he doubtless made no further attempt at the *Memoirs* at this time. This is further substantiated by a reference in one of his letters. On Dec. 28, 1791, the historian had asked Lord Sheffield for the letters which the latter had received from him in order to use them in his autobiography. On May 30, 1792, he wrote to his English friend,

> "Miss Moss delivered the letters into my hands, but I doubt whether they will be of much service to me. The work appears far more difficult in the execution than in the idea, and, as I am now taking leave for some time of the library, I shall not make much progress in the *Memoirs* of p[ersona] p[ropria] till I am on English ground."[3]

As he wrote again on Jan. 6, 1793,

[1] *Gentleman's Magazine*, LXV, 5.

[2] See p. xxx.

[3] *Letters*, II, 302.

"Of the *Memoirs* little has been done, and with that little I am not satisfied; they must be postponed till a mature season, and I much doubt whether the book and the author can ever see the light at the same time," [1]

the conclusion is forced upon us that Gibbon's last attempt at his life, Memoir F, was composed in the early part of 1792.

Summing up the facts so far given, the dates of the various sketches may be set down as follows: Memoir A was written in the winter of 1788–1789; Memoir C in the early part of 1789, and Memoir B before May or June of the same year. Memoir D must have been prepared in the last half of 1790, while Memoir E, completed March 2, 1791, must have been begun as early as the last part of 1790. The notes to Memoir E are possibly as late as the last part of 1791. Memoir F was begun and finished in the early months of 1792, probably before the first of March.

III. HOW THE MEMOIRS HAVE BEEN EDITED.

From what has been said, it will be clear that the fullest and best account of Gibbon's life must be made from five of the six autobiographic sketches in the following manner. It must begin with Memoir F, the last and best sketch for the early life, and must include the greater part of E, the last and best for the later life. Following F must come Memoir B, from the point where F ends. The remainder of the life must be furnished by Memoir C. Even this might seem to be a curious patch-work, yet so nicely do the parts indicated dovetail together, that no word of Gibbon need be changed, and no considerable omissions are necessary.[2]

[1] *Letters*, II, 359.

[2] Three sentences, which are given essentially in earlier texts, are omitted, and placed in footnotes to pp. 91, 158, 189.

This method was followed in the main by the earliest editor of Gibbon's *Memoirs*,[1] the first Lord Sheffield. Lord Sheffield, however, did not print everything in the order indicated. For example, while Memoir B was clearly written after Memoir C, and should have been followed in all points not included in E, a long account of Gibbon's military life[2] was replaced by the briefer and less satisfactory account given in C. Besides, Lord Sheffield took large liberties of excision, especially when he thought a passage might reflect upon the character of his dead friend, or upon some person then living.[3] Again, he did not hesitate to alter words and even occasional sentences, and especially to insert into the Memoir he was following at the time a passage from any of the other texts. Some of the most remarkable portions of the famous autobiography were thus made by piecing together parts from various sketches.[4] Finally, Lord Sheffield sometimes inserted Gib-

[1] The *Miscellaneous Works of Edward Gibbon, Esq., with Memoirs of his Life and Writings, Composed by Himself, Illustrated from his Letters, with Occasional Notes and Narrative, by John Lord Sheffield.* London, 1796. Second edition, with some additions and some other changes, 1814.

[2] See *Memoirs*, p. 112 *ff.*

[3] It is now known that Lord Sheffield did not rely wholly upon his own judgment in omitting portions of the autobiography. In a letter by his daughter Maria occurs the following, under date of Aug. 28, 1794: "Mr. Hayley, Mr. More, and Miss Poole are closeted reading Mr. Gibbon's *Memoirs*, etc., and Mr. Hayley thinks a great deal must be omitted in publication."—*The Girlhood of Maria Josepha Holroyd, Recorded in Letters of a Hundred Years Ago.* Edited by J. H. Adeane. London, 1896, p. 303. The Mr. Hayley is the poet and friend of Gibbon (see *Memoirs*, p. 155 and note). It is a curious coincidence that Mr. Bowdler, not unlikely the one who later "purified" Gibbon's *History*, was also a guest at Sheffield Place at this time.

[4] How true this is can only be appreciated by a close comparison of the first or second edition with the reprint of the manuscripts. Some idea of it may be gained from notes to 88, 16; 88, 27; 144, 23. See

bon's notes in the text, sometimes placed them at the foot of the page, as Gibbon apparently intended, and sometimes omitted them altogether. The parts of Memoir E as printed in the early editions are a medley of notes and original text which has often puzzled the reader.[1] Not only did Lord Sheffield edit the *Memoirs* in this most remarkable manner, but he directed in his will that no further publication should be made of Gibbon's papers.[2]

Such liberties with the writings of a great man, though in this case suggested by Lord Sheffield's friendship and desire not to give pain to others, have seldom been taken and have much less frequently been justified. Particularly in an autobiography does the man reveal his character, not simply in the facts he relates, but also in the manner in which he expresses himself. In such a work every word is important, every phrase, every turn of expression. It is particularly fortunate, therefore, that we now have restored

also an address by Frederic Harrison in *Proceedings of the Gibbon Commemoration*, p. 18.

[1] See a noteworthy example at 165, 31.

[2] For this reason all subsequent issues of the *Memoirs* have been mere reprints of the first or second editions of Lord Sheffield, at least so far as text is concerned. As indicated in the footnote to p. xlviii, the second edition differed in text from the first in a number of passages, and this has not always been noted by editors. Many editions, therefore, are based on Lord Sheffield's first, rather than on his second text. Some of the other editions of the *Memoirs* are important. A third issue in one volume of Lord Sheffield's second edition appeared in 1837. In 1839, Milman edited the *Memoirs* with some additional notes. The latter also, when writing a sketch of the historian for his edition of the *Decline and Fall*, was allowed to inspect the manuscript memoirs, but with the understanding that he should publish no new matter. The novelist Howells reprinted the *Memoirs*, with an introductory essay in 1877. A reprint of Sheffield's first edition appeared in the *Chandos Classics* in 1889, and an edition by Henry Morley (*Carisbrooke Library*) in 1890.

to us all that Gibbon wrote concerning his life, in the exact form in which he left it. In 1894, a century after Gibbon's death, such interest was excited in the commemoration of the historian's life and work,[1] that the present Earl of Sheffield was induced to allow the *Memoirs* to be printed verbatim,[2] thus restoring to its integrity what has been long recognized as one of the most interesting of autobiographies. Upon that edition, by the kindness of the English editor and publisher, the present edition is based. It follows the various partial Memoirs exactly, so far as each can be used.[3] In addition, the most important parts of the other Memoirs are given in the notes, so that the reader has before him all that is best in the six sketches already described.

A question arose as to what to do with Gibbon's notes, but it finally seemed best to place them with others at the end of the volume. This was deemed advisable because to some manuscripts there are no notes at all, and those appended to others vary greatly in completeness and in value. Those belonging to Memoir F are mere jottings which Gibbon no doubt intended to elaborate, while those to Memoir E are fairly complete. Besides, in a continuous memoir, some of the notes to earlier parts of E must be

[1] See *Proceedings of the Gibbon Commemoration.*

[2] *The Autobiographies of Edward Gibbon.* Edited by John Murray. London, 1896.

[3] In this edition, Memoir F ends at line 18 on page 69; Memoir B at line 8, page 140; Memoir C at the beginning of the paragraph on page 163. The rest of the *Memoirs* is from E. It hardly need be said that the spelling, punctuation, and capitals of Gibbon's unrevised manuscript are not reproduced. The text has been modernized in these particulars. In every other respect, however, the reprint of the manuscripts has been exactly followed. Even the slightest variations have been explained in the notes, or have been indicated by brackets in the text.

added to passages from Memoir F, and again, original notes must be made to explain many allusions. All notes are therefore grouped together at the back of the book.

The beginning of Memoir F is somewhat abrupt. As usually printed, the *Memoirs* proper have been prefaced by an introduction on autobiography in general and on the natural interest in ancestry. This introductory passage, however, is one of Lord Sheffield's most curious pieces of patch-work. It begins with a paragraph from Memoir A, which gives the misleading reference to Gibbon's fifty-second year as the time of writing his life, dovetails together various parts of A, and the fragment already mentioned,[1] and closes with part of the introduction to Memoir B. As none of these introductory passages is complete, and as it was impossible to adopt Lord Sheffield's patch-work, it seemed best to omit them all in reprinting the *Memoirs*. Yet each of them merits some place as best expressing the purpose and plan of the historian in writing his life, and they are therefore printed here in the form in which they were written. The first is from the beginning of Memoir A.[2]

In the fifty-second year of my age, after the completion of a toilsome and successful work, I now propose to employ some moments of my leisure in reviewing the simple transactions of a private and literary life. Truth, naked, unblushing truth, the first virtue of more serious history, must be the sole recommendation of this personal narrative. The style shall be simple and familiar; but style is the image of character, and the habits of correct writing may produce without labor or design the appearances of art

[1] See p. xxxvi. The order of sentences in this fragment were so changed that the editor of the *Autobiographies* indicated a considerable portion of it as hitherto unpublished. In some other instances, the hitherto unpublished parts are not accurately marked by Murray.

[2] Murray, pp. 353–356.

and study. My own amusement is my motive and will be my reward; and if these sheets are communicated to some discreet and indulgent friends, they will be secreted from the public eye till the author shall be removed from the reach of criticism or ridicule. The reasons and examples which may furnish some apology will be reserved for the last chapter of these *Memoirs*, when the order of time will lead me to account for this vain undertaking.

A philosopher may reasonably despise the pride of ancestry; and, if the philosopher himself be a plebeian, his own pride will be gratified by the indulgence of such contempt. It is an obvious truth that parts and virtue cannot be transmitted with the inheritance of estates and titles, and that even the claim of our legal descent must rest upon a basis perhaps not sufficiently firm, the unspotted chastity of all our female progenitors. Yet in every age and country the common sense or common prejudice of mankind has agreed to respect the son of a respectable father, and each successive generation is supposed to add a new link to the chain of hereditary splendor. Wherever the distinction of birth is allowed to form a superior order in the state, education and example should always, and will often, produce among them a dignity of sentiment and propriety of conduct which is guarded from dishonor by their own and the public esteem. If we read of some illustrious line so ancient that it has no beginning, so worthy that it ought to have no end, we sympathize in its various fortunes; nor can we blame the generous enthusiasm, or even the harmless vanity, of those who are associated to the honors of its name. In the study of past events, our curiosity is stimulated by the immediate or indirect reference to ourselves. Within its own precincts a local history is always popular, and the connection of a family is more clear and intimate than that of a kingdom, a province, or a city. For my own part, could I draw my pedigree from a general, a statesman, or a celebrated author, I should study their lives or their writings with the diligence of filial love, and I suspect from this casual relation some emotions of pleasure — shall I say of vanity? — might arise in my breast. Yet I will add that I should take more delight in their personal merit than in the memory of their titles or possessions, that I should be more affected by literary than by martial fame; and that I would rather descend from Cicero than from Marius, from Chaucer than from one of the first companions of the Garter. The family of Confucius is in my opinion the noblest upon earth. Seventy authentic generations have elapsed from that philosopher to the present chief of his posterity, who reckons one hundred and thirty-five degrees from the Emperor Hoang-ti, the father, as it is believed, of an illustrious line which has now flourished in China four thousand four hundred and twenty-five years. I have exposed my private feelings, as I shall always do without scruple or reserve. Let every reader, whether noble or plebeian, examine his own conscience on the same subject.

That these sentiments are just or at least natural I am the more inclined to believe, since I do not feel myself interested in the cause, since I can derive from my ancestry neither glory nor shame. I had long and modestly acquiesced in the knowledge of my two immediate predecessors, a country gentleman and a wealthy merchant. Beyond these I found neither tradition nor memorial, and as our genealogy was never a topic of family conversation, it might seem probable that my grandfather, the director of the South Sea Company, was himself a son of the earth who by his industry — his honest industry perhaps — had raised himself from the workhouse or the cottage. It is not two years since I acquired in a foreign land some domestic intelligence of my own family, and this intelligence was conveyed to Switzerland from the heart of Germany. I had formed an acquaintance with Mr. Langer, a lively and ingenious scholar, while he resided at Lausanne as preceptor to the hereditary Prince of Brunswick. On his return to his proper station of librarian to the ducal library of Wolfenbüttel, he accidentally found among some literary rubbish a small old English volume of heraldry inscribed with the name of John Gibbon. From the title only Mr. Langer judged that it might be an acceptable present to his friend; and he judged rightly, for I soon convinced myself that the author was not only my namesake but my kinsman. To his book I am indebted for the best and most curious information; but in my last visit to

England I was tempted to indulge a curiosity which had been excited by this odd discovery. Some wills, parish registers, and monumental inscriptions were consulted at my request, and my inquiries were assisted by Mr. Brooke, the Somerset herald, whose knowledge deserves my applause and whose friendly industry is entitled to my thanks.

The second introductory passage is found at the beginning of Memoir B.[1]

A sincere and simple narrative of my own life may amuse some of my leisure hours, but it will expose me, and perhaps with justice, to the imputation of vanity. Yet I may judge, from the experience both of past and of present times, that the public is always curious to know the men who have left behind them any image of their minds. The most scanty accounts are compiled with diligence and perused with eagerness, and the student of every class may derive a lesson or an example from the lives most similar to his own. The author of an important and successful work may hope without presumption that he is not totally indifferent to his numerous readers. My name may hereafter be placed among the thousand articles of a *Biographia Britannica*, and I must be conscious that no one is so well qualified as myself to describe the series of my thoughts and actions. The authority of my masters, of the grave Thuanus and the philosophic Hume, might be sufficient to justify my design; but it would not be difficult to produce a long list of ancients and moderns who, in various forms, have exhibited their own portraits. Such portraits are often the most interesting, and sometimes the only interesting parts of their writings; and, if they be sincere, we seldom complain of the minuteness or prolixity of these personal memorials. The lives of the younger Pliny, of Petrarch, and of Erasmus, are expressed in the *Epistles* which they themselves have given to the world; the *Essays* of Montaigne and Sir William Temple bring us home to the houses and bosoms of the authors; we smile without contempt at the headstrong passions of Benvenuto Cellini,

[1] Murray, pp. 104–105.

and the gay follies of Colley Cibber. The *Confessions* of St. Austin and Rousseau disclose the secrets of the human heart; the *Commentaries* of the learned Huet have survived his *Evangelical Demonstration;* and the *Memoirs* of Goldoni are more truly dramatic than his Italian comedies. The heretic and the churchman are strongly marked in the characters and fortunes of Whiston and Bishop Newton, and even the dulness of Michael de Marrolles and Anthony Wood acquires some value from the faithful representation of men and manners. That I am the equal or superior of some of these biographers, the efforts of modesty or affectation cannot force me to dissemble.

The last introduction, a disconnected fragment found among Gibbon's papers, reads as follows:[1]

A lively desire of knowing and recording our ancestors so generally prevails, that it must depend upon the influence of some common principle in the minds of men. Our imagination is always active to enlarge the narrow circle in which nature has confined us. Fifty or an hundred years may be allotted to an individual, but we stretch forward beyond death with such hopes as religion and philosophy will suggest, and we fill up the silent vacancy that precedes our birth, by associating ourselves to the authors of our existence. We seem to have lived in the persons of our forefathers. It is the labor and reward of vanity to extend the term of this ideal longevity, and few there are who can sincerely despise in others an advantage of which they are secretly ambitious to partake. The knowledge of our own family from a remote period will be always esteemed as an abstract preëminence, since it can never be promiscuously enjoyed; but the longest series of peasants and mechanics would not afford much gratification to the pride of their descendants. We wish to discover our ancestors, but we wish to discover them possessed of ample fortunes, adorned with honorable titles, and holding an eminent rank in the class of hereditary nobles which has been maintained for the wisest and most beneficial purposes in almost every climate of the globe, and in almost every form of political society. If any of these have

[1] Murray, pp. 417–419.

been conspicuous above their equals by personal merit and glorious achievements, the generous feelings of the heart will sympathize in an alliance with such characters; nor does the man exist who would not peruse with warmer curiosity the life of an hero from whom his name and blood were lineally derived. The satirist may laugh, the philosopher may preach, but reason herself will respect the prejudices and habits which have been consecrated by the experience of mankind.

Our calmer judgment will rather tend to moderate than to suppress the pride of an ancient and worthy race. But in the estimate of honor we should learn to value the gifts of nature above those of fortune, to esteem in our ancestors the qualities that best promote the interest of society, and to pronounce the descendant of a king less truly noble than the offspring of a man of genius whose writing will instruct or delight the latest posterity. The family of Confucius is, in my opinion, the most illustrious in the world. After a painful ascent of eight or ten centuries, our barons and princes of Europe are lost in the darkness of the middle age; but in the vast equality of the empire of China the posterity of Confucius has maintained above two thousand two hundred years its peaceful honors and perpetual succession, and the chief of the family is still revered by the sovereign and the people as the living image of the wisest of mankind. The nobility of the Spencers has been illustrated and enriched by the trophies of Marlborough, but I exhort them to consider the *Faerie Queene* as the most precious jewel of their coronet:

> "Ne lesse praisworthie are the sisters three,
> The honor of the noble familie,
> Of which I meanest boast my selfe to be."

Our immortal Fielding was of a younger branch of the Earls of Denbigh who draw their origin from the Counts of Hapsburg, the lineal descendants of Eltrico, in the seventh century Duke of Alsace. Far different have been the fortunes of the English and German divisions of the family of Hapsburg. The former, the knights and sheriffs of Leicestershire, have slowly risen to the dignity of a peerage: the latter, the emperors of Germany and kings of Spain, have threatened the liberty of the old, and invaded the treasures of the new world. The successors of Charles the Fifth may disdain their humble brethren of England, but the romance of *Tom Jones*, that exquisite picture of human manners, will outlive the palace of the Escurial and the imperial eagle of the house of Austria.

What name Gibbon would have given his autobiography, if he had completed it to his satisfaction, must remain unknown. The titles of the various sketches differ somewhat, and Memoirs D and F are without any titles. On the outside of Memoir A Gibbon wrote "The Memoirs of the Life of Edward Gibbon, with various observations and excursions by himself," and within "Memoirs of my own life." Memoir C, which was next written, is called "Memoirs of the Life and Writings of Edward Gibbon." Memoirs B and E bear the simple title "My own Life." For his editions Lord Sheffield took the title of Memoir C, but modified it to "Memoirs of my Life and Writings." The full title of Memoir C has been restored in this edition.

In most of the manuscripts left by the historian there are no divisions, as of chapters. But Memoir A begins with Chapter I, and Memoir F is divided into three chapters without title, corresponding to the first three divisions of the present edition. Besides, Memoir C is divided into three sections, the second beginning at his return from Lausanne, and the third after his father's death. Lord Sheffield made no divisions in the book, except to indicate one or two breaks, the first between the introduction and the biography proper, for which as we have seen there was good reason, the second between Memoirs F and B. The divisions in this edition were made by the present editor, not so much on the basis of those in the original sketches, as of the subject matter of the various parts.

IV. THE LAST YEARS OF GIBBON'S LIFE.

The older statements as to the time at which the *Memoirs* end are somewhat misleading. Lord Sheffield, the first editor, in continuing the account of Gibbon's life says that they end "soon after his [Gibbon's] return to Switzerland in the year 1788."[1] In the continuation which Milman added to his edition,[2] he says, "Gibbon's autobiography does not extend beyond the year 1789." We now know that Memoir E, which furnishes all that Gibbon has told us of his later life, bears the date March 2, 1791. Even without this date, internal evidence might have corrected both Lord Sheffield and Milman, since Gibbon alludes to "Mr. Burke's creed on the Revolution in France,"[3] which must refer to the latter's *Reflections on the Revolution in France.* The essay was not published until November, 1790, and could hardly have reached the historian before the last of that year or the beginning of the next. On the other hand, the annals of the last years of Gibbon's life are but notes which he doubtless meant to extend "in that mature season"[4] which never came. For this reason it may be well to refer to some of the events following Gibbon's return from England in the fall of 1788, after seeing through the press the last three volumes of his *History.*

During the four years following his English visit Gibbon lived in the enjoyment of one who had completed his life work. He read the books he loved, he saw much of his friends, he enjoyed the flattery of those who felt honored by his life among them. But this happy period was not without its sorrows. On his return from England he found

[1] *Miscellaneous Works*, I, 277.
[2] See Milman's edition, p. 184.
[3] See note to *Memoirs*, 185, 22.
[4] See p. xlvii.

his lifelong friend in a decline, and in July, 1789, Deyverdun was parted from him forever. The loss was a severe one for Gibbon. His letters mention it frequently. Even his efforts to remedy the loss are proof of its effect upon him. At one time he thought of returning to England,[1] at another, of taking his niece, Charlotte Porten, to live with him. He was even led to think — though not too seriously it would seem — of matrimony.[2] It has been frequently said that Gibbon proposed to Mme. de Crousaz, afterwards Mme. de Montolieu.[3] Lord Sheffield's daughter Maria thought him desperately in love with "Mme. da Silva, a pretty Portuguese, who had been some time in England."[4] It could not have been serious, for Gibbon playfully refers to it in one of the letters to Maria Holroyd, as follows: "As Mrs. Wood is about to leave us, I must either cure or die, and upon the whole, I believe the former will be most expedient."[5] Perhaps he may have spoken of marriage to Mme. Necker, of whom he saw much while she and her husband were in Switzerland, after M. Necker's fall. At any rate, Mme. Necker wrote in June, 1792:

"Beware, Monsieur, of forming a late attachment. The marriage which makes one happy in mature age is that which is contracted in youth. Then only is the union perfect, tastes are communicated, sentiments are diffused, ideas become common, intellectual faculties are mutually molded. The whole life is double, the whole life is a prolongation of youth; for the impressions of the soul command the eyes, and the beauty which is no more still

[1] *Letters*, II, 200.

[2] *Ibid.*, II, 215, 220, 248.

[3] The story was told by Mme. de Genlis in *Souvenirs de Félicie*, p. 279, but was denied by the lady herself (Rossel, *Histoire Littéraire de le Suisse*, II, 275). It occasioned a skit by George Colman the younger, called The Luminous Historian, or Learning in Love (*Eccentricities for Edinburgh*, pp. 67–91).

[4] *The Girlhood of Maria Josepha Holroyd*, pp. 115, 116.

[5] *Ibid.*, p. 105.

preserves her empire. But you, Monsieur, in all the vigor of your thought, when all your manner of life is decided, could not without a miracle find a woman worthy of you. . . . You are married to fame, and the friends who cherish you are not jealous of a union the luster of which reflects even upon them."[1]

Deyverdun died at the beginning of July, 1789. Ten days later the Bastile fell, and the hailstorm of the French Revolution began. Gibbon in the quiet of Lausanne was an intent spectator. He wrote at this time of the great opportunity in France for governmental reform, but he soon became hopeless as to the outcome of the Revolution.

"How many years," he wrote, "must elapse before France can recover any vigor or resume her station among the powers of Europe! As yet, there is no symptom of a great man, a Richelieu or a Cromwell, arising either to restore the monarchy or to lead the commonwealth."[2]

Finally, the principles of the Revolution spread to Switzerland, Geneva was threatened, and Gibbon went so far as to make preparations for flight.[3] But his peace was not seriously disturbed, and he still looked on from a distance, more than ever an aristocrat and friend of established government.

Meanwhile, Gibbon's pen was not entirely idle. In 1790, he began the *Antiquities of the House of Brunswick*.[4] In the same year or the next he wrote an essay "*On the Position of the Meridonial Line and an Inquiry into the Supposed Circumnavigation of Africa by the Ancients*.[5] In the summer

[1] *Miscellaneous Works*, II, 450.

[2] *Letters*, II, 210.

[3] *Ibid*., II, 319: "For my part till Geneva falls, I do not think of retreat; but at all events I am provided with two strong horses, and a hundred louis in gold."

[4] *Miscellaneous Works*, III, 359; see also *Letters*, II, 228 *ff*.

[5] *Miscellaneous Works*, V, 170.

of 1791 the separation from his English friends was relieved by a visit from Lord Sheffield and his family. The English travelers posted through France, saw Paris in July of that terrible year, stayed two months at Lausanne, and again posted back to England on the German side of the Rhine through the armies of the *émigrés*.[1] The visit of the Sheffields was a great pleasure to Gibbon, yet their departure left him lonelier than ever. He planned to return their visit the following year, but was prevented by the danger of a passage through France in the summer and fall of 1792. During this year he saw more than ever of the Neckers, who had returned to Geneva. He spent the month of March with them at Coppet, and frequently made shorter visits. But while friends were numerous, some of the most highly esteemed were also passing away. Sir Joshua Reynolds died in February, 1792; Lord North, to whom he had dedicated the last three volumes of his *History*, in August; and M. de Severy, one of his warmest friends at Lausanne, in February, 1793.

The new year found Gibbon meditating another literary venture. For some time he had been engaged on his own *Memoirs*, and had once hinted to his publisher a supplement to his *History*[2] — a project which was never seriously undertaken. Now, however, he proposed to his friend Sheffield another plan. On Jan. 6, 1793, he wrote:

"I have long revolved in my mind another scheme of biographical writing — the lives, or rather the characters, of the most eminent persons in arts and arms, in church and state, who have flourished in Britain from the reign of Henry VIII to the present period. This work, extensive as it may be, would be an amusement rather than a toil. The materials are accessible in our own language, and for the most part ready to my hands. But the sub-

[1] *Letters*, II, 261 *ff.*; see also *The Girlhood of Maria Josepha Holroyd*, 88 *ff.*

[2] *Letters*, II, 241.

ject, which would afford a rich display of human nature and domestic history, would powerfully address itself to the feelings of every Englishman. The taste or fashion of the times seems to delight in picturesque decorations, and this series of British portraits might aptly be accompanied by the respective heads, taken from originals and engraved by the best masters." [1]

But this and all other plans were destined to an unexpected check. In April, Lady Sheffield suddenly died. When the intelligence reached Gibbon, which was not until the twenty-fifth of the month, owing to the long delays occasioned by the continental war, he felt the loss as keenly as if it had been that of a sister. Indeed, the letter of sympathy and consolation which he wrote to his friend Lord Sheffield has long been a striking proof, even to those who are not partial toward him, that the historian was capable of the warmest affection for his friends. In spite of the difficulties of a journey through territory in the hands of combatants, Gibbon determined to hasten to his friend and offer the consolation of personal condolence. In less than a fortnight he was on his way. He left Lausanne on the day following his fifty-seventh birthday, traveled by the longer route of Frankfort and Brussels, and reached England the last of May. He remained with the Sheffields until October, with the exception of brief visits to other friends, one to the poet Hayley, and a longer one to his stepmother who had long resided at Bath. He was, through the summer, in excellent spirits, and apparently in excellent health.

In this last summer, so far as we know, the historian was not seriously engaged on any work for future publication. As shown in another place, he was endeavoring to gain further information respecting his family in order to use it

[1] *Letters*, II, 359.

in his *Memoirs.*[1] This, as we found, did not proceed far, owing to circumstances already mentioned. But besides this, Gibbon was lending his last assistance to an undertaking in which he had been long interested, and which was now apparently to reach a successful issue. Long before, in a note to the third volume of the *Decline and Fall,* he had expressed a hope that England would imitate other modern nations in publishing the manuscript materials of her early history. Many times thereafter, as he tells us, he had urged the same project on literary men and publishers. His attention had been more recently attracted to it by seeing in the *Gentleman's Magazine,* which contained the communications concerning his own family, some letters on the same important object.[2] These letters were signed Philistor, and not until he reached England in 1793 did the historian learn that the writer was Mr. John Pinkerton, a Scotch historian and antiquary already favorably known. Gibbon at once conceived the idea of having Pinkerton edit the early English historical writers, proposed a meeting, and succeeded in arranging for publishing the work. The historian declined to appear as co-editor, owing to his "speedy return to the continent" and his inability to do an adequate share of the labor.[3] But he agreed to write the Prospectus, and allow it to appear with his name, besides writing a general preface and a preface to each volume. This Prospectus, headed *An Address Recommending Mr. John Pinkerton as a person well qualified for conducting the Publication of the "Scriptores Rerum Anglicarum," our Latin Memorials of the Middle Ages,*[4] was

[1] See p. xxxi; compare also *Miscellaneous Works,* II, 488 *ff.*

[2] These had appeared in 1788, in the same volume in which were Sir Egerton Brydges's communications on the Gibbon family. Gibbon, as we know, did not see this volume until February, 1792; see p. xxx.

[3] *Miscellaneous Works,* II, 494. [4] *Ibid.,* III, 559.

the last work to which he set his pen, and was left incomplete at his death on the very day on which it was to have been published.

The latter event came unexpectedly to both himself and his friends. When Gibbon left Sheffield Place at the beginning of October, 1793, there was no suspicion that his own expectation of ten or fifteen years of life might not be fulfilled. Yet a long neglected disorder now required attention. In November he wrote to Lord Sheffield, "I must at length withdraw the veil before my state of health, though the naked truth may alarm you more than a fit of the gout."[1] He immediately placed himself in the hands of skilful surgeons in London. The operation which was necessary was apparently successful, and he could write to his stepmother (November 21):

> "You may justly reproach me with the long neglect of a growing complaint, but I am now in the hands of the most skilful physicians and surgeons, who have given me immediate relief and promise me a safe and radical cure. With their approbation I live as usual and dine abroad every day, and in a fortnight, when my friends return from Brighton, I shall meet them at S[heffield] P[lace] and remain there till after Christmas.[2]

The historian was at Sheffield Place, as he intended, for the holidays of 1793, but was again forced to see his physicians in London early in January, 1794. On the fourteenth of that month his friend Sheffield left him in good spirits and apparently on the road to recovery. On the fifteenth he saw his friends, talked of the probable "duration of his life," and "said that he thought himself a good life for ten, twelve, or perhaps twenty years."[3] The next morning he felt better, he said, than for three months past. But

[1] *Letters*, II, 393. [2] *Ibid.*, II, 394.

[3] *Miscellaneous Works*, I, 422.

even then his hours were numbered. He grew rapidly weaker, and before one o'clock on the sixteenth of January, 1794, the great historian breathed his last. So unexpected had been the event, that with the exception of the publisher Elmsley, at whose house he died, no friend or relative was present. His last words in the language of his adopted country were addressed to his French servant: "Pourquoi est-ce que vous me quittez?"

At the death of Gibbon, there was slight recognition of his eminent services as an historian or his excellent qualities as a man. He had offended his countrymen by his reflections on the church, and to a lesser degree by his self-determined exile to Switzerland. His fame, too, was to be a gradual growth, as the greatness of his life work was to be appreciated in spite of his peculiar views. It is not strange, therefore, that without any demonstration the great historian was laid to rest in the family tomb of his friend Sheffield in the little church at Fletching, Sussex. There, too, his worth is memorialized in an elaborate Latin epitaph, written by the learned Dr. Parr, which reads as follows:

EDVARDUS GIBBON

CRITICUS ACRI INGENIO ET MULTIPLICI DOCTRINA ORNATUS
IDEMQUE HISTORICORUM QUI FORTUNAM
IMPERII ROMANI
VEL LABENTIS ET INCLINATI VEL EVERSI ET FUNDITUS DELETI
LITTERIS MANDAVERINT
OMNIUM FACILE PRINCEPS
CUJUS IN MORIBUS ERAT MODERATIO ANIMI
CUM LIBERALI QUADAM SPECIE CONJUNCTA
IN SERMONE

MULTA GRAVITATI COMITAS SUAVITER ADSPERSA
IN SCRIPTIS
COPIOSUM SPLENDIDUM
CONCINNUM ORBE VERBORUM
ET SUMMO ARTIFICIO DISTINCTUM
ORATIONIS GENUS
RECONDITAE EXQUISITAEQUE SENTENTIAE
ET IN MONUMENTIS RERUM POLITICARUM OBSERVANDIS
ACUTA ET PERSPICAX PRUDENTIA
VIXIT ANNOS LVI MENS. VII DIES XXVIII
DECESSIT XVII CAL. FEB. ANNO SACRO
MDCCLXXXXIV
ET IN HOC MAUSOLEO SEPULTUS EST
EX VOLUNTATE JOHANNIS DOMINI SHEFFIELD
QUI AMICO BENE MERENTI ET CONVICTORI HUMANISSIMO
H. TAB. P. C.

V. GIBBON'S STYLE.

The incomplete state of Gibbon's *Memoirs*, as already shown, makes it manifestly unfair to estimate the style as one might that of a finished production. Only the first part, as here printed,[1] can be regarded as approaching the form in which Gibbon would have left his autobiography, had he completed it to his satisfaction, while the last part is at best only a sketch. The sketchy character of Memoir E,[2] which closes the account of Gibbon's life, will be evident from a glance at its shorter paragraphs and their more abrupt beginning. No exhaustive treatment of Gibbon's style will therefore be attempted. Yet, with the incom-

[1] *Memoirs*, pp. 1–69. [2] *Ibid.*, pp. 163 *ff.*

pleteness of the book fully in mind, it will be right to examine some elements of Gibbon's manner of writing, as well as some previous estimates of its power and its defects.

Much of the early criticism of Gibbon's style is severe in the extreme. Most of this severity is due, without doubt, to a confusion of the man and his much abused *History* with the style itself. The unjustifiable prejudice of the last century could see nothing commendable in the historian. The character, as well as the spirit of this early criticism, is fully illustrated by the slighting words of Coleridge: "Gibbon's style is detestable, but his style is not the worst thing about him." An early reviewer of the last three volumes of the *Decline and Fall* criticised Gibbon as follows:

> "His style is generally correct and elegant, but in the structure and run of the sentences so much like the French that one would almost think it a translation from that language; and it is perhaps the easiest book extant to translate into it. A severe critic might discover some few instances of affectation in the use of new modish words and phrases, and not infrequent redundancies of expression for the sake of giving a better rounding and cadence to the periods. His language, in short, is rather too finely, not to say affectedly polished. . . . The present performance seems to me rather calculated to corrupt than to improve the English language."[1]

The celebrated Porson, who entered the controversy against Travis after his attack on Gibbon, makes more definite his criticism:

> "Though his style is generally correct and elegant, he sometimes draws out the thread of his verbosity finer than the staple of his argument. In endeavoring to avoid vulgar terms he frequently dignifies trifles, and clothes common thoughts in a splendid dress that would be rich enough for the noblest ideas. . . . Sometimes, in his anxiety to vary the phrase he becomes obscure; and instead of calling his personages by their names defines them by

[1] *Gentleman's Magazine*, LVIII, 475.

their birth, alliance, office, or other circumstances of their history. . . . Sometimes epithets are added which the tenor of the sentence renders unnecessary."[1]

On the other hand, later critics have found much to praise in Gibbon's manner of composition. A reviewer of Guizot's and Milman's editions of the *History* says:

"To the style, doubtless deficient in simplicity of diction, ease of movement, or variety of form, he [Lord Brougham] is hardly just; for no English writer abounds with more pregnant evidence of the splendor, power, and copiousness of our tongue — none more elegant, more energetic in its expression. . . . Indeed, it may be asserted of him, as Johnson did of Pope's Homer — and encomium could scarcely proceed further — that there exists not a happy combination of words in the English language, not one of which it is susceptible, that is not exemplified in the *Decline and Fall*. And on the other hand, that while habitually magniloquent and stately he could bend, as the subject required it, is sufficiently testified by the playful or familiar, we will not say graceful, diction of his correspondence."[2]

The latter estimate is certainly nearer that which has been received through this century. Copiousness of vocabulary, ornateness of diction, stateliness of movement must always be credited to the historian's best writing. No doubt fondness for balance and rhythm in sentence structure sometimes carried Gibbon too far from simplicity of expression. But the earlier severity of the critic has been seldom justified by the candid reader. The *History*, if it ever becomes obsolete as to its facts, will yet be read with pleasure and advantage as a splendid example of measured and graceful prose.

Compared with the *History*, the *Memoirs*, as frequently noted, are somewhat simpler and more conversational, just

[1] *Gentleman's Magazine*, LX, 919.

[2] *Dublin Review*, VIII, 405.

as Gibbon's letters are somewhat simpler and more lively than the *Memoirs*.[1] The latter thus hold a middle ground in style between the dignified *History* and the unconventional correspondence, itself no doubt directly imaging Gibbon's conversation. It is true the elaborate manner is sometimes employed where simplicity might have been more effective. Compare, for example, such sentences as these: "As soon as the use of speech had prepared my infant reason for the admission of knowledge, I was taught the arts of reading, writing, and vulgar arithmetic."[2] "In my ninth year, in a lucid interval of comparative health, my father adopted the convenient and customary mode of English education, and I was sent to Kingston-upon-Thames, to a school of about seventy boys, which was kept by Dr. Woodeson and his assistants."[3] Yet such sentences are rather the exception to the general rule of more direct and simple statement.

As an eighteenth century writer, Gibbon naturally shows some usages in words and expressions which have since become antiquated. Some of these are interesting in comparison with writers of the nineteenth century. A few words appear in older meanings, as *lively* (p. lv) for *living*, *disgusting* (27, 19) for *unpleasant*, *curiosity* (35, 15; 40, 30)

[1] This has not always been admitted. Bagehot, in *Literary Studies*, writes: "A wit said of Gibbon's autobiography, that he did not know the difference between himself and the Roman empire. He has narrated his progressions from London to Buriton, and from Buriton to London in the same monotonous, majestic periods that record the fall of states and empires." — Review of Smith's Gibbon, p. 1. Similarly Saintsbury, in a brief notice of Gibbon (Craik's *English Prose*, IV, 458): "These remarks of necessity apply most to the *Decline and Fall*, but the manner of Gibbon is one and indivisible, and the *Autobiography*, the *Miscellaneous Works*, and even the letters exhibit no very different characteristics." With neither of these statements, I venture to say, can there ever be general agreement.

[2] *Memoirs*, p. 27.

[3] *Ibid.*, p. 31.

for *intellectual eagerness*, *science* (72, 11) for *learning*, *miracles* (142, 24) for *wonders*, *date* (180, 17) for *duration*. Some idioms are also seldom or never used to-day. Such are *associate to* (p. lii), *initiate in* (32, 10), *dislike to the study* (41, 25), *facility of* (141, 27). A few inflectional forms are slightly different, as *acquaintance* (96, 2 and often) for *acquaintances*, *shrunk* (105, 5) and *sung* (137, 9) for *shrank* and *sang*, *are become* (2, 29; 51, 10) for *have become*, *was grown* (10, 22), *was expired* (10, 33) for *had grown*, *had expired*. The form *an* instead of *a* is also regularly used before words beginning with *h*, as *an hundred* (p. lv), *an heretic* (58, 23).

Besides the above points of usage, the most common difference from that of to-day is lack of concord between verbs or pronouns and the nouns with which they are used. A few examples will suffice to show the practice. "Wherever the distinction of birth is allowed to form a superior *order* in the state, education and example should always, and will often, produce among *them*, etc." "Could I draw my pedigree from *a general*, *a statesman*, or *a celebrated author*, I should study *their* lives and *their* writings, etc." These are both from a single paragraph of the introduction to Memoir A.[1] Note also such examples as "*a popular* and even a parliamentary *clamor* demanded *their* victims" (9, 7), and "of any given number *the greater part are* extinguished before their ninth year" (25, 33). Such examples are not rare in Gibbon, as indeed in many eighteenth century writers.

It was early pointed out that Gibbon's style shows certain unusual influences of French idiom, no doubt owing to his employment of French through life, in both speaking and writing. Yet the *Memoirs* show few conclusive examples of this influence. The most common indication

[1] See p. li.

of it is in the use of the definite article where it would be omitted in English, as in "*the* Venetian history" (11, 3), "*the* mathematics" (79, 30), "*the* Roman history" (91, 1). Besides the use of *infant* (57, 12) for *young*, *assemblies* (73, 14) for *social gatherings* are perhaps reproductions of foreign usage, while the idioms *assist at* (136, 28; 165, 26) for *attend*, and *several English* (175, 25) for *several Englishmen* are certainly French rather than English.

In sentence structure, Gibbon had a fondness for parallelism, and for frequent balance of word by word. Good examples are the following: "I arrived at Oxford with a stock of erudition that might have puzzled a doctor, and a degree of ignorance of which a schoolboy might have been ashamed" (43, 22); "Her fortune was humble, but her family was respectable" (87, 29); "I sighed as a lover; I obeyed as a son" (see note to 88, 27). More striking still is Gibbon's use of a long and elaborate sentence. The proportion of simple sentences, for example, is unusually small even for an eighteenth century writer. This longer sentence is usually made up of several clauses forming a series bearing upon the same fact or principle, or of one or more premises and a conclusion. The number of clauses is usually three, two of which are introductory; but occasionally four, or even more are bound together in a similar manner. Typical examples are: "The law requires some abilities; the church imposes some restraints; and before our army and navy, our civil establishments and Indian empire had opened so many paths of fortune, the mercantile profession was more frequently chosen by youths of a liberal race and education who aspired to create their own independence" (2, 16). "Against irresistible rapine the use of fraud is almost legitimate; in the dexterous anticipation of a conveyance some fragments of property might escape; debts of honor will not be annulled by any positive law, and the frequent imposition of oaths had enlarged and fortified the Jacobite conscience" (12, 2).

The more elaborate sentence structure of Gibbon explains also the long paragraph which he regularly employs. The short paragraph, serving as introduction to a new division of the subject, is seldom found in his writing. This no doubt bears a certain relation to the sparing use of the simple sentence. Yet the longer paragraph of Gibbon cannot be charged with lack of unity or unnatural sequence of thought, so that it can seldom be broken up into separate parts. Indeed, Gibbon's paragraph structure everywhere bears evidence of the careful attention which we know from his *Memoirs* that he regularly gave to this unit of discourse.[1]

As to the higher qualities of style, Gibbon shows on every page his fondness for ornateness in words and expressions. This tendency to the ornate, sometimes excessive it must be admitted, is exemplified in every form. Apt, striking, and picturesque epithets are usual, and these are paralleled by similar descriptive phrases and clauses. Yet all this adds a vividness and glow to the prose of Gibbon, so that it is not too much to say the historian will always be read with pleasure, as illustrating the power and dignity of the English language.

[1] *Memoirs*, p. 168.

CHRONOLOGICAL OUTLINE OF GIBBON'S LIFE.

1737. April 27—May 8, Gibbon born.

1746. January. Placed at school, Kingston-upon-Thames.

1749. January. Goes to Westminster School.

1752. January. Placed with Mr. Francis at Esher, Surrey. April 3. Entered gentleman commoner at Magdalen, Oxford.

1753. June 30. Settled at Lausanne.

1758. April. Returned to England.

1759. June 12. Accepted commission as captain in militia. Quebec taken September 13. Johnson's *Rasselas*, Goldsmith's *Essay on the Present State of Polite Learning in Europe*, Sterne's *Tristram Shandy*, Burke's *Annual Register*, vol. I, published.

1760. Accession of George III, and embodying of militia May 10.

1761. Published his *Essai sur l'Étude de la Littérature.* Ministry of Lord Bute.

1763. January. Gibbon revisits the continent. Peace signed at Paris, February 10. Grenville ministry. Gibbon reached Lausanne in May.

1764. April. Gibbon visits Italy. October 15, determines to write the *History of the Decline and Fall.*

1765. June 25. Gibbon returns to England a second time. Stamp Act passed March 22. Rockingham ministry.

1766. Chatham ministry. Goldsmith's *Vicar of Wakefield*, Lessing's *Laocoon* published.

1767. Gibbon and Deyverdun publish *Mémoires Littéraires de la Grand Bretagne.*

1768. Grafton ministry. *Mémoires Littéraires* discontinued.

1770. North ministry. Boston Massacre. Burke's *Thoughts on the Present Discontents* published. Gibbon printed his *Critical Observations on the Sixth Book of the Æneid.* His father died November 10.

1772. Gibbon settled in London, aged thirty-five.

1774. Gibbon became a member of the Literary Club, and member of parliament for Liskeard in Cornwall, October 10. Burke *On American Taxation* published April 19. Louis XIV died May 10. Continental Congress met at Philadelphia September 5.

1775. Burke *On Conciliation with America*, published March 22. Johnson's *Taxation no Tyranny* printed. Battle of Lexington, April 19.

1776. Gibbon published the first volume of his *History*. Adam Smith's *Wealth of Nations*, Paine's *Common Sense*, published. Declaration of Independence, July 4. Hume died August 25. Necker made director of finance in France in October.

1777. Gibbon visits the Neckers at Paris. Burke's *Letter to the Sheriffs of Bristol*. La Fayette joins the Americans in July.

1778. France makes treaty with the United States.

1779. Gibbon made one of the Lords Commissioners of Trade and Plantations. Cowper (and Newton's) *Olney Hymns*, Lessing's *Nathan der Weise*. Spain joins France against England.

1780. Gibbon lost his seat in parliament. Crabbe's *Candidate*.

1781. Second and third volumes of the *Decline and Fall* published. Gibbon made member of parliament for Lymington. Cornwallis surrendered at Yorktown, October 19. Schiller's *Die Räuber* published.

1782. Gibbon lost his place as Lord Commissioner. Rockingham ministry. Cowper's *Moral Satires*, Priestley's *Corruptions of Christianity* published.

1783. Gibbon settles at Lausanne. Peace signed at Paris September 3. Coalition ministry of Fox and North. Pitt ministry.

1784. The fourth volume of the *Decline and Fall* finished in June. Johnson died.

1785. The fifth volume of the *Decline and Fall* finished in May. Burns's *Poems* published. Impeachment of Hastings.

1787. Gibbon finished the *Decline and Fall* June 27. Visited England (July) and remained till the following year. Goethe's *Iphigenia*, Schiller's *Don Carlos*.

1788. Last three volumes of the *Decline and Fall* published May 8, Gibbon's fifty-first birthday. Memoir A written.

1789. Deyverdun died July 4. Bastile falls, July 14. Bowles's *Sonnets* published. Memoirs C and B written.

1790. Burke's *Reflections on the French Revolution*, Goethe's *Faust* published. Memoir D written.

1791. Memoir E completed March 2. Lord Sheffield and family visited Gibbon at Lausanne. Boswell's *Johnson*, Paine's *Rights of Man*. Flight of Louis XVI from Paris.

1792. Burke's *Appeal from New to Old Whigs*. September massacres in Paris. Memoir F written.

1793. Gibbon hastened to England on the death of Lady Sheffield in April. Execution of Louis XVI and Marie Antoinette. Wordsworth's *Evening Walk* and *Descriptive Sketches*, Godwin's *Political Justice* published.

1794. Death of Gibbon in London, January 16.

MEMOIRS

OF THE

LIFE AND WRITINGS OF EDWARD GIBBON.

[THE GIBBON FAMILY.]

My family is originally derived from the county of Kent, whose inhabitants have maintained, from the earliest antiquity, a provincial character of civility, courage, and freedom. The southern district of the country, which borders on Sussex and the sea, was formerly overspread with the great forest Anderida, and even now retains the denomination of the Weald or Woodland. In this district, and in the hundred and parish of Rolvenden, the Gibbons were possessed of lands in the year one thousand three hundred and twenty-six; and the elder branch of the family, without much increase or diminution of property, still adheres to its native soil. Fourteen years after the first appearance of his name, John Gibbon is recorded as the Marmorarius, or architect, of King Edward the Third. The strong and stately castle of Queenborough, which guarded the entrance of the Medway, was a monument of his skill, and the grant of an hereditary toll on the passage from Sandwich to Stonar in the Isle of Thanet is the reward of no vulgar artist. In the visitations of the heralds, the Gibbons are frequently mentioned; they held the rank of esquire in an age when that title was less promiscuously assumed. One of them, under the reign of Queen Elizabeth, was captain of the militia of Kent, and a free school in the neighboring town of Benenden proclaims the charity and opulence of its founder. But time, or their own obscurity, has cast a veil of oblivion over the virtues and vices of my Kentish ancestors. Their character or station confined them to the labors and pleasures of a rural life, nor is it in my power to follow the advice of the poet, in an inquiry after a name:

> "Go! search it there, where to be born, and die,
> Of rich and poor makes all the history,"

so recent is the institution of our parish registers. In the beginning of the seventeenth century a younger branch of the Gibbons of Rolvenden migrated from the country to the city, and from this branch I do not blush to descend. The law requires some abilities; the church imposes some restraints; and before our army and navy, our civil establishments, and Indian empire had opened so many paths of fortune the mercantile profession was more frequently chosen by youths of a liberal race and education who aspired to create their own independence. Our most respectable families have not disdained the counting-house, or even the shop. Their names are enrolled in the Livery and Companies of London, and in England, as well as in the Italian commonwealths, heralds have been compelled to declare that gentility is not degraded by the exercise of trade.

The armorial ensigns, which in the times of chivalry adorned the crest and shield of the soldier, are now become an empty decoration, which every man who has money to build a carriage may paint according to his fancy on the panels. My family arms are the same which were borne by the Gibbons of Kent in an age when the College of Heralds religiously guarded the distinctions of blood and name, — a lion rampant, gardant, between three scallop shells argent, on a field azure. I should not, however, have been tempted to blazon my coat of arms, the most useless of all coats, were it not connected with a whimsical anecdote. About the reign of James the First the three harmless scallop shells were changed by Edmund Gibbon, Esq., into three ogresses, or female cannibals, with a design of stigmatizing three ladies, his kinswomen, who had provoked him by an unjust lawsuit. But this singular mode of revenge, for which he obtained the sanction of Sir William Seagar, king-at-arms, soon expired with its author, and on his own monument in the Temple church the monsters vanish, and the three scallop shells resume their proper and hereditary place.

Our alliances by marriage it is not disgraceful to mention. Bluemantle Pursuivant, who will soon be introduced to the reader's acquaintance, enumerates the Phillips de la Weld in Tenterden, the Whetnalls of East Peckham, the Edgars of Suffolk, the Cromers, the Bercleys of Beauston, the Hextalls, the Ellenbriggs, the Calverleys, the Whetnalls of Cheshire — modestly checking his pen lest he should seem to indulge the pride of pedigree, *nam genus et proavos*, etc. As such pride would be ridiculous, it would be scarcely less ridiculous to disclaim it, and I shall simply observe that the Gibbons have been immediately or remotely connected with several worthy families of the old gentry of England. The *Memoirs of the Count de Gramont*, a favorite book of every man and woman of taste, immortalize the Whetnalls, or Whitnells, of Peckham — "la blanche Whitnell et le triste Peckham." But the insipid charms of the lady and the dreary solitude of the mansion were sometimes enlivened by Hamilton and love; and had not our alliance preceded her marriage I should be less confident of my descent from the Whetnalls of Peckham. The Cromers in the fifteenth century were twice sheriffs of Kent and twice lord mayors of London. But the chief honor of my ancestry is James Fiennes, Baron Say and Sele, and Lord High Treasurer of England in the reign of Henry the Sixth, from whom by the Phillips, the Whetnalls, and the Cromers I am lineally descended in the eleventh degree. His dismission and imprisonment in the Tower were insufficient to appease the popular clamor, and the Treasurer, with his son-in-law Cromer, was beheaded (1450) after a mock trial by the Kentish insurgents. The black list of his offenses, as it is exhibited in Shakespeare, displays the ignorance and envy of a plebeian tyrant. Besides the vague reproaches of selling Maine and Normandy to the Dauphin, the Treasurer is specially accused of luxury for riding on a foot-cloth, and of treason for speaking French, the language of our enemies. "Thou hast most traitorously corrupted the youth of the realm," says Jack Cade to the unfortunate lord, "in erecting a grammar school; and whereas before our forefathers had no other books than the score and the tally, thou hast caused printing to be used; and contrary to the king, his crown, and dignity, thou hast built a paper mill. It will be proved to thy face that thou hast men about thee who usually talk of a noun and a verb and such abominable words as no Christian ear can endure to hear." Our dramatic poet is generally more attentive to character than to history, and I much fear that the art of printing was not introduced into England till several years after Lord Say's death. But of some of these meritorious crimes I should hope to find my ancestor guilty, and a man of letters may be proud of his descent from a patron and martyr of learning.

In the beginning of the last century Robert Gibbon, Esq., of Rolvenden in Kent (who died in 1618) had a son of the same name of Robert, who settled in London in trade and became a member of the Clothworkers Company. His wife was a daughter of the Edgars, who flourished above four hundred years in the county of Suffolk, and produced an eminent and wealthy sergeant-at-law, Sir Gregory Edgar, in the reign of Henry the Seventh. Of the sons of Robert Gibbon (who died in 1643), Matthew did not aspire above the station of a linen-draper in Leadenhall Street, in the parish of St. Andrew's, but John has given the public some curious memorials of his existence, his character, and his family. He was born the third of November, in the year 1629. His education was liberal, at a grammar school and afterwards in Jesus College at Cambridge, and he celebrates the retired content which he enjoyed at Allesborough in Worcestershire, in the house of Thomas, Lord Coventry, where John Gibbon was employed as a domestic tutor, the same office which Mr. Hobbes exercised in the Devonshire family. But the spirit of my kinsman soon immerged into more active life. He visited foreign countries as a soldier and a traveler, acquired the knowledge ot the French and Spanish languages, passed some time in the Isle of Jersey, crossed the Atlantic, and resided upwards of a twelvemonth (1659) in the rising colony of Virginia. In this remote province his taste, or, rather, passion, for heraldry found a singular gratification at a war dance of the native Indians. As they moved in measured steps, brandishing their tomahawks, his curious eye contemplated their little shields of bark and their naked bodies, which were painted with the colors and symbols of his favorite science. "At which [says he] I exceedingly wondered, and concluded that heraldry was ingrafted naturally into the sense of human race. If so, it deserves a greater esteem than nowadays is put upon it." His return to England after the Restoration was soon followed by his marriage, his settlement in an house in St. Catherine's Cloister near the Tower, which devolved to my grandfather, and his introduction into the Herald's College (in 1671) by the style and title of Blue-mantle pursuivant at arms. In this office he enjoyed near fifty years the rare felicity of uniting, in the same pursuit, his duty and inclination; his name is remembered in the College, and many of his letters are still preserved. Several of the most respectable characters of the age, Sir William Dugdale, Mr. Ashmole, Dr. John Betts, and Dr. Nehemiah Grew, were his friends, and in the society of such men John Gibbon may be recorded without disgrace as the member of an astrological club. The study of hereditary honors is favorable to the royal prerogative, and my kinsman, like most of his family, was a high Tory in church and state. In the latter end of the reign of Charles the Second his pen was exercised in the cause of the Duke of York. The republican faction he most cordially detested, and as each animal is conscious of its proper arms, the herald's revenge was emblazoned on a most diabolical escutcheon. But the triumph of the Whig government checked the preferment of Blue-mantle, and he was even suspended from his office till his tongue could learn to pronounce the oath of abjuration. His life was prolonged to the age of ninety, and in the expectation of the inevitable though uncertain hour, he wishes to preserve the blessings of health, competence, and virtue. In the year 1682 he published at London his *Introductio ad Latinam Blasoniam*, an original attempt which Camden had desiderated, to define in a Roman idiom the terms and attributes of a Gothic institution. His manner is quaint and affected, his order is confused, but he displays some wit, more reading, and still more enthusiasm, and if an enthusiast be often absurd, he is never languid. An English text is perpetually interspersed with Latin sentences in prose and verse, but in his own poetry he claims an exemption from the laws of prosody. Amidst a profusion of genealogical knowledge my kinsman could not be forgetful of his own name, and to him I am indebted for almost the whole of my information concerning the Gibbon family. From this small work, a duodecimo of one hundred and sixty-five pages, the author expected immortal fame, and at the conclusion of his labor he sings in a strain of self-exultation:

> "Usque huc corrigitur Romana Blasonia per me;
> Verborumque dehinc barbara forma cadat.
> Hic liber, in meritum si forsitan incidet usum,
> Testis rite meæ sedulitatis erit.
> Quicquid agat Zoilus, ventura fatebitur ætas
> Artis quod fueram non Clypearis inops."

Such are the hopes of authors! In the failure of those hopes John Gibbon has not been the first of his profession, and very possibly may not be the last of his name.

His brother Matthew Gibbon, the linen-draper of Leadenhall Street, had one daughter and two sons, — my grandfather Edward, who was born in the year 1666, and Thomas, afterwards Dean of Carlisle. According to the mercantile creed that the best book is a profitable ledger, the writings of John the herald would be much less precious than those of his nephew Edward. But an author professes at least to write for the public benefit, and the slow balance of trade can only be pleasing to those persons to whom it is advantageous. The successful industry of my grandfather raised him above the level of his immediate ancestors. He appears to have launched into various and extensive dealings. Even his opinions were subordinate to his interest, and I find him in Flanders clothing King William's troops, while he would have contracted with more pleasure, though not perhaps at a cheaper rate, for the service of King James. During his residence abroad his concerns at home were managed by his mother, Hester, an active and notable woman. Her second husband was a widower of the name of Acton. They united the children of their first nuptials. After his marriage with the daughter of Richard Acton, goldsmith in Leadenhall Street, he gave his own sister to Sir Whitmore Acton of Aldenham, and I am thus connected by a triple alliance with that ancient and loyal family of Shropshire baronets. It consisted about that time of seven brothers, all of gigantic stature, one of whom, a pigmy of six feet two inches, confessed himself the last and least of the seven, adding in the true spirit of party that such men were not born since the Revolution. Under the Tory administration of the four last years of Queen Anne (1710–1714) Mr. Edward Gibbon was appointed one of the Commissioners of the Customs. He sat at that Board with Prior; but the merchant was better qualified for his station than the poet, since Lord Bolingbroke has been heard to declare that he had never conversed with a man who more clearly understood the commerce and finances of England. In the year 1716 he was elected one of the directors of the South Sea Company, and his books exhibited the proof that, before his acceptance of this fatal office, he had acquired an independent fortune of sixty thousand pounds.

But his fortune was overwhelmed in the shipwreck of the year twenty, and the labors of thirty years were blasted in a single day. Of the use or abuse of the South Sea scheme, of the guilt or innocence of my grandfather and his brother directors, I am neither a competent nor a disinterested judge. Yet the equity of modern times must condemn the violent and arbitrary proceedings, which would have disgraced the cause of justice, and would render injustice still more odious. No sooner had the nation awakened from its golden dream than a popular and even a parliamentary clamor demanded their victims, but it was acknowledged on all sides that the South Sea directors, however guilty, could not be touched by any known laws of the land. The speech of Lord Molesworth, the author of *The State of Denmark*, may show the temper, or rather the intemperance, of the House of Commons. "Extraordinary crimes," exclaimed that ardent Whig, "call aloud for extraordinary remedies. The Roman lawgivers had not foreseen the possible existence of a parricide. But as soon as the first monster appeared, he was sewed in a sack and cast headlong into the river, and I shall be content to inflict the same treatment on the authors of our present ruin." His motion was not literally adopted, but a bill of pains and penalties was introduced, a retroactive statute to punish the offenses which did not exist at the time they were committed. Such a pernicious violation of liberty and law can only be excused by the most imperious necessity, nor could it be defended on this occasion by the plea of impending danger or useful example. The legislature restrained the persons of the directors, imposed an exorbitant security for their appearance, and marked their characters with a previous note of ignominy; they were compelled to deliver, upon oath, the strict value of their estates, and were disabled from making any transfer or alienation of any part of their property. Against a bill of pains and penalties it is the common right of every subject to be heard by his counsel at the bar. They prayed to be heard; their prayer was refused, and their oppressors, who required no evidence, would listen to no defense. It had been at first proposed that one-eighth of their respective estates should be allowed for the future support of the directors; but it was speciously urged that, in the various shades of opulence and guilt, such an equal proportion would be too light for many and for some might possibly be too heavy. The character and conduct of each man were separately weighed. But, instead of the calm solemnity of a judicial inquiry, the fortune and honor of three and thirty Englishmen were made the topic of hasty conversation, the sport of a lawless majority, and the basest member of the committee, by a malicious word or a silent vote, might indulge his general spleen or personal animosity. Injury was aggravated by insult, and insult was embittered by pleasantry. Allowances of twenty pounds, or one shilling, were facetiously moved. A vague report that a director had formerly been concerned in another project, by which some unknown persons had lost their money, was admitted as a proof of his actual guilt. One man was ruined because he had dropped a foolish speech that his horses should feed upon gold; another because he was grown so proud that one day at the Treasury he had refused a civil answer to persons much above him. All were condemned, absent and unheard, in arbitrary fines and forfeitures which swept away the greatest part of their substance. Such bold oppression can scarcely be shielded by the omnipotence of parliament; and yet it may be seriously questioned whether the judges of the South Sea directors were the true and legal representatives of their country. The first parliament of George the First had been chosen (1715) for three years; the term had elapsed, their trust was expired, and the four additional years (1718–1722) during which they continued to sit were derived not from the people, but from themselves — from the strong measure of the septennial bill, which can only be paralleled by *il serrar di consiglio* of the Venetian history. Yet candor will own that to the same parliament every Englishman is deeply indebted; the septennial act, so vicious in its origin, has been sanctioned by time, experience, and the national consent. Its first operation secured the House of Hanover on the throne, and its permanent influence maintains the peace and stability of government. As often as a repeal has been moved in the House of Commons I have given in its defense a clear and conscientious vote.

My grandfather could not expect to be treated with more lenity than his companions. His Tory principles and connections rendered him obnoxious to the ruling powers. His name is reported in a suspicious secret, and his well-known abilities could not plead the excuse of ignorance or error. In the first proceedings against the South Sea directors Mr. Gibbon is one of the few who were taken into custody, and in the final sentence the measure of his fine proclaims him eminently guilty. The total estimate which he delivered on oath to the House of Commons amounted to one hundred and six thousand, five hundred and forty-three pounds, five shillings, and six pence, exclusive of antecedent settlements. Two different allowances of fifteen and of ten thousand pounds were moved for Mr. Gibbon, but on the question being put it was carried without a division for the smaller sum; and as a philosopher I should mention, without a sigh, the irreparable loss of above ninety-six thousand pounds, of which, in a single moment and by an arbitrary vote, I have been ultimately deprived. The provision reserved for his wife could not be very considerable, but the valuable gift which he afterwards received from his friend and companion, Mr. Francis Acton, was understood in the family to be the restitution of an honorable trust. Against irresistible rapine the use of fraud is almost legitimate; in the dexterous anticipation of a conveyance some fragments of property might escape; debts of honor will not be annulled by any positive law, and the frequent imposition of oaths had enlarged and fortified the Jacobite conscience. On these ruins, with the skill and credit of which parliament had not been able to despoil him, my grandfather at a mature age erected the edifice of a new fortune. The labors of sixteen years were amply rewarded, and I have reason to believe that the second temple was not much inferior to the first. A large stock of money was vested in the funds and in trade, and his warehouses at Cadiz were replenished with naval stores for which he had contracted to supply the court of Madrid. But he had realized a very considerable property in Sussex, Hampshire, Buckinghamshire, and the New River Company, and had acquired a spacious house, with gardens and lands, at Putney in Surrey, where he resided in decent hospitality. His portraits represent a stern and sensible countenance; his children trembled in his presence; tradition informs me that the independent visitors who might have smiled at his anger were awed by his frown; and, as he was the richest or wisest or oldest of his neighbors, he soon became the oracle and the tyrant of a petty kingdom. His own wrongs had not reconciled him to the House of Hanover; his wishes might be expressed in some harmless toasts, but he was disqualified from all public trust, and in the daily devotions of the family the name of the king for whom they prayed was prudently omitted. My grandfather died at Putney in December, 1736, at the age of seventy, leaving Edward, his only son, and two daughters, Hester and Catherine.

My father, Edward Gibbon, was born in October, 1707. At the age of thirteen he could scarcely feel that he was disinherited by act of parliament, and as he advanced towards manhood new prospects of fortune opened on his view. A parent is most attentive to supply in his children the deficiencies of which he is conscious in himself. My grandfather's knowledge was derived from a strong understanding and the experience of the ways of men, but my father enjoyed the benefits of a liberal education as a scholar and a gentleman. At Westminster School, and afterwards at Emanuel College in Cambridge, he passed through a regular course of academical discipline, and the care of his learning and morals was intrusted to his private tutor, the celebrated Mr. William Law. But the mind of a saint is above or below the present world, and while the pupil proceeded on his travels the tutor remained at Putney, the much-honored friend and spiritual director of the whole family. My father resided some time at Paris to acquire the fashionable exercises, and, as his temper was warm and social, he indulged in those pleasures for which the strictness of his former education had given him a keener relish. He afterwards visited several provinces of France; but his excursions were neither long nor remote, and the slender knowledge which he had gained of the French language was gradually obliterated. His passage through Besançon is marked by a singular consequence in the chain of human events. In a dangerous illness Mr. Gibbon was attended, at his own request, by one of his kinsmen of the name of Acton, the younger brother of a younger brother, who had applied himself to the study of physic. During the slow recovery of his patient the physician himself was attacked by the malady of love. He married his mistress, renounced his country and religion, settled at Besançon, and became the father of three sons, the eldest of whom, General Acton, is conspicuous in Europe as the principal minister of the King of the Two Sicilies. By an uncle whom another stroke of fortune had transplanted to Leghorn he was educated in the naval service of the Emperor, and his valor and conduct in the command of the Tuscan frigates protected the retreat of the Spaniards from Algiers. On my father's return to England he was chosen at the general election of 1734 to serve in parliament for the borough of Petersfield, a burgage tenure of which my grandfather possessed a weighty share till he alienated (I know not why) such important property. Prejudice and society connected his son with the Tories, or, as they were pleased to style themselves, the country gentlemen. With them he gave many a vote; with them he drank many a bottle. Without acquiring the fame of an orator or statesman, he eagerly joined in the great opposition which, after a seven years' chase, hunted down Sir Robert Walpole; and in the pursuit of an unpopular minister he gratified a private revenge against the oppressor of his family in the South Sea persecution.

The union to which I owe my birth was a marriage of inclination and esteem. Mr. James Porten, a merchant of London, resided with his family at Putney, in a house adjoining to the bridge and churchyard where I have passed many happy hours of my childhood. Of his son Stanier, and of a daughter Catherine who preserved her maiden name, I shall hereafter speak. Another daughter married Mr. Darrel of Richmond, and her two sons are opulent and worthy. The youngest and handsomest of the three sisters was Judith, my mother. In the society of Putney the two families lived in friendly and frequent intercourse. The familiar habits of the young people improved into a tender attachment, and their mutual affection, according to the difference of the sexes, was ardently professed and modestly acknowledged. These sentiments were justified by a more perfect knowledge of each other. My father's constancy was neither chilled by absence nor dissolved by pleasure, and after his return from his travels and his election into parliament he seriously resolved to unite himself forever with the object of his choice.

> "Notitiam primosque gradus vicinia fecit;
> Tempore crevit amor, tædæ quoque juræ coissent
> Sed vetuere patres. Quod non potuere vetare,
> Ex æquo captis ardebant mentibus ambo."

Such is the beginning of a love tale at Babylon or at Putney. On the present occasion, however, the opposition of the two fathers was not equally strenuous or sincere. The slender fortunes and dubious credit of Mr. Porten would have been pleased with such an alliance, but he was provoked by a sense of honor to imitate the reluctance of his wealthy and ambitious neighbor. The usual consequences ensued, — harsh threats and tender protestations, frowns and sighs, the seclusion of the lady, the despair of the lover, clandestine correspondence and stolen interviews. At the distance of forty years my Aunt Catherine Porten could relate with pleasure the innocent artifices which she practiced to second or screen her beloved sister, and I have found among my father's papers many letters of both parties that breathe a spirit of constancy and love. All their acquaintance, the whole neighborhood of Putney, was favorable to their wishes. My paternal grandfather yielded a tardy and ungracious consent, and as soon as the marriage ceremony had been performed the young couple was received into his house on the hard terms of implicit obedience and a precarious maintenance. Yet such were the charms and talents of my mother, with such soft dexterity did she follow and lead the morose humor of the old tyrant, that in a few months she became his favorite. Could he have embraced the first child, of which she was pregnant at the time of his decease, it is probable that a will executed in anger would have been canceled by affection, and that he would have moderated the shares of his two daughters, whom, in resentment to his son, he had enriched beyond the measure of female inheritance.

Of my two wealthy aunts on the father's side, Hester persevered in a life of celibacy, while Catherine became the wife of Mr. Edward Elliston, a captain in the service of the East India Company, whom my grandfather styles his nephew in his will. Both Mr. and Mrs. Elliston were dead before the date of my birth, or at least of my memory, and their only daughter and heiress will be mentioned in her proper place. These two ladies are described by Mr. Law under the names of Flavia and Miranda, the pagan and Christian sister. The sins of Flavia, which excluded her from the hope of salvation, may not appear to our carnal apprehension of so black a dye. Her temper was gay and lively; she followed the fashion in her dress, and indulged her taste for company and public amusements; but her expense was regulated by economy, she practiced the decencies of religion, nor is she accused of neglecting the essential duties of a wife or a mother. The sanctity of her sister, the original or the copy of Miranda, was indeed of a higher cast. By austere penance Miss Hester Gibbon labored to atone for the faults of her youth, for the profane vanities into which she had been led or driven by authority and example. But no sooner was she mistress of her own actions and plentiful fortune than the pious virgin abandoned forever the house of a brother from whom she was alienated by the interest of this world and of the next. With her spiritual guide and a widow lady of the name of Hutchinson, she retired to a small habitation at Cliffe in Northamptonshire, where she lived almost half a century, surviving many years the loss of her two friends. It is not my design to enumerate or extenuate the Christian virtues of Miranda as they are described by Mr. Law. Her charity, even in its excess, commands our respect. "Her fortune," says the historian, "is divided between herself and several other poor people, and she has only her part of relief from it." The sick and lame, young children and aged persons, were the first objects of her benevolence; but she seldom refused to give alms to a common beggar, "and instead" (I resume Mr. Law's words) "of driving him away as a cheat because she does not know him, she relieves because he is a stranger and unknown to her. Excepting her victuals, she never spent ten pounds a year upon herself. If you was to see her, you would wonder what poor body it was that was so surprisingly neat and clean. She eats and drinks only for the sake of living and with so regular an abstinence that every meal is an exercise of self-denial, and she humbles her body every time that she is forced to feed it." Her only study was the Bible, with some legends and books of piety, which she read with implicit faith. She prayed five times each day and, as singing, according to *The Serious Call*, is an indispensable part of devotion, she rehearsed the psalms and hymns of thanksgiving which she now, perhaps, may chant in a full chorus of saints and angels. Such is the portrait and such was the life of that holy virgin who by gods was Miranda called and by men Miss Hester Gibbon. Of the pains and pleasures of a spiritual life I am ill qualified to speak; yet I am inclined to believe that her lot, even on earth, has not been unhappy. Her penance was voluntary and, in her own eyes, meritorious. Her time was filled by regular occupations, and, instead of the insignificance of an old maid, she was surrounded by dependents, poor and abject as they were, who implored her bounty and imbibed her lessons. In the course of these *Memoirs* I shall not forget to introduce my personal acquaintance with the saint.

At an advanced age, about the year 1761, Mr. Law died in the house — I may not say in the arms — of his beloved Miranda. In our family he has left the reputation of a worthy and pious man, who believed all that he professed and practiced all that he enjoined. The character of a non-juror, which he maintained to the last, is a sufficient evidence of his principles in church and state, and the sacrifice of interest to conscience will be always respectable. His theological writings, which our domestic connection has tempted me to peruse, preserve an imperfect sort of life, and I can pronounce with more confidence and knowledge on the merits of the author. His last compositions are darkly tinctured with the incomprehensible visions of Jacob Behmen, and his discourse on the absolute unlawfulness of stage entertainments is sometimes quoted for a ridiculous intemperance of sentiment and language. "The actors and spectators must all be damned; the playhouse is the porch of hell, the place of the devil's abode, where he holds his filthy court of evil spirits; a play is the devil's triumph, a sacrifice performed to his glory, as much as in the heathen temples of Bacchus or Venus," etc. But these sallies of religious frenzy must not extinguish the praise which is due to Mr. William Law as a wit and a scholar. His argument on topics of less absurdity is specious and acute, his manner is lively, his style forcible and clear, and had not his vigorous mind been clouded by enthusiasm, he might be ranked with the most agreeable and ingenious writers of the times. While the Bangorian controversy was a fashionable theme he entered the lists on the subject of Christ's kingdom and the authority of the priesthood. Against the plain account of the sacrament of the Lord's Supper he resumed the combat with Bishop Hoadley, the object of Whig idolatry and Tory abhorrence; and at every weapon of attack and defense the non-juror, on the ground which is common to both, approves himself at least equal to the prelate. On the appearance of *The Fable of the Bees*, he drew his pen against the licentious doctrine that private vices are public benefits, and morality as well as religion must join in his applause. Mr. Law's master work, *The Serious Call*, is still read as a popular and powerful book of devotion. His precepts are rigid, but they are founded on the gospel; his satire is sharp, but it is drawn from the knowledge of human life, and many of his portraits are not unworthy of the pen of La Bruyère. If he finds a spark of piety in his reader's mind, he will soon kindle it to a flame; and a philosopher must allow that he exposes, with equal severity and truth, the strange contradiction between the faith and practice of the Christian world. Hell fire and eternal damnation are darted from every page of the book, and it is indeed somewhat whimsical that the fanatics who most vehemently inculcate the love of God should be those who despoil him of every amiable attribute.

[EARLY LIFE AND EDUCATION.]

I was born at Putney in Surrey, the twenty-seventh of April, OS., the eighth of May, NS., in the year one thousand seven hundred and thirty-seven, within a twelvemonth after my father's marriage with Judith Porten, his first wife. From my birth I have enjoyed the right of primogeniture; but I was succeeded by five brothers and one sister, all of whom were snatched away in their infancy. They died so young and I was myself so young at the time of their deaths that I could not then feel nor can I now estimate their loss, the importance of which could only have been ascertained by future contingencies. The shares of fortune to which younger children are reduced by our English laws would have been sufficient, however, to oppress my inheritance, and the compensation of their friendship must have depended on the uncertain event of character and conduct, on the affinity or opposition of our reciprocal sentiments. My five brothers, whose names may be found in the parish register of Putney, I shall not pretend to lament; but from my childhood to the present hour I have deeply and sincerely regretted my sister, whose life was somewhat prolonged, and whom I remember to have seen an amiable infant. The relation of a brother and a sister, especially if they do not marry, appears to me of a very singular nature. It is a familiar and tender friendship with a female much about our own age, an affection perhaps softened by the secret influence of sex, but pure from any mixture of sensual desire, — the sole species of Platonic love that can be indulged with truth and without danger.

About four months before the birth of their eldest son my parents were delivered from a state of servitude, and my father inherited a considerable estate, which was magnified in his own eyes by flattery and hope. The prospect of Spanish gold from our naval contract with the court of Madrid was suddenly overclouded about three years after my grandfather's decease. The public faith had been pledged for the security of the English merchants. Their effects were seized (in 1740) on the first hostilities between the two nations. After the return of peace (in 1749 and 1763), the contractors or their representatives demanded the restitution of their property with a large claim of damages and interest. But the Catholic kings absolved themselves from the engagements of their predecessors. The helpless strangers were referred by the ministers to the judges and from the judges to the ministers, and this antiquated debt has melted away in oblivion and despair. Such a stroke could not have been averted by any foresight or care, but the arts of industry were not devolved from the father to the son, and several undertakings which had been profitable in the hands of the merchant became barren or adverse in those of the gentleman. At the general election of 1741 Mr. Gibbon and Mr. Delmé stood an expensive and successful contest against Mr. Dummer and Mr. Henly, afterwards Lord Chancellor and Earl of Northington. The Whig candidates had a majority of the resident voters, but the corporation was firm in the Tory interest. A sudden creation of one hundred and seventy new freemen turned the scale, and a supply was readily obtained of respectable volunteers, who flocked from all parts of England to support the cause of their political friends. The new parliament opened with the victory of an opposition which was fortified by strong clamor and strange coalitions. From the event of the first divisions, Sir Robert Walpole perceived that he could no longer lead a majority in the House of Commons and prudently resigned, after a reign of one-and-twenty years, the scepter of the state (1742). But the fall of an unpopular minister was not succeeded, according to general expectation, by a millennium of happiness and virtue. Some courtiers lost their places; some patriots lost their characters. Lord Orford's offenses vanished with his power, and, after a short vibration, the Pelham government was fixed on the old basis of the Whig aristocracy. In the year 1745 the throne and the constitution were attacked by a rebellion which does not reflect much honor on the national spirit, since the English friends of the Pretender wanted courage to join his standard, and his enemies, — the bulk of the people, — allowed him to advance into the heart of the kingdom. Without daring, perhaps without desiring to aid the rebels, my father invariably adhered to the Tory opposition. In the most critical season he accepted, for the service of the party, the office of alderman in the city of London; but the duties were so repugnant to his inclination and habits that he resigned his gown at the end of a few months. The second parliament in which he sat was prematurely dissolved (1747), and, as he was unable or unwilling to maintain a second contest for Southampton, the life of the senator expired in that dissolution.

At home my father possessed the inestimable treasure of an amiable and affectionate wife, the constant object during a twelve years' marriage of his tenderness and esteem. My mother's portraits convey some idea of her beauty; the elegance of her manners has been attested by surviving friends, and my Aunt Porten could descant for hours on the talents and virtues of her amiable sister. A domestic life would have been the choice and the felicity of my mother, but she vainly attempted to check with a silken rein the passions of an independent husband. The world was open before him, his spirit was lively, his appearance splendid, his aspect cheerful, his address polite; he gracefully moved in the highest circles of society, and I have heard him boast that he was the only member of opposition admitted into the old club at White's, where the first names of the country were often rejected. Yet such was the pleasing flexibility of his temper that he could accommodate himself with ease and almost with indifference to every class — to a meeting of lords or farmers, of citizens or fox hunters, and, without being admired as a wit, Mr. Gibbon was everywhere beloved as a companion and esteemed as a man. But in the pursuit of pleasure his happiness, alas, and his fortune were gradually injured. Economy was superseded by fashion; his income proved inadequate to his expense; his house at Putney, in the neighborhood of London, acquired the dangerous fame of hospitable entertainment. Against the more dangerous temptation of play he was not invulnerable, and large sums were silently precipitated into that bottomless pit. Few minds have sufficient resources to support the weight of idleness, and had he continued to walk in the path of mercantile industry my father might have been a happier, and his son would be a richer man.

Of these public and private scenes and of the first years of my own life I must be indebted, not to memory, but to information. Our fancy may create and describe a perfect Adam, born in the mature vigor of his corporeal and intellectual faculties.

> "As new waked from soundest sleep,
> Soft on the flowery herb I found me laid
> In balmy sweat, which with his beams the sun

Soon dried, and on the reeking moisture fed.
Straight toward heav'n my wondering eyes I turned
And gazed awhile the ample sky, till raised
By quick instinctive motion, up I sprung
As thitherward endeavoring, and upright
Stood on my feet; about me round I saw
Hill, dale, and shady woods, and sunny plains,
And liquid lapse of murmuring streams; by these,
Creatures that lived and moved and walked and flew,
Birds on the branches warbling: all things smiled;
With fragrance and with joy my heart o'erflowed.
Myself I then perused, and limb by limb
Surveyed, and sometimes went and sometimes ran
With supple joints, as lively vigor led;
But who I was, or where, or from what cause,
Knew not; to speak I tried and forthwith spake;
My tongue obeyed, and readily could name
Whate'er I saw."

It is thus that the poet has animated his statue. The theologian must infuse a miraculous gift of science and language, the philosopher might allow more time for the gradual exercise of his new senses, but all would agree that the consciousness and memory of Adam might proceed in a regular series from the moment of his birth. Far different is the origin and progress of human nature, and I may confidently apply to myself the common history of the whole species. Decency and ignorance cast a veil over the mystery of generations, but I may relate that after floating nine months in a liquid element I was painfully transported into the vital air. Of a new-born infant it cannot be predicated "he thinks, therefore he is"; it can only be affirmed "he suffers, therefore he feels." But in this imperfect state of existence I was still unconscious of myself and of the universe, my eyes were open without the power of vision, and, according to M. de Buffon, the rational soul, that secret and incomprehensible energy, did not manifest its presence till after the fortieth day. During the first year I was below the greatest part of the brute creation, and must inevitably have perished had I been abandoned to my own care. Three years at least had elapsed before I acquired our peculiar privileges,—the facility of erect motion and the intelligent use of articulate and discriminating sounds. Slow is the growth of the body; that of the mind is still slower. At the age of seven years I had not attained to one half of the strength and proportions of manhood, and could the mental powers be measured with [the] same accuracy, their deficiency would be found far more considerable. The exercise of the understanding combines the past with the present, but the youthful fibers are so tender, the cells are so minute, that the first impressions are obliterated by new images, and I strive without much success to recollect the persons and objects which might appear at the time most forcibly to affect me. The local scenery of my education is, however, before my eyes. My father's contest for Southampton, when I must have been between three and four years old, and my childish revenge in shouting after being whipped the names of his opponents, is the first event that I seem to remember. But even that belief may be elusive, and I may only repeat the hearsay of a riper season. In the entire period of ten or twelve years from our birth our pains and pleasures, our actions and designs are remotely connected with our present mode of existence; and, according to a just computation, we should begin to reckon our life from the age of puberty.

The death of a new-born child before that of its parents may seem an unnatural, but it is strictly a probable, event, since of any given number the greater part are extinguished before their ninth year, before they possess the faculties of the mind or body. Without accusing the profuse waste or imperfect workmanship of nature, I shall only observe that this unfavorable chance was multiplied against my infant existence. So feeble was my constitution, so precarious my life, that in the baptism of each of my brothers, my father's prudence successively repeated my Christian name of Edward, that in case of the departure of the eldest son this patronymic appellation might be still perpetuated in the family;

"Uno avulso non deficit alter."

To preserve and to rear so frail a being, the most tender assiduity was scarcely sufficient, and my mother's attention was somewhat diverted by her frequent pregnancies, by an exclusive passion for her husband and by the dissipation of the world, in which his taste and authority obliged her to mingle. But the maternal office was supplied by my aunt, Miss Catherine Porten, at whose name I feel a tear of gratitude trickling down my cheek. A life of celibacy transferred her vacant affection to her sister's first child. My weakness excited her pity; her attachment was fortified by labor and success, and if there are any, as I trust there are some, who rejoice that I live, to that dear and excellent woman they must hold themselves indebted. Many anxious and solitary days did she consume in the patient trial of every mode of relief and amusement. Many wakeful nights did she sit by my bedside in trembling expectation that each hour would be my last. My poor aunt has often told me with tears in her eyes how I was nearly starved by a nurse that had lost her milk, how long she herself was apprehensive lest my crazy frame, which is now of common shape, should remain forever crooked and deformed. From one dangerous malady, the smallpox, I was indeed rescued by the practice of inoculation which had been recently introduced into England and was still opposed by medical, religious, and even political prejudice. But it is only against the smallpox that a preservative has been found. I was successively afflicted by lethargies and fevers, by opposite tendencies to a consumptive and a dropsical habit, by a contraction of my nerves, a fistula in my eye, and the bite of a dog most vehemently suspected of madness; and in the list of my sufferings from my birth to the age of puberty few physical ills would be omitted. From Sir Hans Sloane and Dr. Mead to Ward and the Chevalier Taylor, every practitioner was called to my aid. The fees of doctors were swelled by the bills of apothecaries and surgeons. There was a time when I swallowed more physic than food, and my body is still marked with the indelible scars of lances, issues, and caustics. Of the various and frequent disorders of my childhood my own recollection is dark, nor do I wish to expatiate on so disgusting a topic. I will not follow the vain example of Cardinal Querini, who has filled half a volume of his memoirs with medical consultations on his particular case, nor shall I imitate the naked frankness of Montaigne, who exposes all the symptoms of his malady and the operation of each dose of physic on his nerves and bowels. It may not, however, be useless to observe that in this early period the care of my mind was too frequently neglected for that of my health. Compassion always suggested an excuse for the indulgence of the master, or the idleness of the pupil, and the chain of my education was broken as often as I was recalled from the school of learning to the bed of sickness.

As soon as the use of speech had prepared my infant reason for the admission of knowledge, I was taught the arts of reading, writing, and vulgar arithmetic. So remote is the date, so vague is the memory of their origin in myself, that were not the error corrected by analogy I should be tempted to conceive them as innate. In the improved state of society in which I have the good fortune to exist, these attainments are so generally diffused that they no longer constitute the liberal distinctions of scholars and gentlemen. The operations of writing and reading must seem on an abstract view to require the labor of genius, — to transform articulate sounds into visible signs by the swift and almost spontaneous motion of the hand, to render visible signs into articulate sounds by the voluntary and rapid utterance of the voice. Yet experience has proved that these operations of such apparent difficulty, when they are taught to all, may be learned by all, and that the meanest capacity in the most tender age is not inadequate to the task. Between the sister arts there exists, however, a material difference; the one is connected with mental intelligence, the other with manual dexterity. The excellence of reading, if the vocal organ be not defective, the propriety of the cadence, the tones and the pauses, is always in just proportion to the knowledge, taste, and feelings of the reader. But an illiterate scribe may delineate a correct and elegant copy of penmanship, while the sense and style of the philosopher or poet are most awkwardly scrawled in such ill-formed and irregular characters that the authors themselves, after a short interval, will be incapable of deciphering them. My own writing is of a middle cast, legible rather than fair, but I may observe that age and long practice which are often productive of negligence have rather improved than corrupted my hand. The science of numbers, the third element of our primitive education, may be esteemed the best scale to measure the degrees of the human understanding. A child or a peasant performs with ease and assurance the four first rules of arithmetic; the profound mysteries of algebra are reserved for the disciples of Newton and Bernoulli. In my childhood I was praised for the readiness with which I could multiply and divide by memory alone two sums of several figures. Such praise encouraged my growing talent, and had I persevered in this line of application I might have acquired some fame in mathematical studies.

After this previous institution at home or at a day school at Putney, I was delivered at the age of seven (April, 1744) into the hands of Mr. John Kirkby, who exercised about eighteen months the office of my domestic tutor. His own words, which I shall here transcribe, inspire in his favor a sentiment of pity and esteem. "During my abode in my native county of Cumberland in quality of an indigent curate, I used now and then in a summer when the pleasantness of the season invited, to take a solitary walk to the sea-shore which lies about two miles from the town where I lived. Here I would amuse myself, one while in viewing at large the agreeable prospect which surrounded me, and another while, confining my sight to nearer objects, in admiring the vast variety of beautiful shells thrown upon the beach, some of the choicest of which I always picked up to divert my little ones upon my return. One time among the rest, taking such a journey in my head, I sat down upon the declivity of the beach with my face to the sea, which was now come up within a few yards of my feet; when immediately the sad thoughts of the wretched condition of my family, and the unsuccessfulness of all endeavors to amend it, came crowding into my mind, which drove me into a deep melancholy and ever and anon forced tears from my eyes." Distress at last forced him to leave the country. His learning and virtue introduced him to my father, and at Putney he might have found at least a temporary shelter had not an act of indiscretion again driven him into the world. One day reading prayers in the parish church, he most unluckily forgot the name of King George. His patron, a loyal subject, dismissed him with some reluctance, and a decent reward, and how the poor man ended his days I have never [been] able to learn. Mr. John Kirkby is the author of two small volumes, the *Life of Automathes* (London, 1745), and an *English and Latin Grammar* (London, 1746), which, as a testimony of gratitude, he dedicated (November 5th, 1745) to my father. The books are before me; from them the pupil may judge the preceptor, and upon the whole the judgment will not be unfavorable. The grammar is executed with accuracy and skill, and I know not whether any better existed at the time in our language; but the *Life of Automathes* aspires to the honors of a philosophical fiction. It is the story of a youth, the son of a shipwrecked exile, who lives alone on a desert island from infancy to the age of manhood. A hind is his nurse; he inherits a cottage, with many useful and curious instruments; some ideas remain of the education of his two first years; some arts are borrowed from the beavers of a neighboring lake; some truths are revealed in supernatural visions. With these helps and his own industry, Automathes becomes a self-taught though speechless philosopher who had investigated with success his own mind, the natural world, the abstract sciences, and the great principles of morality and religion. The author is not entitled to the merit of invention, since he has blended the English story of Robinson Crusoe with the Arabian romance of Hai Ebn Yokhdan which he might read in the Latin version of Pocock.

In the *Automathes* I cannot praise either the depth of thought or elegance of style; but the book is not devoid of entertainment or instruction, and among several interesting passages I would select the discovery of fire, which produces by accidental mischief the discovery of conscience. A man who had thought so much on the subjects of language and education was surely no ordinary preceptor. My childish years and his hasty departure prevented me from enjoying the full benefit of his lessons, but they enlarged my knowledge of arithmetic, and left a clear impression of the English and Latin rudiments.

In my ninth year (January, 1746), in a lucid interval of comparative health, my father adopted the convenient and customary mode of English education, and I was sent to Kingston-upon-Thames, to a school of about seventy boys which was kept by Dr. Wooddeson and his assistants. Every time I have since passed over Putney Common, I have always noticed the spot where my mother as we drove along in the coach admonished me that I was now going into the world and must learn to think and act for myself. The expression may appear ludicrous, yet there is not in the course of life a more remarkable change than the removal of a child from the luxury and freedom of a wealthy house, to the frugal diet and strict subordination of a school; from the tenderness of parents and the obsequiousness of servants, to the rude familiarity of his equals, the insolent tyranny of his seniors, and the rod, perhaps, of a cruel and capricious pedagogue. Such hardships may steel the mind and body against the injuries of fortune, but my timid reserve was astonished by the crowd and tumult of the school. The want of strength and activity disqualified me for the sports of the play-field; nor have I forgot how often in the year forty-six I was reviled and buffeted for the sins of my Tory ancestors. By the common methods of discipline, at the expense of many tears and some blood.

I purchased the knowledge of the Latin syntax; and not long since I was possessed of the dirty volumes of Phædrus and Cornelius Nepos which I painfully construed and darkly understood. The choice of these authors is not injudicious. The *Lives* of Cornelius Nepos, the friend of Atticus and Cicero, are composed in the style of the purest age. His simplicity is elegant, his brevity copious; he exhibits a series of men and manners; and with such illustrations as every pedant is not indeed qualified to give, this classic biographer may initiate a young student in the history of Greece and Rome. The use of fables or apologues has been approved in every age from ancient India to modern Europe. They convey in familiar images the truths of morality and prudence, and the most childish understanding — I advert to the scruples of Rousseau — will not suppose either that beasts do speak, or that men may lie. A fable represents the genuine characters of animals, and a skillful master might extract from Pliny and Buffon some pleasing lessons of natural history, a science well adapted to the taste and capacity of children. The Latinity of Phædrus is not exempt from an alloy of the silver age, but his manner is concise, terse, and sententious. The Thracian slave discreetly breathes the spirit of a freeman, and when the text is sound, the style is perspicuous. But his fables, after a long oblivion, were first published by Peter Pithou from a corrupt manuscript. The labors of fifty editors confess the defects of the copy, as well as the value of the original, and a schoolboy may have been whipped for misapprehending a passage which Bentley could not restore and which Burmann could not explain.

My studies were too frequently interrupted by sickness, and after a real or nominal residence at Kingston School of near two years, I was finally recalled (December, 1747) by my mother's death, which was occasioned in her thirty-eighth year by the consequences of her last labor. As I had seldom enjoyed the smiles of maternal tenderness, she was rather the object of my respect than of my love. Some natural tears were soon wiped. I was too young to feel the importance of my loss, and the image of her person and conversation is faintly imprinted in my memory. The affectionate heart of my aunt, Catherine Porten, bewailed a sister and a friend, but my poor father was inconsolable and the transport of grief seemed to threaten his life or his reason. I can never forget the scene of our first interview some weeks after the fatal event; the awful silence, the room hung with black, the mid-day tapers, his sighs and tears; his praises of my mother, a saint in heaven; his solemn adjuration that I would cherish her memory and imitate her virtues, and the fervor with which he kissed and blessed me as the sole surviving pledge of their loves. The storm of passion insensibly subsided into calmer melancholy. But he persevered in the use of mourning much beyond the term which has been fixed by decency and custom. Three years after my mother's death his situation is described by Mr. Mallet, who then resided at Putney, and with whose family my father had formed a very intimate connection. In a pleasing little composition entitled the *Wedding Day*, Cupid and Hymen undertake the office of inviting some chosen friends to celebrate the ninth anniversary (October 2, 1750) of the poet's nuptials. Cupid flies eastward to London.

> "His brother too with sober cheer,
> For the same end did westward steer;
> But first a pensive love forlorn,
> Who three long weeping years has borne
> His torch reversed, and all around,
> Where once it flamed with cypress bound,

Sent off to call a neighboring friend,
On whom the mournful train attend;
And bid him this one day at least,
For such a pair, at such a feast,
Strip off the sable vest and wear
His once gay look and happier air."

At a convivial meeting of his friends, Mr. Gibbon might affect or enjoy a gleam of cheerfulness; but his plan of happiness was forever destroyed, and after the loss of his companion he was left alone in a world of which the business and pleasure were to him irksome or insipid. After some unsuccessful trials he renounced the tumult of London and the hospitality of Putney, and buried himself in the rural or rather rustic solitude of Buriton from which during several years he seldom emerged. It must not, however, be dissembled that the sorrowful widower was urged to this resolution by the growing perplexity of his affairs. His fortune was impaired, his debts had multiplied, and as long as his son was a minor he could not disengage his estate from the legal fetters of an entail. Had my mother lived he must soon have retired into the country, with more comfort indeed but without the credit of a pious and disinterested motive. Shall I presume to add that a secret inconstancy, which always adhered to his disposition, might impel him at once to sink the man of fashion in the character and occupations of a Hampshire farmer?

As far back as I can remember the house, near Putney bridge and churchyard, of my maternal grandfather appears in the light of my proper and native home. It was there that I was allowed to spend the greatest part of my time in sickness or in health, during my school vacations and my parents' residence in London, and finally after my mother's death. Three months after that event, in the spring of 1748, the commercial ruin of her father Mr. James Porten was accomplished and declared. He suddenly absconded, but as his effects were not sold nor the house evacuated till the Christmas following, I enjoyed during the whole year the society of my aunt without much consciousness of her impending fate. I feel a melancholy pleasure in commemorating my obligations to that excellent woman Miss Catherine Porten, the true mother of my mind as well as of my health. Her natural good sense was improved by the perusal of the best books in the English language, and if her reason was sometimes clouded by prejudice, her sentiments were never disguised by hypocrisy or affectation. Her indulgent tenderness, the frankness of her temper, and my innate rising curiosity soon removed all distance between us. Like friends of an equal age we freely conversed on every topic, familiar or abstruse, and it was her delight and reward to observe the first shoots of my young ideas. Pain and languor were often soothed by the voice of instruction and amusement, and to her kind lessons I ascribe my early and invincible love of reading, which I would not exchange for the treasures of India. I should perhaps be astonished, were it possible to ascertain the date at which a favorite tale was engraved by frequent repetition, in my memory — the cavern of the winds; the palace of felicity; and the fatal moment, at the end of three months or centuries, when Prince Adolphus is overtaken by Time, who had worn out so many pair of wings in the pursuit. Before I left Kingston School I was well acquainted with Pope's *Homer* and the *Arabian Nights Entertainments*, two books which will always please by the moving picture of human manners and specious miracles. The verses of Pope accustomed my ear to the sound of poetic harmony; in the death of Hector and the shipwreck of Ulysses, I tasted the new emotions of terror and pity, and seriously disputed with my aunt on the vices and virtues of the heroes of the Trojan war. From Pope's *Homer* to Dryden's *Virgil* was an easy transition; but I know not how, from some fault in the author, the translator, or the reader, the pious Æneas did not so forcibly seize on my imagination, and I derived more pleasure from Ovid's *Metamorphoses*, especially in the fall of Phaëton and the speeches of Ajax and Ulysses. My grandfather's flight unlocked the door of a tolerable library, and I turned over many English pages of poetry and romance, of history and travels. Where a title attracted my eye, without fear or awe I snatched the volume from the shelf, and Miss Porten, who indulged herself in moral and religious speculations, was more prone to encourage than to check a curiosity above the strength of a boy. This year (1748), the twelfth of my age, I shall note as the most propitious to the growth of my intellectual stature.

After such satisfaction as could be given to his creditors, the relics of my grandfather's fortune afforded a bare annuity for his own maintenance, and his daughter my worthy aunt, who had already passed her fortieth year, was left naked and destitute. Her not more wealthy relations were not absolutely without bowels, but her noble spirit scorned a life of obligation and dependence and after revolving several schemes, she preferred the humble industry of keeping a boarding-house for Westminster School where she laboriously earned a competence for her old age. This singular opportunity of blending the advantages of private and public education decided my father. After the Christmas holidays, in January 1749, I accompanied Miss Porten to her new house in College street and was immediately entered in the school, of which Dr. John Nicoll was at [that] time head-master. At first I was alone; but my aunt's resolution was praised, her character was esteemed, her friends were numerous and active. In the course of some years she became the mother of forty or fifty boys, for the most part of family and fortune, and as her primitive habitation was too narrow, she built and occupied a spacious mansion in Dean's Yard. I shall always be ready to join in the common opinion that our public schools, which have produced so many eminent characters, are the best adapted to the genius and constitution of the English people. A boy of spirit may acquire a previous and practical experience of the world, and his playfellows may be the future friends of his heart or his interest. In a free intercourse with his equals, the habits of truth, fortitude, and prudence will insensibly be matured. Birth and riches are measured by the standard of personal merit, and the mimic scene of a rebellion has displayed in their true colors the ministers and patriots of the rising generation. Our seminaries of learning do not exactly correspond with the precept of a Spartan king, "that the child should be instructed in the arts which will be useful to the man," since a finished scholar may emerge from the head of Westminster or Eton, in total ignorance of the business and conversation of English gentlemen in the latter end of the eighteenth century. But these schools may assume the merit of teaching all that they pretend to teach, the Latin and Greek languages. They deposit in the hands of a disciple the keys of two valuable chests, nor can he complain, if they are afterwards lost or neglected by his own fault. The necessity of leading in equal ranks so many unequal powers of capacity and application, will prolong to eight or ten years the juvenile studies which might be dispatched in half that time by the skillful master of a single pupil. Yet even the repetition of exercise and discipline contributes to fix in a vacant mind the verbal science of grammar and prosody, and the private or voluntary student who possesses the sense and spirit of the classics, may offend by a false quantity the scrupulous ear of a well-flogged critic. For myself, I must be content with a very small share of the civil and literary fruits of a public school. In the space of two years (1749, 1750), interrupted by danger and debility, I painfully climbed into the third form, and my riper age was left to acquire the beauties of the Latin and the rudiments of the Greek tongue. Instead of audaciously mingling in the sports, the quarrels, and the connections of our little world, I was still cherished at home under the maternal wing of my aunt, and my removal from Westminster long preceded the approach of manhood. In our domestic society I formed, however, an intimate acquaintance with a young nobleman of my own age, and vainly flattered myself that our sentiments would prove as lasting as they seemed to be mutual. On my return from abroad, his coldness repelled such faint advances as my pride allowed me to make, and in our different walks of life we gradually became strangers to each other. Yet his private character, for Lord H[untingtower] has never affected a public name, leaves me no room to accuse the propriety and merit of my early choice.

The violence and variety of my complaints, which had excused my frequent absence from Westminster School, at length engaged Miss Porten, with the advice of physicians, to conduct me to Bath. At the end of the Michaelmas vacation (1750) she quitted me with reluctance, and I remained several months under the care of a trusty maid-servant. A strange nervous affection, which alternately contracted my legs and produced without any visible symptoms the most excruciating pain, was ineffectually opposed by the various methods of bathing and pumping. From Bath I was transported to Winchester, to the house of a physician, and after the failure of his medical skill we had again recourse to the virtues of the Bath waters. During the intervals of these fits, I moved with my father to Buriton and Putney, and a short unsuccessful trial was attempted to renew my attendance at Westminster School. But my infirmities could not be reconciled with the hours and discipline of a public seminary, and instead of a domestic tutor, who might have watched the favorable moments and gently advanced the progress of my learning, my father was too easily content with such occasional teachers as the different places of my residence could supply. I was never forced, and seldom was I persuaded, to admit these lessons; yet I read with a clergyman at Bath some odes of Horace and several episodes of Virgil, which gave me an imperfect and transient enjoyment of the Latin poets. It might now be apprehended that I should continue for life an illiterate cripple, but as I approached my sixteenth year nature displayed in my favor her mysterious energies. My constitution was fortified and fixed, and my disorders, instead of growing with my growth and strengthening with my strength, most wonderfully vanished. I have never possessed or abused the insolence of health, but since that time few persons have been more exempt from real or imaginary ills, and till I am admonished by the gout the reader shall no more be troubled with the history of any bodily complaints. My unexpected recovery again encouraged the hope of my education, and I was placed at Esher in Surrey, in the house of the Reverend Mr. Philip Francis, in a pleasant spot which promised to unite the various benefits of air, exercise, and study (January, 1752). Mr. Francis was recommended, I believe by the Mallets, as a scholar and a wit. His two tragedies have been coldly received, but his version of Demosthenes, which I have not seen, supposes some knowledge of Greek literature, and he had executed with success and applause the arduous task of a complete translation of Horace in English verse. Besides a young gentleman whose name I do not remember, our family consisted only of myself and his son, who has since been conspicuous in the supreme Council of India, from whence he is returned to England with an ample fortune. It was stipulated that his father should always confine himself to a small number and, with so able a preceptor in this private academy, the time which I had lost might have been speedily retrieved. But the experience of a few weeks was sufficient to discover that Mr. Francis's spirit was too lively for his profession, and while he indulged himself in the pleasures of London his pupils were left idle at Esher, in the custody of a Dutch usher of low manners and contemptible learning. From such careless or unworthy hands I was indignantly rescued, but my father's perplexity, rather than his prudence, was urged to embrace a singular and desperate measure. Without preparation or delay he carried me to Oxford, and I was matriculated in the university as a gentleman commoner of Magdalen College, before I accomplished the fifteenth year of my age (April 3, 1752).

The curiosity which had been implanted in my infant mind was still alive and active, but my reason was not sufficiently informed to understand the value, or to lament the loss, of three precious years from my entrance at Westminster to my admission at Oxford. Instead of repining at my long and frequent confinement to the chamber or the couch, I secretly rejoiced in those infirmities which delivered me from the exercises of the school and the society of my equals. As often as I was tolerably exempt from danger and pain, reading, free desultory reading, was the employment and comfort of my solitary hours. At Westminster my aunt sought only to amuse and indulge me; in my stations at Bath and Winchester, at Buriton and Putney, a false compassion respected my sufferings, and I was allowed without control or advice to gratify the wanderings of an unripe taste. My indiscriminate appetite subsided by degrees in the historic line, and since philosophy has exploded all innate ideas and natural propensities, I must ascribe this choice to the assiduous perusal of the *Universal History* as the octavo volumes successively appeared. This unequal work and a treatise of Hearne, the *Ductor Historicus*, referred and introduced me to the Greek and Roman historians, to as many at least as were accessible to an English reader. All that I could find were greedily devoured, from Littlebury's lame *Herodotus* and Spelman's valuable *Xenophon*, to the pompous folios of Gordon's *Tacitus* and a ragged *Procopius* of the beginning of the last century. The cheap acquisition of so much knowledge confirmed my dislike to the study of languages, and I argued with Miss Porten, that were I master of Greek and Latin, I must interpret to myself in English the thoughts of the original, and that such extemporary versions must be inferior to the elaborate translations of professed scholars — a silly sophism which could not easily be confuted by a person ignorant of any other language than her own. From the ancient I leaped to the modern world. Many crude lumps of Speed, Rapin, Mézeray, Davila, Machiavel, Father Paul, Bower, etc., passed through me like so many novels, and I swallowed with the same voracious appetite the descriptions of India and China, of Mexico and Peru. Our family collection was decently furnished. The circulating libraries of London and Bath afforded a rich treasure. I borrowed many books and some I contrived to purchase from my scanty allowance. My father's friends who visited the boy were astonished at finding him surrounded with a heap of folios of whose titles they were ignorant and on whose contents he could pertinently discourse.

My first introduction to the historic scenes which have since engaged so many years of my life, must be ascribed to an accident. In the summer of 1751, I accompanied my father on a visit to Mr. Hoare's in Wiltshire. But I was less delighted with the beauties of Stourhead, than with discovering in the library a common book, the continuation of Echard's *Roman History*, which is indeed executed with more skill and taste than the previous work. To me the reigns of the successors of Constantine were absolutely new, and I was immersed in the passage of the Goths over the Danube, when the summons of the dinner-bell reluctantly dragged me from my intellectual feast. This transient glance served rather to irritate than to appease my curiosity, and no sooner was I returned to Bath than I procured the second and third volumes of Howell's *History of the World*, which exhibit the Byzantine period on a larger scale. Mahomet and his Saracens soon fixed my attention, and some instinct of criticism directed me to the genuine sources. Simon Ockley, an original in every sense, first opened my eyes, and I was led from one book to another till I had ranged round the circle of oriental history. Before I was sixteen, I had exhausted all that could be learned in English of the Arabs and Persians, the Tartars and Turks, and the same ardor urged me to guess at the French of d'Herbelot, and to construe the barbarous Latin of Pocock's *Abulfaragius*. Such vague and multifarious reading could not teach me to think, to write, or to act, and the only principle that darted a ray of light into the indigested chaos, was an early and rational application to the order of time and place. The maps of Cellarius and Wells imprinted in my mind the picture of ancient geography; from Strauchius I imbibed the elements of chronology; the tables of Helvicus and Anderson, the annals of Usher and Prideaux, distinguished the connection of events and I engraved the multitude of names and dates in a clear and indelible series. But in the discussion of the first ages I overleaped the bounds of modesty and use. In my childish balance I presumed to weigh the systems of Scaliger and Petavius, of Marsham and Newton, which I could seldom study in the originals; the dynasties of Assyria and Egypt were my top and cricket ball, and my sleep has been disturbed by the difficulty of reconciling the Septuagint with the Hebrew computation. I arrived at Oxford with a stock of erudition that might have puzzled a doctor, and a degree of ignorance of which a schoolboy would have been ashamed.

At the conclusion of this first period of my life, I am tempted to enter a protest against the trite and lavish praise of the happiness of our boyish years, which is echoed with so much affectation in the world. That happiness I have never known, that time I have never regretted; and were my poor aunt still alive, she would bear testimony to the early and constant uniformity of my sentiments. It will indeed be replied, that I am not a competent judge; that pleasure is incompatible with pain; that joy is excluded from sickness, and that the felicity of a schoolboy consists in the perpetual motion of thoughtless and playful agility, in which I was never qualified to excel. My name, it is most true, could never be enrolled among the sprightly race, the idle progeny of Eton or Westminster, who delight to cleave the water with pliant arm, to urge the flying ball, and to chase the speed of the rolling circle. But I would ask the warmest and most active hero of the play-field whether he can seriously compare his childish with his manly enjoyments; whether he does not feel, as the most precious attribute of his existence, the vigorous maturity of sensual and spiritual powers which nature has reserved for the age of puberty. A state of happiness arising only from the want of foresight and reflection shall never provoke my envy. Such degenerate taste would tend to sink us in the scale of beings from a man to a child, a dog, and an oyster, till we had reached the confines of brute matter which can not suffer because it can not feel. The poet may gaily describe the short hours of recreation, but he forgets the daily tedious labors of the school, which is approached each morning with anxious and reluctant steps. Degrees of misery are proportioned to the mind rather than to the object — *parva leves capiunt animos* — and few men in the trials of life have experienced a more painful sensation than the poor schoolboy with an imperfect task who trembles on the eve of the black Monday. A school is the cavern of fear and sorrow. The mobility of the captive youths is chained to a book and a desk. An inflexible master commands their attention which every moment is impatient to escape. They labor, like the soldiers of Persia, under the scourge, and their education is nearly finished before they can apprehend the sense or utility of the harsh lessons which they are forced to repeat. Such blind and absolute dependence may be necessary, but can never be delightful. Freedom is the first wish of our heart, freedom is the first blessing of our nature, and unless we bind ourselves with the voluntary chains of interest or passion, we advance in freedom as we advance in years.

[LIFE AT OXFORD.]

A traveler who visits Oxford or Cambridge is surprised and edified by the apparent order and tranquillity that prevail in the seats of the English muses. In the most celebrated universities of Holland, Germany, and Italy, the students, who swarm from different countries, are loosely dispersed in private lodgings at the houses of the burghers. They dress according to their fancy and fortune, and in the intemperate quarrels of youth and wine their swords, though less frequently than of old, are sometimes stained with each other's blood. The use of arms is banished from our English universities; the uniform habit of the academics, the square cap and black gown, is adapted to the civil and even clerical profession, and from the doctor in divinity to the undergraduate, the degrees of learning and age are externally distinguished. Instead of being scattered in a town, the students of Oxford and Cambridge are united in colleges; their maintenance is provided at their own expense, or that of the founders, and the stated hours of the hall and chapel represent the discipline of a regular and, as it were, a religious community. The eyes of the traveler are attracted by the size or beauty of the public edifices, and the principal colleges appear to be so many palaces which a liberal nation has erected and endowed for the habitation of science. My own introduction to the University of Oxford forms a new era in my life, and at the distance of forty years I still remember my first emotions of surprise and satisfaction. In my fifteenth year I felt myself suddenly raised from a boy to a man. The persons, whom I respected as my superiors in age and academical rank, entertained me with every mark of attention and civility, and my vanity was flattered by the velvet cap and silk gown which discriminate a gentleman commoner from a plebeian student. A decent allowance, more money than a schoolboy had ever seen, was at my own disposal, and I might command among the tradesmen of Oxford an indefinite and dangerous latitude of credit. A key was delivered into my hands, which gave me the free use of a numerous and learned library; my apartment consisted of three elegant and well-furnished rooms in the new building, a stately pile, of Magdalen College, and the adjacent walks, had they been frequented by Plato's disciples, might have been compared to the Attic shade on the banks of the Ilissus. Such was the fair prospect of my entrance (April 3, 1752) into the University of Oxford.

A venerable prelate, whose taste and erudition must reflect honor on the society in which they were formed, has drawn a very interesting picture of his academical life. "I was educated," says Bishop Lowth, "in the University of Oxford. I enjoyed all the advantages, both public and private, which that famous seat of learning so largely affords. I spent many years in that illustrious society, in a well-regulated course of useful discipline and studies, and in the agreeable and improving commerce of gentlemen and of scholars; in a society where emulation without envy, ambition without jealousy, contention without animosity, incited industry and awakened genius;

where a liberal pursuit of knowledge, and a generous freedom of thought, was raised, encouraged, and pushed forward by example, by commendation, and by authority. I breathed the same atmosphere that the Hookers, the Chillingworths, and the Lockes had breathed before; whose benevolence and humanity were as extensive as their vast genius and comprehensive knowledge; who always treated their adversaries with civility and respect; who made candor, moderation, and liberal judgment as much the rule and law as the subject of their discourses. And do you reproach me with my education in this place, and with my relation to this most respectable body which I shall always esteem my greatest advantage and my highest honor?" I transcribe with pleasure this eloquent passage, without examining what benefits or what rewards were derived by Hooker, or Chillingworth, or Locke, from their academical institution; without inquiring, whether in this angry controversy the spirit of Lowth himself is purified from the intolerant zeal which Warburton had ascribed to the genius of the place. The expression of gratitude is a virtue and a pleasure. A liberal mind will delight to cherish and celebrate the memory of its parents, and the teachers of science are the parents of the mind. I applaud the filial piety which it is impossible for me to imitate, since I must not confess an imaginary debt, to assume the merit of a just or generous retribution. To the University of Oxford I acknowledge no obligation, and she will as cheerfully renounce me for a son, as I am willing to disclaim her for a mother. I spent fourteen months at Magdalen College; they proved the fourteen months the most idle and unprofitable of my whole life. The reader will pronounce between the school and the scholar, but I cannot affect to believe that nature had disqualified me for all literary pursuits. The specious and ready excuse of my tender age, imperfect preparation, and hasty departure, may doubtless be alleged, nor do I wish to defraud such excuses of their proper weight. Yet in my sixteenth year I was not devoid of capacity or application. Even my childish reading had displayed an early though blind propensity for books, and the shallow flood might have been taught to flow in a deep channel and a clear stream. In the discipline of a well-constituted academy, under the guidance of skillful and vigilant professors, I should gradually have risen from translations to originals, from the Latin to the Greek classics, from dead languages to living science. My hours would have been occupied by useful and agreeable studies, the wanderings of fancy would have been restrained, and I should have escaped the temptations of idleness which finally precipitated my departure from Oxford.

Perhaps in a separate annotation I may coolly examine the fabulous and real antiquities of our sister universities, a question which has kindled such fierce and foolish disputes among their fanatic sons. In the meanwhile it will be acknowledged that these venerable bodies are sufficiently old to partake of all the prejudices and infirmities of age. The schools of Oxford and Cambridge were founded in a dark age of false and barbarous science, and they are still tainted with the vices of their origin. Their primitive discipline was adapted to the education of priests and monks, and the government still remains in the hands of the clergy, an order of men whose manners are remote from the present world, and whose eyes are dazzled by the light of philosophy. The legal incorporation of these societies by the charters of popes and kings had given them a monopoly of the public instruction, and the spirit of monopolists is narrow, lazy, and oppressive. Their work is more costly and less productive than that of independent artists, and the new improvements so eagerly grasped by the competition of freedom, are admitted with slow and sullen reluctance in those proud corporations, above the fear of a rival and below the confession of an error. We may scarcely hope that any reformation will be a voluntary act, and so deeply are they rooted in law and prejudice, that even the omnipotence of parliament would shrink from an inquiry into the state and abuses of the two universities.

The use of academical degrees, as old as the thirteenth century, is visibly borrowed from the mechanic corporations, in which an apprentice, after serving his time, obtains a testimonial of his skill and a license to practice his trade and mystery. It is not my design to depreciate those honors, which could never gratify or disappoint my ambition, and I should applaud the institution if the degrees of bachelor or licentiate were bestowed as the reward of manly and successful study, if the name and rank of doctor or master were strictly reserved for the professors of science who have approved their title to the public esteem. The mysterious faculty of theology must not be scanned by a profane eye. The cloak of reason sits awkwardly on our fashionable divines, and in the ecclesiastical studies of the fathers and councils their modesty will yield to the Catholic universities. Our English civilians and canonists have never been famous. Their real business is confined to a small circle, and the double jurisprudence of Rome is overwhelmed by the enormous profession of common lawyers who, in the pursuit of honors and riches, disdain the mock majesty of our budge doctors. We are justly proud of the skill and learning of our physicians. Their skill is acquired in the practice of the hospitals. They seek their learning in London, in Scotland, or on the continent, and few patients would trust their pulse to a medical student if he had passed the fourteen years of his novitiate at Oxford or Cambridge, whose degrees, however, are exclusively admitted in the Royal College. The arts are supposed to include the liberal knowledge of philosophy and literature, but I am informed that some tattered shreds of the old logic and metaphysics compose the exercises for a bachelor's and master's degree, and that modern improvements, instead of introducing a more rational trial, have only served to relax the forms which are now the object of general contempt.

In all the universities of Europe except our own, the languages and sciences are distributed among a numerous list of effective professors. The students according to their taste, their calling, and their diligence, apply themselves to the proper masters, and in the annual repetition of public and private lectures, these masters are assiduously employed. Our curiosity may inquire what number of professors has been instituted at Oxford?—for I shall now confine myself to my own university. By whom are they appointed, and what may be the probable chances of merit or incapacity? How many are stationed to the three faculties, and how many are left for the liberal arts? What is the form, and what the substance of their lessons? But all these questions are silenced by one short and singular answer, "that in the University of Oxford, the greater part of the public professors have for these many years given up altogether even the pretense of teaching." Incredible as the fact may appear, I must rest my belief on the positive and impartial evidence of a philosopher who had himself resided at Oxford. Dr. Adam Smith assigns as the cause of their indolence, that instead of being paid by voluntary contributions, which would urge them to increase the number and to deserve the gratitude of their pupils, the Oxford professors are secure in the enjoyment of a fixed stipend, without the necessity of labor or the apprehension of control. It has indeed been observed, nor is the observation absurd, that except in experimental sciences, which demand a costly apparatus and a dexterous hand, the many valuable treatises that have been published on every subject of learning may now supersede the ancient mode of oral instruction. Were this principle true in its utmost latitude, I should only infer that the offices and salaries, which are become useless, ought without delay to be abolished. But there still remains a material difference between a book and a professor. The hour of the lecture enforces attendance; attention is fixed by the presence, the voice, and the occasional questions of the teacher; the most idle will carry something away, and the more diligent will compare the instructions which they have heard in the school, with the volumes which they peruse in their chamber. The advice of a skillful professor will adapt a course of reading to every mind and every situation. His learning will remove difficulties and solve objections, his authority will discover, admonish, and at last chastise the negligence of his disciples, and his vigilant inquiries will ascertain the steps of their literary progress. Whatsoever science he professes he may illustrate in a series of discourses, composed in the leisure of his closet, pronounced on public occasions, and finally delivered to the press. I observe with pleasure, that in the University of Oxford Dr. Lowth, with equal eloquence and erudition, has executed this task in his incomparable *Prælectiones* on the poetry of the Hebrews.

The college of St. Mary Magdalen (it is vulgarly pronounced Maudlin) was founded in the fifteenth century by a bishop of Winchester, and now consists of a president, forty fellows, and a number of inferior students. It is esteemed one of the largest and most wealthy of our academical corporations, which may be compared to the Benedictine abbeys of Catholic countries; and I have loosely heard that the estates belonging to Magdalen College, which are leased by those indulgent landlords at small quit-rents and occasional fines, might be raised in the hands of private avarice to an annual revenue of near thirty thousand pounds. Our colleges are supposed to be schools of science as well as of education, nor is it unreasonable to expect that a body of literary men, addicted to a life of celibacy, exempt from the care of their own subsistence, and amply provided with books, should devote their leisure to the prosecution of study, and that some effects of their studies should be manifested to the world. The shelves of their library groan under the weight of the Benedictine folios, of the editions of the Fathers, and the collections of the middle ages which have issued from the single abbey of St. Germain de Prés at Paris. A composition of genius must be the offspring of one mind; but such works of industry as may be divided among many hands and must be continued during many years are the peculiar province of a laborious community. If I inquire into the manufactures of the monks of Magdalen, if I extend the inquiry to the other colleges of Oxford and Cambridge, a silent blush or a scornful frown will be the only reply. The fellows or monks of my time were decent easy men, who supinely enjoyed the gifts of the founder. Their days were filled by a series of uniform employments — the chapel and the hall, the coffee-house and the common room — till they retired, weary and well satisfied, to a long slumber. From the toil of reading, or thinking, or writing, they had absolved their conscience, and the first shoots of learning and ingenuity withered on the ground, without yielding any fruit to the owners or the public. The only student was a young fellow (a future bishop) who was deeply immersed in the follies of the Hutchinsonian system. The only author was an half-starved chaplain — Ballard was his name — who begged subscriptions for some *Memoirs* concerning the learned ladies of Great Britain. As a gentleman commoner I was admitted to the society of the fellows, and fondly expected that some questions of literature would be the amusing and instructive topics of their discourse. Their conversation stagnated in a round of college business, Tory politics, personal stories, and private scandal; their dull and deep potations excused the brisk intemperance of youth, and their constitutional toasts were not expressive of the most lively loyalty for the House of Hanover. A general election was now approaching; the great Oxfordshire contest already blazed with all the malevolence of party zeal. Magdalen College was devoutly attached to the old interest, and the names of Wenman and Dashwood were more frequently pronounced than those of Cicero and Chrysostom. The example of the senior fellows could not inspire the undergraduates with a liberal spirit, a studious emulation, and I cannot describe, as I never knew, the discipline of the college. Some duties may possibly have been imposed on the poor scholars, whose ambition aspired to the peaceful honors of a fellowship (*ascribi quietis ordinibus . . . Deorum*); but no independent members were admitted below the rank of a gentleman commoner, and our velvet cap was the cap of liberty. A tradition prevailed that some of our predecessors had spoken Latin declamations in the hall, but of this ancient custom no vestige remained; the obvious methods of public exercises and examinations were totally unknown, and I have never heard that either the president or the society interfered in the private economy of the tutors and their pupils.

The silence of the Oxford professors, which deprives the youth of public instruction, is imperfectly supplied by the tutors, as they are styled, of the several colleges. Instead of confining themselves to a single science, which had satisfied the ambition of Burmann or Bernoulli, they teach, or promise to teach, either history or mathematics or ancient literature or moral philosophy; and as it is possible that they may be defective in all, it is highly probable that of some they will be ignorant. They are paid, indeed, by private contributions, but their appointment depends on the head of the house. Their diligence is voluntary and will consequently be languid, while the pupils themselves and their parents are not indulged in the liberty of choice or change. The first tutor into whose hands I was resigned appears to have been one of the best of the tribe. Dr. Waldegrave was a learned and pious man, of a mild disposition, strict morals, and abstemious life, who seldom mingled in the politics or the jollity of the college. But his knowledge of the world was confined to the university; his learning was of the last, rather than the present age; his temper was indolent; his faculties, which were not of the first rate, had been relaxed by the climate, and he was satisfied, like his fellows, with the slight and superficial discharge of an important trust. As soon as my tutor had sounded the insufficiency of his disciple in school-learning, he proposed that we should read every morning from ten to eleven the comedies of Terence. The sum of my improvement in the University of Oxford is confined to three or four Latin plays; and even the study of an elegant classic, which might have been illustrated by a comparison of ancient and modern theatres, was reduced to a dry and literal interpretation of the author's text. During the first weeks I constantly attended these lessons in my tutor's room; but as they appeared equally devoid of profit and pleasure, I was once tempted to try the experiment of a formal apology. The apology was accepted with a smile. I repeated the offense with less ceremony; the excuse was admitted with the same indulgence. The slightest motive of laziness or indisposition, the most trifling avocation at home or abroad, was allowed as a worthy impediment, nor did my tutor appear conscious of my absence or neglect. Had the hour of lecture been constantly filled, a single hour was a small portion of my academic leisure. No plan of study was recommended for my use; no exercises were prescribed for his inspection, and at the most precious season of youth, whole days and weeks were suffered to elapse without labor or amusement, without advice or account. I should have listened to the voice of reason and of my tutor; his mild behavior had gained my confidence. I preferred his society to that of the younger students, and in our evening walks to the top of Heddington hill, we freely conversed on a variety of subjects. Since the days of Pocock and Hyde, oriental learning has always been the pride of Oxford, and I once expressed an inclination to study Arabic. His prudence discouraged this childish fancy, but he neglected the fair occasion of directing the ardor of a curious mind. During my absence in the summer vacation, Dr. Waldegrave accepted a college living at Washington in Sussex, and on my return I no longer found him at Oxford. From that time I have lost sight of my first tutor; but at the end of thirty years (1781) he was still alive, and the practice of exercise and temperance had entitled him to an healthy old age.

The long recess between the Trinity and Michaelmas terms empties the colleges of Oxford, as well as the courts of Westminster. I spent, at my father's house at Buriton in Hampshire, the two months of August and September, which in the year 1752 were curtailed, to my great surprise, of eleven days by the alteration of the style. It is whimsical enough, that as soon as I left Magdalen College my taste for books began to revive; but it was the same blind and boyish taste for the pursuit of exotic history. Unprovided with original learning, unformed in the habits of thinking, unskilled in the arts of composition, I resolved — to write a book. The title of this first essay, *The Age of Sesostris*, was perhaps suggested by Voltaire's *Age of Louis XIV*, which was new and popular; but my sole object was to investigate the probable date of the life and reign of the conqueror of Asia. I was then enamored of Sir John Marsham's *Canon Chronicus*, an elaborate work of whose merits and defects I was not yet qualified to judge. According to his specious though narrow plan, I settled my hero about the time of Solomon, in the tenth century before the Christian era. It was therefore incumbent on me, unless I would adopt Sir Isaac Newton's shorter chronology, to remove a formidable objection, and my solution, for a youth of fifteen, is not devoid of ingenuity. In his version of the Sacred Books, Manetho the high priest has identified Sethosis, or Sesostris, with the elder brother of Danaus, who landed in Greece, according to the Parian Marble, fifteen hundred and ten years before Christ. But in my supposition the high priest is guilty of a voluntary error; flattery is the prolific parent of falsehood, and falsehood, I will now add, is not incompatible with the sacerdotal character. Manetho's *History of Egypt* is dedicated to Ptolemy Philadelphus, who derived a fabulous or illegitimate pedigree from the Macedonian kings of the race of Hercules. Danaus is the ancestor of Hercules; and after the failure of the elder branch, his descendants the Ptolemies are the sole representatives of the royal family, and may claim by inheritance the kingdom which they hold by conquest. Such were my juvenile discoveries; at a riper age I no longer presume to connect the Greek, the Jewish, and the Egyptian antiquities, which are lost in a distant cloud. Nor is this the only instance in which the belief and knowledge of the child are superseded by the more rational ignorance of the man. During my stay at Buriton, my infant labor was diligently prosecuted without much interruption from company or country diversions, and I already heard the music of public applause. The discovery of my own weakness was the first symptom of taste. On my return to Oxford, the *Age of Sesostris* was wisely relinquished; but the imperfect sheets remained twenty years at the bottom of a drawer, till in a general clearance of papers (November, 1772) they were committed to the flames.

After the departure of Dr. Waldegrave, I was transferred with the rest of his live stock to a senior fellow, whose literary and moral character did not command the respect of the college. Dr. Winchester well remembered that he had a salary to receive, and only forgot that he had a duty to perform. Instead of guiding the studies and watching over the behavior of his disciple, I was never summoned to attend even the ceremony of a lecture; and except one voluntary visit to his rooms, during the eight months of his titular office the tutor and pupil lived in the same college as strangers to each other. The want of experience, of advice, and of occupation, soon betrayed me into some improprieties of conduct, ill-chosen company, late hours, and inconsiderate expense. My growing debts might be secret; but my frequent absence was visible and scandalous, and a tour to Bath, a visit into Buckinghamshire, and four excursions to London in the same winter, were costly and dangerous frolics. They were indeed without a meaning, as without an excuse. The irksomeness of a cloistered life repeatedly tempted me to wander; but my chief pleasure was that of traveling, and I was too young and bashful to enjoy, like a manly Oxonian in town, the taverns and bagnios of Covent Garden. In all these excursions I eloped from Oxford, I returned to college; in a few days I eloped again, as if I had been an independent stranger in a hired lodging, without once hearing the voice of admonition, without once feeling the hand of control. Yet my time was lost, my expenses were multiplied, my behavior abroad was unknown. Folly as well as vice should have awakened the attention of my superiors, and my tender years would have justified a more than ordinary degree of restraint and discipline.

[CONVERSION TO ROMAN CATHOLICISM.]

It might at least be expected that an ecclesiastical school should inculcate the orthodox principles of religion, but our venerable mother had contrived to unite the opposite extremes of bigotry and indifference. An heretic, or unbeliever, was a monster in her eyes, but she was always, or often, or sometimes, remiss in the spiritual education of her own children. According to the statutes of the university every student, before he is matriculated, must subscribe his assent to the thirty-nine articles of the church of England, which are signed by more than read, and read by more than believe them. My insufficient age excused me, however, from the immediate performance of this legal ceremony; and the vice-chancellor directed me to return, so soon as I should have accomplished my fifteenth year, recommending me, in the meanwhile, to the instruction of my college. My college forgot to instruct; I forgot to return, and was myself forgotten by the first magistrate of the university. Without a single lecture, either public or private, either Christian or Protestant, without any academical subscription, without any Episcopal confirmation, I was left by the dim light of my catechism to grope my way to the chapel and communion table, where I was admitted without a question how far, or by what means, I might be qualified to receive the sacrament. Such almost incredible neglect was productive of the worst mischiefs. From my childhood I had been fond of religious disputation; my poor aunt has been often puzzled by my objections to the mysteries which she strove to believe, nor had the elastic spring been totally broken by the weight of the atmosphere of Oxford. The blind activity of idleness urged me to advance without armor into the dangerous mazes of controversy, and at the age of sixteen I bewildered myself in the errors of the church of Rome.

The progress of my conversion may tend to illustrate, at least, the history of my own mind. It was not long since Dr. Middleton's *Free Inquiry* had sounded an alarm in the theological world; much ink and much gall had been spilt in the defense of the primitive miracles, and the two dullest of their champions were crowned with academic honors by the University of Oxford. The name of Middleton was unpopular, and his proscription very naturally tempted me to peruse his writings, and those of his antagonists. His bold criticism, which approaches the precipice of infidelity, produced on my mind a singular effect, and had I persevered in the communion of Rome,

I should now apply to my own fortune the prediction of the Sibyl,

> "Via prima salutis,
> Quod minime reris, Graia, pandetur ab urbe."

The elegance of style and freedom of argument were repelled by a shield of prejudice. I still revered the characters, or rather the names of the saints and fathers whom Dr. Middleton exposes, nor could he destroy my implicit belief, that the gift of miraculous powers was continued in the church during the first four or five centuries of Christianity. But I was unable to resist the weight of historical evidence that, within the same period, most of the leading doctrines of popery were already introduced in theory and practice; nor was my conclusion absurd, that miracles are the test of truth, and that the church must be orthodox and pure which was so often approved by the visible interposition of the Deity. The marvelous tales which are so boldly attested by the Basils and Chrysostoms, the Austins and Jeromes, compelled me to embrace the superior merits of celibacy; the institution of the monastic life; the use of the sign of the cross, of holy oil, and even of images; the invocation of saints; the worship of relics; the rudiments of purgatory in prayers for the dead, and the tremendous mystery of the sacrifice of the body and blood of Christ, which insensibly swelled into the prodigy of transubstantiation. In these dispositions, and already more than half a convert, I formed an unlucky intimacy with a young gentleman of our college, whose name I shall spare. With a character less resolute Mr. —— had imbibed the same religious opinions, and some popish books, I know not through what channel, were conveyed into his possession. I read, I applauded, I believed; the English translations of two famous works of Bossuet, Bishop of Meaux, the

Exposition of the Catholic Doctrine and the *History of the Protestant Variations*, achieved my conversion, and I surely fell by a noble hand. I have since examined the originals with a more discerning eye, and shall not hesitate to pronounce that Bossuet is indeed a master of all the weapons of controversy. In the *Exposition*, a specious apology, the orator assumes with consummate art the tone of candor and simplicity; and the ten-horned monster is transformed, at his magic touch, into the milk-white hind who must be loved as soon as she is seen. In the *History*, a bold and well-aimed attack, he displays with an happy mixture of narrative and argument the faults and follies, the changes and contradictions of our first reformers; whose variations — as he dexterously contends — are the mark of heretical error, while the perpetual unity of the Catholic church is the sign and test of infallible truth. To my actual feelings it seems incredible that I could ever believe that I believed in transubstantiation. But my conqueror oppressed me with the sacramental words, *Hoc est corpus meum*, and dashed against each other the figurative half-meanings of the Protestant sects. Every objection was resolved into omnipotence, and after repeating at St. Mary's the Athanasian creed, I humbly acquiesced in the mystery of the real presence.

"To take up half on trust, and half to try,
Name it not faith, but bungling bigotry,
Both knave and fool, the merchant we may call,
To pay great sums, and to compound the small,
For who would break with Heaven, and would not break for all?"

No sooner had I settled my new religion than I resolved to profess myself a Catholic. Youth is sincere and impetuous, and a momentary glow of enthusiasm had raised me above all temporal considerations.

By the keen Protestants, who would gladly retaliate the example of persecution, a clamor is raised of the increase of popery; and they are always loud to declaim against the toleration of priests and Jesuits, who pervert so many of his majesty's subjects from their religion and allegiance. On the present occasion, the fall of one or more of her sons directed this clamor against the university, and it was confidently affirmed that popish missionaries were suffered, under various disguises, to introduce themselves into the colleges of Oxford. But the love of truth and justice enjoins me to declare, that as far as relates to myself this assertion is false, and that I never conversed with a priest, or even with a papist, till my resolution from books was absolutely fixed. In my last excursion to London, I addressed myself to a Roman Catholic bookseller in Russell street, Covent Garden, who recommended me to a priest of whose name and order I am at present ignorant. In our first interview he soon discovered that persuasion was needless, and after sounding the motives and merits of my conversion, he consented to admit me into the pale of the church, and at his feet on the eighth of June, 1753, I solemnly, though privately, abjured the errors of heresy. The seduction of an English youth of family and fortune was an act of as much danger as glory; but he bravely overlooked the danger, of which I was not then sufficiently informed. "Where a person is reconciled to the see of Rome, or procures others to be reconciled, the offense," says Blackstone, "amounts to high treason." And if the humanity of the age would prevent the execution of this sanguinary statute, there were other laws of a less odious cast, which condemned the priest to perpetual imprisonment, and transferred the proselyte's estate to his nearest relation. An elaborate controversial epistle, approved by my director and addressed to my father, announced and justified the step which I had taken. My father was neither a bigot nor a philosopher, but his affection deplored the loss of an only son, and his good sense was astonished at my strange departure from the religion of my country. In the first sally of passion he divulged a secret which prudence might have suppressed, and the gates of Magdalen College were forever shut against my return. Many years afterwards when the name of Gibbon was become as notorious as that of Middleton, it was industriously whispered at Oxford that the historian had formerly "turned papist." My character stood exposed to the reproach of inconstancy, and this invidious topic would have been handled without mercy by my opponents, could they have separated my cause from that of the university. For my own part, I am proud of an honest sacrifice of interest to conscience. I can never blush, if my tender mind was entangled in the sophistry that seduced the acute and manly understandings of Chillingworth and Bayle, who afterwards emerged from superstition to skepticism.

While Charles the First governed England, and was himself governed by a Catholic queen, it cannot be denied that the missionaries of Rome labored with impunity and success in the court, the country, and even the universities. One of the sheep,

> "Whom the grim wolf with privy paw
> Daily devours apace, and nothing said,"

is Mr. William Chillingworth, Master of Arts and Fellow of Trinity College, who, at the ripe age of twenty-eight years, was persuaded to elope from Oxford to the English seminary at Douay in Flanders. Some disputes with Fisher, a subtle Jesuit, might first awaken him from the prejudices of education; but he yielded to his own victorious argument, "that there must be somewhere an infallible judge, and that the church of Rome is the only Christian society which either does or can pretend to that character." After a short trial of a few months, Mr. Chillingworth was again tormented by religious scruples; he returned home, resumed his studies, unraveled his mistakes, and delivered his mind from the yoke of authority and superstition. His new creed was built on the principle that the Bible is our sole judge, and private reason our sole interpreter; and he ably maintains this principle in the *Religion of a Protestant*, a book (1634) which, after startling the doctors of Oxford, is still esteemed the most solid defense of the Reformation. The learning, the virtue, the recent merits of the author, entitled him to fair preferment; but the slave had now broke his fetters, and the more he weighed, the less was he disposed to subscribe the thirty-nine articles of the church of England. In a private letter he declares, with all the energy of language, that he could not subscribe them without subscribing his own damnation, and that if ever he should depart from this immovable resolution, he would allow his friends to think him a madman, or an atheist. As the letter is without a date, we cannot ascertain the number of weeks or months that elapsed between this passionate abhorrence and the Salisbury register which is still extant, — "*Ego Gulielmus Chillingworth, . . . omnibus hisce articulis, . . . et singulis in iisdem contentis, volens et ex animo subscribo, et consensum meum iisdem præbeo; 20 die Juli 1638.*" But, alas! "the chancellor and prebendary of Sarum soon deviated from his own subscription. As he more deeply scrutinized the article of the Trinity, neither Scripture nor the primitive fathers could long uphold his orthodox belief, and he could not but confess, that the doctrine of

Arius is either the truth or at least no damnable heresy." From this middle region of the air, the descent of his reason would naturally rest on the firmer ground of the Socinians, and if we may credit a doubtful story and the popular opinion, his anxious inquiries at last subsided in philosophic indifference. So conspicuous, however, were the candor of his nature and the innocence of his heart, that this apparent levity did not affect the reputation of Chillingworth. His frequent changes proceeded from too nice an inquisition into truth. His doubts grew out of himself; he assisted them with all the strength of his reason; he was then too hard for himself, but finding as little quiet and repose in those victories, he quickly recovered by a new appeal to his own judgment, so that in all his sallies and retreats, he was in fact his own convert.

Bayle was the son of a Calvinist minister in a remote province of France, at the foot of the Pyrenees. For the benefit of education, the Protestants were tempted to risk their children in the Catholic universities; and in the twenty-second year of his age, young Bayle was seduced by the arts and arguments of the Jesuits of Toulouse. He remained about seventeen months (19th March, 1669–19th August, 1670) in their hands, a voluntary captive, and a letter to his parents, which the new convert composed or subscribed (15th April, 1670), is darkly tinged with the spirit of popery. But nature had designed him to think as he pleased, and to speak as he thought; his piety was offended by the excessive worship of creatures, and the study of physics convinced him of the impossibility of transubstantiation, which is abundantly refuted by the testimony of our senses. His return to the communion of a falling sect was a bold and disinterested step that exposed him to the rigor of the laws, and a speedy flight to Geneva protected him from the resentment of his spiritual tyrants, unconscious as they were of the full value of the prize which they had lost. Had Bayle adhered to the Catholic church, had he embraced the ecclesiastical profession, the genius and favor of such a proselyte might have aspired to wealth and honors in his native country. But the hypocrite would have found less happiness in the comforts of a benefice, or the dignity of a mitre, than he enjoyed at Rotterdam in a private state of exile, indigence, and freedom. Without a country, or a patron, or a prejudice, he claimed the liberty and subsisted by the labors of his pen. The inequality of his voluminous works is explained and excused by his alternately writing for himself, for the booksellers, and for posterity, and if a severe critic would reduce him to a single folio, that relic, like the books of the Sybil, would become still more valuable. A calm and lofty spectator of the religious tempest, the philosopher of Rotterdam condemned with equal firmness the persecution of Louis the Fourteenth, and the republican maxims of the Calvinists; their vain prophecies, and the intolerant bigotry which sometimes vexed his solitary retreat. In reviewing the controversies of the times, he turned against each other the arguments of the disputants. Successively wielding the arms of the Catholics and Protestants, he proves that neither the way of authority, nor the way of examination can afford the multitude any test of religious truth, and dexterously concludes that custom and education must be the sole grounds of popular belief. The ancient paradox of Plutarch, that atheism is less pernicious than superstition, acquires a tenfold vigor, when it is adorned with the colors of his wit and pointed with the acuteness of his logic. His *Critical Dictionary* is a vast repository of facts and opinions, and he balances the false religions in his skeptical scales, till the opposite quantities — if I may use the language of algebra — annihilate each other. The wonderful power which he so boldly exercised, of assembling doubts and objections, had tempted him jocosely to assume the title of the νεφεληγερέτα Ζεύς, the cloud-compelling Jove, and in a conversation with the ingenious Abbé (afterwards Cardinal) de Polignac, he freely disclosed his universal Pyrrhonism. "I am most truly," said Bayle, "a Protestant, for I protest indifferently against all systems and all sects."

The academical resentment which I may possibly have provoked, will prudently spare this plain narrative of my studies or rather of my idleness, and of the unfortunate event which shortened the term of my residence at Oxford. But it may be suggested, that my father was unlucky in the choice of a society and the chance of a tutor. It will perhaps be asserted, that in the lapse of forty years many improvements have taken place in the College and the University. I am not unwilling to believe that some tutors might have been found more active than Dr. Waldegrave, and less contemptible than Dr. Winchester. About the same time and in the same walk, a Bentham was still treading in the footsteps of a Burton, whose maxims he had adopted and whose life he has published. The biographer indeed preferred the school-logic to the new philosophy, Burgursdicius to Locke, and the hero appears in his own writings a stiff and conceited pedant. Yet even these men, according to the measure of their capacity, might be diligent and useful, and it is recorded of Burton, that he taught his pupils what he knew; some Latin, some Greek, some ethics and metaphysics; referring them to proper masters for the languages and sciences of which he was ignorant. At a more recent period, many students have been attracted by the merit and reputation of Sir William Scott, then a tutor in University College and now conspicuous in the profession of the civil law. My personal acquaintance with that gentleman has inspired me with a just esteem for his abilities and knowledge, and I am assured that his lectures on history would compose, were they given to the public, a most valuable treatise. Under the auspices of the present Archbishop of York, Dr. Markham, himself an eminent scholar, a more regular discipline has been introduced, as I am told, at Christ Church; a course of classical and philosophical studies is proposed, and even pursued, in that numerous seminary. Learning has been made a duty, a pleasure, and even a fashion, and several young gentlemen do honor to the college in which they have been educated. According to the will of the donor, the profits of the second part of Lord Clarendon's *History* has been applied to the establishment of a riding-school, that the polite exercises might be taught, I know not with what success, in the university. The Vinerian professorship is of far more serious importance; the laws of his country are the first science of an Englishman of rank and fortune, who is called to be a magistrate and may hope to be a legislator. This judicious institution was coldly entertained by the graver doctors, who complained — I have heard the complaint — that it would take the young people from their books; but Mr. Viner's benefaction is not unprofitable, since it has at least produced the excellent *Commentaries* of Sir William Blackstone. The manners and opinions of our universities must follow at a distance the progressive motion of the age, and some prejudices which reason could not subdue have been slowly obliterated by time. The last generation of Jacobites is extinct; "the right divine of kings to govern wrong" is now exploded even at Oxford, and the remains of Tory principles are rather salutary than hurtful at a time when the constitution has nothing to fear from the prerogative of the crown, and can only be injured by popular innovation. But the inveterate evils which are derived from their birth and character must still cleave to our ecclesiastical corporations. The fashion of the present day is not propitious in England to discipline and economy, and even the exceptionable mode of foreign education has been lately preferred by the highest and most respectable authority in the kingdom. I shall only add that Cambridge appears to have been less deeply infected than her sister with the vices of the cloister. Her loyalty to the House of Hanover is of a more early date, and the name and philosophy of her immortal Newton were first honored in his native academy.

[RESIDENCE IN SWITZERLAND.]

After carrying me to Putney to the house of his friend Mr. Mallet, by whose philosophy I was rather scandalized than reclaimed, it was necessary to form a new plan of education, and to devise some method which if possible might effect the cure of my spiritual malady. The gates of Oxford were shut against my return. In every part of England I might be accessible to the seductions of my new friends, and after much debate it was determined from the advice and personal experience of Mr. Eliot, now Lord Eliot, to fix me during some years at Lausanne in Switzerland. M. Frey, a Swiss gentleman of Basel, undertook the conduct of the journey. We left London the 19th of June, crossed the sea from Dover to Calais, traveled post through several provinces of France by the direct road of St. Quentin, Rheims, Langres, and Besançon, and arrived the 30th of June at Lausanne, where I was immediately settled under the roof and tuition of M. Pavilliard, a Calvinist minister.

The first marks of my father's displeasure rather astonished than afflicted me. When he threatened to banish, and disown, and disinherit a rebellious son, I cherished a secret hope that he would not be able or willing to effect his menaces, and the pride of conscience encouraged me to sustain the honorable and important part which I was now acting. My spirits were raised and kept alive by the rapid motion of the journey, the new and various scenes of the continent, and the civility of M. Frey, a man of sense, and who was not ignorant of books or the world. But after he had resigned me into Pavilliard's hands and I was fixed in my new habitation, I had leisure to contemplate the strange and melancholy prospect. My first complaint arose from my ignorance of the language. In my childhood I had once studied the French grammar, and I could imperfectly understand the easy prose of a familiar subject. But when I was thus suddenly cast on a foreign land, I found myself deprived of the use of speech and of hearing, and during some weeks incapable not only of enjoying the pleasures of conversation, but even of asking or answering a question in the common intercourse of life. To an home-bred Englishman every object, every custom was offensive; but the native of any country might have been disgusted with the general aspect of his lodging and entertainment.

The minister's wife, Madame Pavilliard, governed our domestic economy. I now speak of her without resentment, but in sober truth she was ugly, dirty, proud, ill-tempered, and covetous. Our hours of twelve for dinner.

of seven for supper, were arbitrary though inconvenient customs. The appetite of a young man might have overlooked the badness of the materials and cookery, but his appetite was far from being satisfied with the scantiness of our daily meals, and more than one sense was offended by the appearance of the table, which during eight successive days was regularly covered with the same linen. I had now exchanged my elegant apartment in Magdalen College for a narrow gloomy street, the most unfrequented of an unhandsome town, for an old inconvenient house, and for a small chamber ill-contrived and ill-furnished, which on the approach of winter instead of a companionable fire, must be warmed by the dull invisible heat of a stove. From a man I was again degraded to the dependence of a schoolboy. M. Pavilliard managed my expenses, which had been reduced to a diminutive scale: I received a small monthly allowance for my pocket-money, and helpless and awkward as I have ever been, I no longer enjoyed the indispensable comfort of a servant. My condition seemed as destitute of hope as it was devoid of pleasure; I was separated for an indefinite, which appeared an infinite term from my native country, and I had lost all connection with my Catholic friends. I have since reflected with surprise that, as the Romish clergy of every part of Europe maintain a close correspondence with each other, they never attempted by letters or messages to rescue me from the hands of the heretics, or at least to confirm my zeal and constancy in the profession of the faith. Such was my first introduction to Lausanne — a place where I spent nearly five years with pleasure and profit, which I afterwards revisited without compulsion, and which I have finally selected as the most grateful retreat for the decline of my life.

But it is the peculiar felicity of youth that the most

unpleasing objects and events seldom make a deep or lasting impression. At the flexible age of sixteen I soon learned to endure, and gradually to adopt, the new forms of arbitrary manners; the real hardships of my situation, the house, the table, and the mistress, were alleviated by time. And to this coarse and scanty fare I am perhaps indebted for the establishment of my constitution. Had I been sent abroad in a more splendid style, such as the fortune and bounty of my father might have supplied, I might have returned home with the same stock of language and science as our countrymen usually import from the continent. An exile and a prisoner as I was, their example betrayed me into some irregularities of wine, of play, and of idle excursions; but I soon felt the impossibility of associating with them on equal terms, and after the departure of my first acquaintance, I held a cold and civil correspondence with their successors. This seclusion from English society was attended with the most solid benefits. In the Pays de Vaud, the French language is used with less imperfection than in most of the distant provinces of France. In Pavilliard's family, necessity compelled me to listen and to speak, and if I was at first disheartened by the apparent slowness, in a few months I was astonished by the rapidity of my progress. My pronunciation was formed by the constant repetition of the same sounds; the variety of words and idioms, the rules of grammar, and distinctions of genders, were impressed in my memory. Ease and freedom were obtained by practice; correctness and elegance by labor; and before I was recalled home, French, in which I spontaneously thought, was more familiar than English to my ear, my tongue, and my pen. The first effect of this opening knowledge was the revival of my love of reading, which had been chilled at Oxford, and I soon turned over without much choice almost all the French books in my tutor's library. Even these amusements were productive of real advantage; my taste and judgment were now somewhat riper. I was introduced to a new mode of style and literature. By the comparison of manners and opinions, my views were enlarged, my prejudices were corrected, and a copious voluntary abstract of the *Histoire de l' Église et de l' Empire* by Lesueur, may be placed in a middle line between my childish and my manly studies. As soon as I was able to converse with the natives, I began to feel some satisfaction in their company. My awkward timidity was polished and emboldened, and I frequented for the first time assemblies of men and women. The acquaintance of the Pavilliards prepared me by degrees for more elegant society. I was received with kindness and indulgence in the best families of Lausanne, and it was in one of these that I formed an intimate, lasting connection with M. Deyverdun, a young man of an amiable temper and excellent understanding. In the arts of fencing and dancing, small indeed was my proficiency, and some expensive months were idly wasted in the riding-school. My unfitness to bodily exercise reconciled me to a sedentary life, and the horse, the favorite of my countrymen, never contributed to the pleasures of my youth.

My obligations to the lessons of M. Pavilliard, gratitude will not suffer me to forget. But truth compels me to own that my best preceptor was not himself eminent for genius or learning. Even the real measure of his talents was underrated in the public opinion. The soft credulity of his temper exposed him to frequent imposition, and his want of eloquence and memory in the pulpit disqualified him for the most popular duty of his office. But he was endowed with a clear head and a warm heart; his innate benevolence had assuaged the spirit of the church; he was rational, because he was moderate. In the course of his studies he had acquired a just though superficial knowledge of most branches of literature; by long practice, he was skilled in the arts of teaching, and he labored with assiduous patience to know the character, gain the affection, and open the mind of his English pupil. As soon as we began to understand each other, he gently led me into the path of instruction. I consented with pleasure that a portion of the morning hours should be consecrated to a plan of modern history and geography, and to the critical perusal of the French and Latin classics, and at each step I felt myself invigorated by the habits of application and method.

The principles of philosophy were associated with the examples of taste, and by a singular chance the book, as well as the man, which contributed the most effectually to my education, has a stronger claim on my gratitude than on my admiration. M. de Crousaz, the adversary of Bayle and Pope, is not distinguished by lively fancy or profound reflection, and even in his own country, at the end of a few years, his name and writings are almost obliterated. But his philosophy had been formed in the school of Locke, his divinity in that of Limborch and Le Clerc. In a long and laborious life, several generations of pupils were taught to think, and even to write; his lessons rescued the Academy of Lausanne from Calvinistic prejudice, and he had the rare merit of diffusing a more liberal spirit among the clergy and people of the Pays de Vaud. His system of logic, which in the last editions has swelled to six tedious and prolix volumes, may be praised as a clear and methodical abridgment of the art of reasoning, from our simple ideas to the most complex operations of the human understanding. This system I studied, and meditated, and abstracted, till I have obtained the free command of an universal instrument, which I soon presumed to exercise on my Catholic opinions. Pavilliard was not unmindful that his first task, his most important duty, was to reclaim me from the errors of popery. The intermixture of sects has rendered the Swiss clergy acute and learned on the topics of controversy, and I have some of his letters in which he celebrates the dexterity of this attack, and my gradual concessions after a firm and well managed defense. I was willing, and I am now willing, to allow him an handsome share of the honor of my conversion. Yet I must observe, that it was principally effected by my private reflections, and I still remember my solitary transport at the discovery of a philosophical argument against the doctine of transubstantiation — that the text of scripture which seems to inculcate the real presence is attested only by a single sense, our sight; while the real presence itself is disproved by three of our senses, the sight, the touch, and the taste. The various articles of the Romish creed disappeared like a dream, and after a full conviction, on Christmas day 1754, I received the sacrament in the church of Lausanne. It was here that I suspended my religious inquiries, acquiescing with implicit belief in the tenets and mysteries which are adopted by the general consent of Catholics and Protestants.

Such, from my arrival at Lausanne during the first eighteen or twenty months (July, 1753 – March, 1755), were my useful studies, the foundation of all my future improvements. But in the life of every man of letters there is an era, from a level, from whence he soars with his own wings to his proper height, and the most important part of his education is that which he bestows on himself. My worthy tutor had the good sense and modesty to discern how far he could be useful. As soon as he felt that I advanced beyond his speed and measure, he wisely left me to my genius, and the hours of lesson were soon lost in the voluntary labor of the whole morning, and sometimes of the whole day. The desire of prolonging my time, gradually confirmed the salutary habit of early rising, to which I have always adhered with some regard to seasons and situations; but it is happy for my eyes and for my health, that my temperate ardor has never been seduced to trespass on the hours of the night. During the last three years of my residence at Lausanne, I may assume the merit of serious and solid application, but I am tempted to distinguish the last eight months of the year 1755, as the period of the most extraordinary diligence and rapid progress. In my French and Latin translations I adopted an excellent method, which from my own success I would recommend to the imitation of students. I chose some classic writer such as Cicero and Vertot, the most approved for purity and elegance of style. I translated, for instance, an epistle of Cicero into French; and after throwing it aside, till the words and phrases were obliterated from my memory, I re-translated my French into such Latin as I could find, and then compared each sentence of my imperfect version, with the ease, the grace, the propriety of the Roman orator. A similar experiment was made on some pages of the *Revolutions* of Vertot; I turned them into Latin, re-turned them after a sufficient interval into my own French, and again scrutinized the resemblance or dissimilitude of the copy and the original. By degrees I was less ashamed, by degrees I was more satisfied with myself; and I persevered in the practice of these double translations, which filled several books, till I had acquired the knowledge of both idioms, and the command at least of a correct style. This useful exercise of writing was accompanied and succeeded by the more pleasing occupation of reading the best authors. Dr. Middleton's *History*, which I then appreciated above its true value, naturally directed me to the writings of Cicero. The most perfect editions, that of Olivet which may adorn the shelves of the rich, that of Ernesti which should lie on the table of the learned, were not in my power. For the familiar epistles I used the text and English commentary of Bishop Ross, but my general edition was that of Verburgius, published at Amsterdam in two large volumes in folio, with an indifferent choice of various notes. I read with application and pleasure all the epistles, all the orations, and the most important treatises of rhetoric and philosophy, and as I read, I applauded the observation of Quintilian, that every student may judge of his own proficiency by the satisfaction which he receives from the Roman orator. Cicero in Latin, and Xenophon in Greek, are indeed the two ancients whom I would first propose to a liberal scholar, not only for the merit of their style and sentiments, but for the admirable lessons, which may be applied almost to every situation of public and private life. Cicero's *Epistles* may in particular afford the models of every form of correspondence, from the careless effusions of tenderness and friendship, to the well-guarded declaration of discreet and dignified resentment. After finishing this great author, a library of eloquence and reason, I formed a more extensive plan of reviewing the Latin classics under the four divisions of, 1. historians, 2. poets, 3. orators, and 4. philosophers, in a chronological series from the days of Plautus and Sallust, to the decline of the language and empire of Rome; and this plan, in the last twenty-seven months of my residence at Lausanne (January, 1756–April, 1758), I nearly accomplished. Nor was this review, however rapid, either hasty or superficial. I indulged myself in a second and even a third perusal of Terence, Virgil, Horace, Tacitus, etc., and studied to imbibe the sense and spirit most congenial to my own. I never suffered a difficult or corrupt passage to escape, till I had viewed it in every light of which it was susceptible. Though often disappointed, I always consulted the most learned or ingenious commentators, Torrentius and Dacier on Horace, Catrou and Servius on Virgil, Lipsius on Tacitus, Meziriac on Ovid, etc., and in the ardor of my inquiries I embraced a large circle of historical and critical erudition. My abstracts of each book were made in the French language; my observations often branched into particular essays, and I can still read without contempt a dissertation of eight folio pages on eight lines (287–294) of the fourth Georgic of Virgil. M. Deyverdun, my friend whose name will be frequently repeated, had joined with equal zeal, though not with equal perseverance in the same undertaking. To him every thought, every composition, was instantly communicated; with him I enjoyed the benefits of a free conversation on the topics of our common studies.

But it is scarcely possible for a mind endowed with any active curiosity to be long conversant with the Latin classics, without aspiring to know the Greek originals whom they celebrate as their masters, and of whom they so warmly recommended the study and imitation;

> "Vos exemplaria Græca
> Nocturna versate manu, versate diurna."

It was now that I regretted the early years which had been wasted in sickness or idleness, or more idle reading;

that I condemned the perverse method of our schoolmasters, who by first teaching the mother-language, might descend with so much ease and perspicuity to the origin and etymology of a derivative idiom. In the nineteenth year of my age I determined to supply this defect, and the lessons of Pavilliard again contributed to smooth the entrance of the way, the Greek alphabet, the grammar, and the pronunciation according to the French accent. As he had possessed only such a stock as was requisite for an ecclesiastic, our first book was St. John's gospel, and [I] should probably have construed the whole of the New Testament, had I not represented the absurdity of adhering to the corrupt dialect of the Hellenist Jews. At my earnest request we presumed to open the Iliad, and I had the pleasure of beholding, though darkly and through a glass, the true image of Homer, whom I had long since admired in an English dress. After my tutor, conscious of his inability, had left me to myself, I worked my way through about half the Iliad, and afterwards interpreted alone a large portion of Xenophon and Herodotus. But my ardor, destitute of aid and emulation, was gradually cooled, and, from the barren task of searching words in a lexicon, I withdrew to the free and familiar conversation of Virgil and Tacitus. Yet in my residence at Lausanne I had laid a solid foundation, which enabled me in a more propitious season to prosecute the study of Grecian literature.

From a blind idea of the usefulness of such abstract science, my father had been desirous, and even pressing, that I should devote some time to the mathematics, nor could I refuse to comply with so reasonable a wish. During two winters I attended the private lectures of Monsieur de Traytorrens, who explained the elements of algebra and geometry as far as the *Conic Sections* of the

Marquis de l'Hôpital, and appeared satisfied with my diligence and improvement. But as my childish propensity for numbers and calculations was totally extinct, I was content to receive the passive impression of my professor's lectures, without any active exercise of my own powers. As soon as I understood the principles, I relinquished forever the pursuit of the mathematics, nor can I lament that I desisted before my mind was hardened by the habit of rigid demonstration, so destructive of the finer feelings of moral evidence, which must, however, determine the actions and opinions of our lives. I listened with more pleasure to the proposal of studying the law of nature and nations, which was taught in the Academy of Lausanne by M. Vicat, a professor of some learning and reputation. But instead of attending his public or private course, I preferred in my closet the lessons of his masters and my own reason. Without being disgusted by the pedantry of Grotius or the prolixity of Puffendorf, I studied in their writings the duties of a man, the rights of a citizen, the theory of justice (it is, alas! a theory), and the laws of peace and war, which have had some influence on the practice of modern Europe. My fatigues were alleviated by the good sense of their commentator Barbeyrac. Locke's *Treatise of Government* instructed me in the knowledge of Whig principles, which are rather founded in reason than in experience; but my delight was in the frequent perusal of Montesquieu, whose energy of style and boldness of hypothesis were powerful to awaken and stimulate the genius of the age. The logic of de Crousaz had prepared me to engage with his master Locke and his antagonist Bayle, of whom the former may be used as a bridle, and the latter as a spur[1] to the curiosity of a young philosopher. According to the

[1] MS. 'bridle,' but 'spur,' as in MS. C., is evidently intended.

nature of their respective works, the schools of argument and objection, I carefully went through the *Essay on Human Understanding*, and occasionally consulted the most interesting articles of the *Philosophic Dictionary*. In the infancy of my reason I turned over, as an idle amusement, the most serious and important treatise; in its maturity, the most trifling performance could exercise my taste or judgment, and more than once I have been led by a novel into a deep and instructive train of thinking. But I cannot forbear to mention three particular books, since they may have remotely contributed to form the historian of the Roman empire. 1. From the *Provincial Letters* of Pascal, which almost every year I have perused with new pleasure, I learned to manage the weapon of grave and temperate irony, even on subjects of ecclesiastical solemnity. 2. The *Life of Julian* by the Abbé de la Bletterie, first introduced me to the man and the times, and I should be glad to recover my first essay on the truth of the miracle which stopped the rebuilding of the temple of Jerusalem. 3. In Giannone's *Civil History of Naples* I observed with a critical eye the progress and abuse of sacerdotal power, and the revolutions of Italy in the darker ages. This various reading, which I now conducted with skill and discretion, was digested according to the precept and model of Mr. Locke into a large commonplace book — a practice, however, which I do not strenuously recommend. The action of the pen will doubtless imprint an idea on the mind as well as on the paper; but I much question whether the benefits of this laborious method are adequate to the waste of time, and I must agree with Dr. Johnson, "that what is twice read is commonly better remembered than what is transcribed."

During two years, if I forget some boyish excursions of a day or a week, I was fixed at Lausanne; but at the end of the third summer, my father consented that I should make the tour of Switzerland with Pavilliard, and our short absence of one month (September 21–October 20, 1755) was a reward and relaxation of my assiduous studies. The fashion of climbing the mountains and viewing the glaciers, had not yet been introduced by foreign travelers who seek the sublime beauties of nature. But the political face of the country is not less diversified by the forms and spirit of so many various republics, from the jealous government of the few to the licentious freedom of the many. I contemplated with pleasure the new prospects of men and manners, though my conversation with the natives would have been more free and instructive, had I possessed the German, as well as the French language. We passed through most of the principal towns of Switzerland — Neufchâtel, Bienne, Soleurre, Arau, Baden, Zürich, Basel, and Berne. In every place we visited the churches, arsenals, libraries, and all the most eminent persons, and after my return I digested my notes in fourteen or fifteen sheets of a French journal, which I dispatched to my father, as a proof that my time and his money had not been misspent. Had I found this journal among his papers, I might be tempted to select some passages; but I will not transcribe the printed accounts, and it may be sufficient to notice a remarkable spot which left a deep and lasting impression on my memory. From Zürich we proceeded on a pilgrimage, not of devotion but of curiosity, to the Benedictine Abbey of Einsiedeln, more commonly styled Our Lady of the Hermits. I was astonished by the profuse ostentation of riches in the poorest corner of Europe. Amidst a savage scene of woods and mountains, a palace appears to have been erected by magic, and it was erected by the potent magic of religion. A crowd of palmers and votaries was prostrate before the altar. The title and worship of the mother of God provoked my indignation, and the lively naked image of superstition suggested to me, as in the same place it had done to Zwinglius, the most pressing argument for the reformation of the church. About two years after this tour, I passed at Geneva an useful and agreeable month; but this excursion, and some short visits in the Pays de Vaud, did not materially interrupt my studious and sedentary life at Lausanne.

My thirst of improvement, and the languid state of science at Lausanne, soon prompted me to solicit a literary correspondence with several men of learning whom I had not an opportunity of personally consulting. 1. In the perusal of Livy (xxx. 44), I had been stopped by a sentence in a speech of Hannibal which cannot be reconciled by any torture with his character or argument. The commentators dissemble, or confess their perplexity. It occurred to me that the change of a single letter, by substituting *otio* instead of *odio*, might restore a clear and consistent sense, but I wished to weigh my emendation in scales less partial than my own. I addressed myself to M. Crevier, the successor of Rollin, and a professor in the University of Paris who had published a large and valuable edition of Livy. His answer was speedy and polite; he praised my ingenuity, and adopted my conjecture, which I must still applaud as easy and happy. 2. I maintained a Latin correspondence, at first anonymous and afterwards in my own name, with Professor Breitinger of Zürich, the learned editor of a Septuagint Bible. In our frequent letters we discussed many questions of antiquity, many passages of the Latin classics. I proposed my interpretations and amendments. His censures, for he did not spare my boldness of conjecture, were sharp and strong, and I was encouraged by the consciousness of my strength, when I could stand in free debate against a critic of such eminence and erudition. 3. I corresponded on similar topics with the celebrated Professor Matthew Gesner of the University of Göttingen, and he accepted as courteously as the two former the invitation of an unknown youth. But his abilities might possibly be decayed; his elaborate letters were feeble and prolix, and when I asked his proper direction, the vain old man covered half a sheet of paper with the foolish enumeration of his titles and offices. 4. These professors of Paris, Zürich, and Göttingen, were strangers whom I presumed to address on the credit of their name; but M. Allamand, minister at Bex, was my personal friend, with whom I maintained a more free and interesting correspondence. He was a master of language, of science, and above all of dispute, and his acute and flexible logic could support with equal address, and perhaps with equal indifference, the adverse sides of every possible question. His spirit was active, but his pen had been indolent. M. Allamand had exposed himself to much scandal and reproach by an anonymous letter (1745) to the Protestants of France, in which he labors to persuade them that public worship is the exclusive right and duty of the state, and that their numerous assemblies of dissenters and rebels are not authorized by the law or the gospel. His style is animated, his arguments specious, and if the papist may seem to lurk under the mask of a Protestant, the philosopher is concealed under the disguise of a papist. After some trials in France and Holland, which were defeated by his fortune or his character, a genius that might have enlightened or deluded the world was buried in a country living, unknown to fame and discontented with mankind. *Est sacrificulus in pago, et rusticos decipit.* As often as private or ecclesiastical business called him to Lausanne,

I enjoyed the pleasure and benefit of his conversation, and we were mutually flattered by our attention to each other. Our correspondence in his absence chiefly turned on Locke's metaphysics, which he attacked and I defended; the origin of ideas, the principles of evidence, and the doctrine of liberty;

"And found no end, in wandering mazes lost."

By fencing with so skillful a master, I acquired some dexterity in the use of my philosophic weapons, but I was still the slave of education and prejudice. He had some measures to keep, and I much suspect that he never showed me the true colors of his secret skepticism.

Before I was recalled from Switzerland, I had the satisfaction of seeing the most extraordinary man of the age, a poet, an historian, a philosopher, who has filled thirty quartos of prose and verse with his various productions, often excellent and always entertaining. Need I add the name of Voltaire? After forfeiting by his own misconduct the friendship of the first of kings, he retired at the age of sixty, with a plentiful fortune, to a free and beautiful country, and resided two winters (1757 and 1758) in the town or neighborhood of Lausanne. My desire of beholding Voltaire, whom I then rated above his real magnitude, was easily gratified. He received me with civility as an English youth, but I cannot boast of any peculiar notice or distinction, *Virgilium vidi tantum*. The ode which [he] composed on his first arrival on the banks of the Leman Lake, *O Maison d'Aristippe! O Jardin d'Epicure*, etc., had been imparted as a secret to the gentleman by whom I was introduced. He allowed me to read it twice; I knew it by heart; and as my discretion was not equal to my memory, the author was soon displeased by the circulation of a copy. In writing this trivial anecdote, I wished to observe whether my memory was impaired, and I have the comfort of finding that every line of the poem is still engraved in fresh and indelible characters. The highest gratification which I derived from Voltaire's residence at Lausanne, was the uncommon circumstance of hearing a great poet declaim his own productions on the stage. He had formed a troupe of gentlemen and ladies, some of whom were not destitute of talents. A decent theatre was framed at Monrepos, a country-house at the end of a suburb; dresses and scenes were provided at the expense of the actors, and the author directed the rehearsals with the zeal and attention of paternal love. In two successive winters his tragedies of *Zaïre*, *Alzire*, *Zulime*, and his sentimental comedy of the *Enfant Prodigue*, were played at the theatre of Monrepos, but it was not without much reluctance and ill humor that the envious bard allowed the representation of the *Iphigénie* of Racine. The parts of the young and fair were distorted by his fat and ugly niece, Madame Denys, who could not, like our admirable Pritchard, make the spectators forget the defects of her age and person. For himself, Voltaire reserved the characters best adapted to his years, Lusignan, Alvaréz, Benassar, Euphemon. His declamation was fashioned to the pomp and cadence of the old stage, and he expressed the enthusiasm of poetry rather than the feelings of nature. My ardor, which soon became conspicuous, seldom failed of procuring me a ticket. The habits of pleasure fortified my taste for the French theatre, and that taste has perhaps abated my idolatry for the gigantic genius of Shakespeare, which is inculcated from our infancy as the first duty of an Englishman. The wit and philosophy of Voltaire, his table and theatre, refined in a visible degree the manners of Lausanne, and however addicted to study, I enjoyed my share of the amusements of society. After the representations of Monrepos I sometimes supped with the actors. I was now familiar in some, and acquainted in many houses, and my evenings were generally devoted to cards and conversation, either in private parties or numerous assemblies.

I hesitate, from the apprehension of ridicule, when I approach the delicate subject of my early love. By this word I do not mean the polite attention of the gallantry without hope or design which has originated from the spirit of chivalry, and is interwoven with the texture of French manners. I do not confine myself to the grosser appetite which our pride may affect to disdain, because it has been implanted by nature in the whole animal creation, *amor omnibus idem*. The discovery of a sixth sense, the first consciousness of manhood, is a very interesting moment of our lives, but it less properly belongs to the memoirs of an individual, than to the natural history of the species. I understand by this passion the union of desire, friendship, and tenderness, which is inflamed by a single female, which prefers her to the rest of her sex, and which seeks her possession as the supreme or the sole happiness of our being. I need not blush at recollecting the object of my choice, and though my love was disappointed of success, I am rather proud that I was once capable of feeling such a pure and exalted sentiment. The personal attractions of Mademoiselle Susan Curchod were embellished by the virtues and talents of the mind. Her fortune was humble, but her family was respectable. Her mother, a native of France, had preferred her religion to her country. The profession of her father did not extinguish the moderation and philosophy of his temper, and he lived content with a small salary and laborious duty in the obscure lot of minister of Crassy, in the mountains that separate the Pays de Vaud from the county of Burgundy. In the solitude of a sequestered village he bestowed a liberal, and even learned, education on his only daughter. She surpassed his hopes by her proficiency in the sciences and languages, and in her short visits to some relations at Lausanne, the wit and beauty and erudition of Mademoiselle Curchod were the theme of universal applause. The report of such a prodigy awakened my curiosity; I saw and loved. I found her learned without pedantry, lively in conversation, pure in sentiment, and elegant in manners, and the first sudden emotion was fortified by the habits and knowledge of a more familiar acquaintance. She permitted me to make her two or three visits at her father's house. I passed some happy days in the mountains of Burgundy, and her parents honorably encouraged a connection which might raise their daughter above want and dependence. In a calm retirement the gay vanity of youth no longer fluttered in her bosom; she listened to the voice of truth and passion, and I might presume to hope that I had made some impression on a virtuous heart. At Crassy and Lausanne I indulged my dream of felicity; but on my return to England I soon discovered that my father would not hear of this strange alliance, and that without his consent I was myself destitute and helpless. After a painful struggle I yielded to my fate. The remedies of absence and time were at length effectual, and my love subsided in friendship and esteem. The minister of Crassy soon afterwards died; his stipend died with him; his daughter retired to Geneva, where by teaching young ladies she earned a hard subsistence for herself and her mother, but in her lowest distress she maintained a spotless reputation, and a dignified behavior. The Duchess of Grafton, now Lady Ossory, has often told me that she had nearly engaged Mademoiselle Curchod as a governess, and her declining a life of servitude was most probably blamed by the wisdom of her short sighted friends. A rich banker of Paris, a citizen of Geneva, had the good fortune and good sense to discover and possess this inestimable treasure, and in the capital of taste and luxury she resisted the temptations of wealth as she had sustained the hardships of indigence. The genius of her husband has exalted him to the most conspicuous station in Europe. In every change of prosperity and disgrace he has reclined on the bosom of a faithful friend, and Mademoiselle Curchod is now the wife of M. Necker, the minister and perhaps the legislator of the French monarchy.

Such as I am, in genius or learning or manners, I owe my creation to Lausanne. It was in that school that the statue was discovered in the block of marble and my own religious folly, my father's blind resolution, produced the effects of the most deliberate wisdom. One mischief, however, and in the eyes of my countrymen a serious and irreparable mischief, was derived from the success of my Swiss education, — I had ceased to be an Englishman. At the flexible period of youth, from the age of sixteen to twenty-one, my opinions, habits, and sentiments were cast in a foreign mold; the faint and distant remembrance of England was almost obliterated; my native language was grown less familiar, and I should have cheerfully accepted the offer of a moderate independent fortune on the terms of perpetual exile. By the good sense and temper of Pavilliard my yoke was insensibly lightened. He left me master of my time and actions; but he could neither change my situation nor increase my allowance, and with the progress of my years and reason I impatiently sighed for the moment of my deliverance. At length, in the spring of the year 1758, my father signified his permission and his pleasure that I should immediately return home. We were then in the midst of a war. The resentment of the French at our taking their ships without a declaration, had rendered that polite nation somewhat peevish and difficult. They denied a passage to English travelers, and the road through Germany was circuitous, toilsome, and perhaps in the neighborhood of the armies exposed to some danger. In this perplexity, two Swiss officers of my acquaintance in the Dutch service, who were returning to their garrisons, offered to conduct me through France as one of their companions; nor did we sufficiently reflect that my borrowed name and regimentals might have been considered, in case of a discovery, in a very serious light. I took my leave of Lausanne on the 11th of April 1758 with a mixture of joy and regret, in the firm resolution of revisiting as a man the persons and places which had been so dear to my youth. We traveled slowly, but pleasantly, in a hired coach over the hills of Franche-Compté and the fertile province of Lorraine, and passed, without accident or inquiry, through several fortified towns of the French frontier. From thence we entered the wild Ardennes of the Austrian duchy of Luxemburg, and after crossing the Meuse at Liege we traversed the heaths of Brabant, and reached on the fifteenth day our Dutch garrison of Bois le Duo. In our passage through Nancy, my eye was gratified by the aspect of a regular and beautiful city, the work of Stanislaus, who after the storms of Polish royalty reposed in the love and gratitude of his new subjects of Lorraine. In our halt at Maestricht I visited M. de Beaufort, a learned critic, who was known to me by his specious arguments against the five first centuries of the Roman History. After dropping my regimental companions, I stepped aside to visit Rotterdam and the Hague. I wished to have observed a country, the monument of freedom and industry, but my days were numbered, and a longer delay would have been ungraceful. I hastened to embark at the Brill, landed the next day at Harwich, and proceeded to London where my father awaited my arrival. The whole term of my first absence from England was four years ten months and fifteen days.

[GIBBON IN ENGLAND AGAIN.]

In the prayers of the church our personal concerns are judiciously reduced to the threefold distinction of mind, body, and estate. The sentiments of the mind excite and exercise our social sympathy. The review of my moral and literary character is the most interesting to myself and to the public; and I may expatiate without reproach on my private studies, since they have produced the public writings, which can alone entitle me to the esteem and friendship of my readers. The pains and pleasures of the body, how important soever to ourselves, are an indelicate topic of conversation.[1] The experience of the world inculcates a discreet reserve on the subject of our estate, and we soon learn that a free disclosure of our riches or poverty would pro-

[1] Here follows a sentence which, in a slightly modified form, Gibbon put later in an earlier part of his Memoirs; see p. 27, l. 19. The sentence here reads: I shall not follow the vain example of Cardinal Querini who has filled half a volume of his memoirs with medical consultations on his own particular case. I shall not imitate the naked frankness of Montaigne who exposes the most disgusting symptoms of his malady, and marks the operation of each remedy on his nerves and bowels.

voke the malice of envy, or encourage the insolence of contempt. Yet I am tempted to glance in a few words on the state of my private circumstances, as I am persuaded that, had I been more indigent or more wealthy, I should not have possessed the leisure or the perseverance to prepare and execute my voluminous history. My father's impatience for my return to England was not wholly of the disinterested kind. I have already hinted that he had been impoverished by his two sisters, and that his gay character and mode of life were less adapted to the acquisition, than the expenditure of wealth. A large and legitimate debt for the supply of naval stores was lost by the injustice of the court of Spain. His elegant hospitality at Putney exceeded the measure of his income. The honor of being chosen a member of the old club at White's had been dearly paid, and a more pernicious species of gaming — the contest for Southampton — exhausted his sickly finances. His retirement into Hampshire on my mother's death was colored by a pious motive. Some years of solitude allowed him to breathe, but it was only by his son's majority that he could be restored to the command of an entailed estate. The time of my recall had been so nicely computed that I arrived in London three days before I was of age. The priests and the altar had been prepared, and the victim was unconscious of the impending stroke. According to the forms and fictions of our law, I levied a fine and suffered a recovery. The entail was cut off, a sum of ten thousand pounds was raised on mortgage for my father's use, and he repaid the obligation by settling on me an annuity for life of three hundred pounds a year. My submission at the time was blind and almost involuntary, but it has been justified by duty and interest to my cooler thoughts, and

I could only regret that the receipt of some appropriated funds was not given into my own hands. My annuity, though somewhat more valuable thirty years ago, was, however, inadequate to the style of a young Englishman of fashion in the most wealthy metropolis of Europe. But I was rich in my indifference, or more properly my aversion, for the active and costly pleasures of my age and country. Some arrears, especially my bookseller's bill, were occasionally discharged, and the extraordinaries of my travels into France and Italy amounted, by previous agreement, to the sum of twelve hundred pounds. But the ordinary scale of my expense was proportioned to my ordinary revenue. My desires were regulated by temper as much as by philosophy, and as soon as my purse was empty I had the courage to retire into Hampshire, where I found in my father's house a liberal maintenance, and in my own studies an inexhaustible source of amusement. With a credit which might have been largely abused, I may assume the singular merit that I never lost or borrowed twenty pounds in the twelve years which elapsed between my return from Switzerland and my father's death.

The only person in England whom I was impatient to see was my Aunt Porten, the affectionate guardian of my tender years. I hastened to her house in College street Westminster, and the evening was spent in the effusions of joy and confidence. It was not without some awe and apprehension that I approached the presence of my father. My infancy, to speak the truth, had been neglected at home; the severity of his look and language at our last parting still dwelt on my memory, nor could I form any notion of his character, or my probable reception. They were both more agreeable than I could expect. The domestic discipline of our ancestors has been relaxed by the philosophy and softness of the age, and if my father remembered that he had trembled before a stern parent, it was only to adopt with his own son an opposite mode of behavior. He received me as a man and a friend. All constraint was banished at our first interview, and we ever afterwards continued on the same terms of easy and equal politeness. He applauded the success of my education; every word and action was expressive of the most cordial affection; and our lives would have passed without a cloud, if his economy had been equal to his fortune, or if his fortune had been equal to his desires. During my absence he had married his second wife, Miss Dorothea Patton, who was introduced to me with the most unfavorable prejudice. I considered his second marriage as an act of displeasure, and the rival who had usurped my mother's bed appeared in the light of a personal and domestic enemy. I will not say that I was apprehensive of the bowl or dagger, or that I had then weighed the sentence of Euripides —

> "'Εχθρὰ γὰρ ἡ 'πιοῦσα μητρυιὰ τέκνοις
> Τοῖς πρόσθ', ἐχίδνης οὐδὲν ἠπιωτέρα."

But I well knew that the *odium novercale* was proverbial in the language of antiquity. The Latin poets always couple with the name of step-mother the hateful epithets of *crudelis*, *sæva*, *scelerata*, and on the road I had often repeated the line of Virgil —

> "Est mihi namque domi pater, est injusta noverca."

But the injustice was in my own fancy, and the imaginary monster was an amiable and deserving woman. I could not be mistaken in the first view of her understanding, her knowledge, and the elegant spirit of her conversation. Her polite welcome, and her assiduous care to study and gratify my wishes, announced at least that the surface would be smooth, and my suspicions of art and falsehood were gradually dispelled by the full discovery of her warm and exquisite sensibility. After some reserve on my side, our minds associated in confidence and friendship, and as Mrs. Gibbon had neither children nor the hopes of children, we more easily adopted the tender names and genuine characters of mother and of son. By the indulgence of these parents, I was left at liberty to consult my taste or reason in the choice of place, of company, and of amusements; and my excursions were only bounded by the limits of the island, and the measure of my income. Some faint efforts were made to procure me an employment of secretary to a foreign embassy, and I listened to a scheme which would again have transported me to the continent. Mrs. Gibbon with seeming wisdom, exhorted me to take chambers in the Temple and devote my leisure to the study of the law. I cannot repent of having neglected her advice. Few men, without the spur of necessity, have resolution to force their way through the thorns and thickets of that gloomy labyrinth. Nature had not endowed me with the bold and ready eloquence which makes itself heard amidst the tumult of the bar,

"Vincentem strepitus, et natum rebus agendis:"

and I should probably have been diverted from the labors of literature without acquiring the fame or fortune of a successful pleader. I had no need to call to my aid the regular duties of a profession. Every day, every hour was agreeably filled nor have I known, like so many of my countrymen, the tediousness of an idle life.

Of the two years (May 1758–May 1760) between my return to England and the embodying of the Hampshire militia, I passed about nine months in London, and the remainder in the country. The metropolis affords many amusements which are open to all. It is itself an astonishing and perpetual spectacle to the curious eye, and each taste, each sense may be gratified by the variety of objects that will occur in the long circuit of a morning walk. I assiduously frequented the theatres at a very prosperous era of the stage, when a constellation of excellent actors, both in tragedy and comedy, was eclipsed by the meridian brightness of Garrick in the maturity of his judgment, and vigor of his performance. The pleasures of a town life, the daily round from the tavern to the play, from the play to the coffee-house, from the coffee-house to the ——, are within the reach of every man who is regardless of his health, his money, and his company. By the contagion of example I was sometimes seduced; but the better habits, which I had formed at Lausanne, induced me to seek a more elegant and rational society, and if my search was less easy and successful than I might have hoped, I shall at present impute the failure to the disadvantages of my situation and character. Had the rank and fortune of my parents given them an annual establishment in London, their own house would have introduced me to a numerous and polite circle of acquaintance. But my father's taste had always preferred the highest and the lowest company, for which he was equally qualified, and after a twelve years' retirement, he was no longer in the memory of the great with whom he had associated. I found myself a stranger in the midst of a vast and unknown city, and at my entrance into life I was reduced to some dull family parties, and some scattered connections which were not such as I should have chosen for myself. The most useful friends of my father were the Mallets. They received me with civility and kindness at first on his account, and afterwards on my own, and — if I may use Lord Chesterfield's word — I was soon domesticated in their house. Mr. Mallet, a name among the English poets, is praised by an unforgiving enemy for the ease and elegance of his conversation, and whatsoever might be the defects of his wife she was not destitute of wit or learning. By his assistance I was introduced to Lady Hervey, the mother of the present Earl of Bristol. Her age and infirmities confined her at home. Her dinners were select; in the evening her house was open to the best company of both sexes and all nations, nor was I displeased at her preference and even affectation of the manners, the language, and the literature of France. But my progress in the English world was in general left to my own efforts, and those efforts were languid and slow. I had not been endowed by art or nature with those happy gifts of confidence and address, which unlock every door and every bosom; nor would it be reasonable to complain of the just consequences of my sickly childhood, foreign education, and reserved temper. While coaches were rattling through Bond street, I have passed many a solitary evening in my lodging with my books. My studies were sometimes interrupted by a sigh which I breathed towards Lausanne, and on the approach of spring I withdrew without reluctance from the noisy and expensive scene of crowds without company, and dissipation without pleasure. In each of the twenty-five years of my acquaintance with London (1758–1783) the prospect gradually brightened, and this unfavorable picture most properly belongs to the first period after my return from Switzerland.

My father's residence in Hampshire, where I have passed many light, and some heavy hours, was at Buriton near Petersfield, one mile from the Portsmouth road and at the easy distance of fifty-eight miles from London. An old mansion in a state of decay had been converted into the fashion and convenience of a modern house, and if strangers had nothing to see, the inhabitants had little to desire. The spot was not happily chosen, at the end of the village and the bottom of the hill, but the aspect of the adjacent grounds was various and cheerful. The downs commanded a noble prospect, and the long hanging woods in sight of the house could not perhaps have been improved by art or expense. My father kept in his own hands the whole of his estate, and even rented some additional land; and whatsoever might be the balance of profit and loss, the farm supplied him with amusement and plenty. The produce maintained a number of men and horses, which were multiplied by the intermixture of domestic and rural servants, and in the intervals of labor the favorite team, an handsome set of bays or grays, was harnessed to the coach. The economy of the house was regulated by the taste and prudence of Mrs. Gibbon. She prided herself in the elegance of her occasional dinners, and from the uncleanly avarice of Madame Pavilliard, I was suddenly transported to the daily neatness and luxury of an English table. Our immediate neighborhood was rare and rustic; but from the verge of our hills as far as Chichester and Goodwood, the western district of Sussex was interspersed with noble seats and hospitable families, with whom we cultivated a friendly, and might have enjoyed a very frequent intercourse. As my stay at Buriton was always voluntary, I was received and dismissed with smiles, but the comforts of my retirement did not depend on the ordinary pleasures of the country. My father could never inspire me with his love and knowledge of farming. When he galloped away on a fleet hunter to follow the Duke of Richmond's foxhounds I saw him depart without a wish to join in the sport, and in the command of an ample manor I valued the supply of the kitchen much more than the exercise of the field. I never handled a gun, I seldom mounted an horse; and my philosophic walks were soon terminated by a shady bench, where I was long detained by the sedentary amusement of reading or meditation. At home I occupied a pleasant and spacious apartment. The library on the same floor was soon considered as my peculiar domain, and I might say with truth, that I was never less alone than when by myself. My sole complaint, which I piously suppressed, arose from the kind restraint imposed on the freedom of my time. By the habit of early rising I always secured a sacred portion of the day, and many scattered moments were stolen and employed by my studious industry. But the family hours of breakfast, of dinner, of tea, and of supper, were regular and long. After breakfast Mrs. Gibbon expected my company in her dressing-room; after tea my father claimed my conversation and the perusal of the newspapers, and in the midst of an interesting work I was often called down to receive the visit of some idle neighbors. Their dinners and visits required in due season a similar return, and I dreaded the period of the full moon, which was usually reserved for our more distant excursions. I could not refuse attending my father in the summer of 1759 to the races at Stockbridge, Reading, and Odiham, where he had entered a horse for the hunter's plate, and I was not displeased with the sight of our Olympic games, the beauty of the spot, the fleetness of the horses, and the gay tumult of the numerous spectators. As soon as the militia business was agitated, many days were tediously consumed in meetings of deputy-lieutenants at Petersfield, Alton, and Winchester. In the close of the same year, 1759, Sir Simeon (then Mr.) Stewart attempted an unsuccessful contest for the county of Southampton, against Mr. Legge, Chancellor of the Exchequer,—a well-known contest, in which Lord Bute's influence was first exerted and censured. Our canvass at Portsmouth and Gosport lasted several days, but the interruption of my studies was compensated in some degree by the spectacle of English manners, and the acquisition of some practical knowledge.

If in a more domestic or more dissipated scene my application was somewhat relaxed, the love of knowledge was inflamed and gratified by the command of books, and I compared the poverty of Lausanne with the plenty of London. My father's study at Buriton was stuffed with much trash of the last age, with much high church divinity and politics which have long since gone to their proper place. Yet it contained some valuable editions of the classics and the fathers, the choice as it should seem of Mr. Law, and many English publications of the times had been occasionally added. From this slender beginning I have gradually formed a numerous and select library, the foundation of my works and the best comfort of my life both at home and abroad. On the receipt of the first quarter, a large share of my allowance was appropriated to my literary wants. I cannot forget the joy with which I exchanged a bank-note of twenty pounds for the twenty volumes of the *Memoirs of the Academy of Inscriptions;* nor would it have been easy, by any other expenditure of the same sum, to have procured so large and lasting a fund of rational amusement. At a time when I most assiduously frequented this school of ancient literature, I thus expressed my opinion of a learned and various collection, which since the year 1759 has been doubled in magnitude, though not equally in merit,— "Une de ces sociétés, qui ont mieux immortalisé Louis XIV qu'une ambition souvent pernicieuse aux hommes, commençoit déjà ces recherches qui réunissent la justesse de l'esprit, l'aménité et l'érudition; où l'on voit tant des découvertes, et quelquefois, ce qui ne cède qu'à peine aux découvertes, une ignorance modeste et savante." The review of my library must be reserved for the period of its maturity, but in this place I may allow myself to observe, that I am not conscious of having ever bought a book from a motive of ostentation; that every volume, before it was deposited on the shelf, was either read or sufficiently examined, and that I soon adopted the tolerating maxim of the elder Pliny, *nullum esse librum tam malum ut non ex aliqua parte prodesset.* I could not yet find leisure or courage to renew the pursuit of the Greek language, except by reading the lessons of the Old and New Testament every Sunday when I attended the family to church. The series of my Latin authors was less strenuously completed, but the acquisition by inheritance or purchase of the best editions of Cicero, Quintillian, Livy, Tacitus, Ovid, etc., afforded a fair opportunity which I seldom neglected. I persevered in the useful methods of abstracts and observation, and a single example may suffice, of a note which had almost swelled into a work. The solution of a passage of Livy (xxxviii. 38,) involved me in the dry and dark treatises of Greaves, Arbuthnot, Hooper, Bernard, Eisenschmid, Gronovius, La Barré, Fréret, etc., and in my French *Essay* (c. xx) I ridiculously send the reader to my own manuscript remarks on the weights, coins, and measures of the ancients, which were abruptly terminated by the militia drum.

As I am now entering on a more ample field of society and study, I can only hope to avoid a vain and prolix garrulity by overlooking the vulgar crowd of my acquaintance, and confining myself to such intimate friends among books and men as are best entitled to my notice by their own merit and reputation, or by the deep impression which they have left on my mind. Yet I will embrace this occasion of recommending to the young student a practice which about this time I adopted myself. After glancing my eye over the design and order of a new book, I suspended the perusal till I had finished the task of self-examination; till I had revolved, in a solitary walk, all that I knew or believed, or had thought on the subject of the whole work, or of some particular chapter. I was then qualified to discern how much the author added to my original stock, and I was sometimes satisfied by the agreement, I was sometimes armed by the opposition of our ideas. The favorite companions of my leisure were our English writers since the Revolution. They breathe the spirit of reason and liberty, and they most seasonably contributed to restore the purity of my own language, which had been corrupted by the long use of a foreign idiom. By the judicious advice of Mr. Mallet, I was directed to the writings of Swift and Addison. Wit and simplicity are their common attributes; but the style of Swift is supported by manly original vigor, that of Addison is adorned by the female graces of elegance and mildness, and the contrast of too coarse or too thin a texture is visible even in the defects of these celebrated authors. The old reproach, that no British altars had been raised to the muse of history, was recently disproved by the first performances of Robertson and Hume, the histories of Scotland and of the Stuarts. I will assume the presumption to say, that I was not unworthy to read them, nor will I disguise my different feelings in the repeated perusals. The perfect composition, the nervous language, the well-turned periods of Dr. Robertson inflamed me to the ambitious hope that I might one day tread in his footsteps; the calm philosophy, the careless, inimitable beauties of his friend and rival, often forced me to close the volume with a mixed sensation of delight and despair.

[FIRST PUBLISHED WORK.]

The design of my first work, the *Essay on the Study of Literature*, was suggested by a refinement of vanity, the desire of justifying and praising the object of a favorite pursuit. In France, to which my ideas were confined, the learning and language of Greece and Rome were neglected by a philosophic age. The guardian of those studies, the Academy of Inscriptions, was degraded to the lowest rank among the three royal societies of Paris; the new appellation of *Érudits* was contemptuously applied to the successors of Lipsius and Casaubon, and I was provoked to hear (see M. d'Alembert, *Discours préliminaire à l'Encyclopédie*) that the exercise of the memory, their sole merit, had been superseded by the nobler faculties of the imagination and the judgment. I was ambitious of proving by my own example, as well as by my precepts, that all the faculties of the mind may be exercised and displayed by [the] study of ancient literature. I began to select and adorn the various proofs and illustrations which had offered themselves in reading the classics, and the first pages or chapters of my essay were composed before my departure from Lausanne. The hurry of the journey and of the first weeks of my English life suspended all thoughts of serious application; but my object was ever before my eyes, and no more than ten days, from the first to the eleventh of July, were suffered to elapse after my summer establishment at Buriton. My essay was finished in about six weeks, and as soon as a fair copy had been transcribed by one of the French prisoners at Petersfield, I looked round for a critic and a judge of my first performance. A writer can seldom be content with the doubtful recompense of solitary approbation, but a youth, ignorant of the world and of himself, must desire to weigh his talents in some scales less partial than his own. My conduct was natural, my motive laudable, my choice of Dr. Maty judicious and fortunate. By descent and education Dr. Maty, though born in Holland, might be considered as a Frenchman, but he was fixed in London by the practice of physic, and an office in the British Museum. His reputation was justly founded on the eighteen volumes of the *Journal Britannique*, which he had supported almost alone with perseverance and success. This humble though useful labor, which had once been dignified by the genius of Bayle and the learning of Le Clerc, was not disgraced by the taste, the knowledge, and the judgment of Maty. He exhibits a candid and pleasing view of the state of literature in England during a period of six years (January 1750–December 1755), and, far different from his angry son, he handles the rod of criticism with the tenderness and reluctance of a parent. The author of the *Journal Britannique* sometimes aspires to the character of a poet and philosopher; his style is pure and elegant, and in his virtues, or even his defects, he may be ranked as one of the last disciples of the school of Fontenelle. His answer to my first letter was prompt and polite. After a careful examination he returned my manuscript, with some animadversion and much applause, and when I visited London in the ensuing winter, we discussed the design and execution in several free and familiar conversations. In a short excursion to Buriton I reviewed my essay according to his friendly advice, and after suppressing a third, adding a third, and altering a third, I consummated my first labor by a short preface which was dated Feb. 3, 1759. Yet I still shrunk from the press with the terrors of virgin modesty; the manuscript was safely deposited in my desk, and as my attention was engaged by new objects, the delay might have been prolonged till I had fulfilled the precept of Horace, *nonumque prematur in annum.* Father Sirmond, a learned Jesuit, was still more rigid, since he advised a young friend to expect the mature age of fifty before he gave himself or his writings to the public (Olivet, *Histoire de l'Académie Françoise*, tom. ii. p. 143). The counsel was singular, but it is still more singular that it should have been approved by the example of the author. Sirmond was himself fifty-five years of age when he published in 1614 his first work, an edition of Sidonius Apollinaris, with many valuable annotations (see his life, before the great edition of his works in five volumes in folio, Paris, 1696, e Typographia Regia).

Two years elapsed in silence, but in the spring of 1761 I yielded to the authority of a parent, and complied like a pious son with the wish of my own heart. My private resolves were influenced by the state of Europe. About this time the belligerent powers had made and accepted overtures of peace; our English plenipotentiaries were named to assist at the Congress of Augsburg, which never met. I wished to attend them as a gentleman or a secretary, and my father fondly believed that the proof of some literary talents might introduce me to public notice, and second the recommendations of my friends. After a last revisal I consulted with Mr. Mallet and Dr. Maty, who approved the design and promoted the execution. Mr. Mallet, after hearing me read my manuscript, received it from my hands and delivered it into those of Becket, with whom he made an agreement in my name — an easy agreement; I required only a certain number of copies and, without transferring my property, I devolved on the bookseller the charges and profits of the edition. Dr. Maty undertook in my absence to correct the sheets. He inserted without my knowledge an elegant and flattering epistle to the author, which is composed, however, with so much art, that in case of a defeat his favorable report might have been ascribed to the indulgence of a friend for the rash attempt of a young English gentleman. The work was printed and published, under the title of *Essai sur l'Étude de la Littérature, à Londres, chez T. Becket et P. A. de Hondt, 1761*, in a small volume in duodecimo. My dedication to my father, a proper and pious address, was composed the twenty-eighth of May; Dr. Maty's letter is dated the 16th of June, and I received the first copy (June 23) at Alresford, two days before I marched with the Hampshire militia. Some weeks afterwards, on the same ground, I presented my book to the late Duke of York, who breakfasted in Colonel Pitt's tent; and, as the regiment was just returned from a field day, the author appeared before his royal highness, somewhat disordered with sweat and dust, in the cap, dress, and accoutrements of a captain of grenadiers. By my father's direction and Mallet's advice, a number of copies were given to several of their acquaintance and my own; to the Duke of Richmond, the Marquis of Carnarvon, the Earls of Litchfield, Waldegrave, Egremont, Shelburne, Bute, Hardwicke, Bath, Granville, and Chesterfield, Lady Hervey, Sir Joseph Yorke, Sir Matthew Fetherstone, Messrs. Walpole, Scott, Wray, etc. Two books were sent to the Count de

Caylus and the Duchesse d'Aiguillon, at Paris; I had reserved twenty for my friends at Lausanne, as the first fruits of my education and a grateful token of my remembrance, and on all these persons I levied an unavoidable tax of civility and compliment. It is not surprising that a work, of which the style and sentiments were so totally foreign, should have been more successful abroad than at home. I was delighted by the copious extracts, the warm commendations, and the flattering predictions of the journals of France and Holland; and the next year (1762) a new edition (I believe at Geneva) extended the fame, or at least the circulation, of the work. In England it was received with cold indifference, little read and speedily forgotten. A small impression was slowly dispersed; the bookseller murmured, and the author (had his feelings been more exquisite) might have wept over the blunders and the baldness of the English translation. The publication of my *History* fifteen years afterwards revived the memory of my first performance, and the *Essay* was eagerly sought in the shops. But I refused the permission which Becket solicited of reprinting it; the public curiosity was imperfectly satisfied by a pirated copy of the booksellers of Dublin, and when a copy of the original edition has been discovered in a sale, the primitive value of half-a-crown has risen to the fanciful price of a guinea or thirty shillings. Such is the power of a name.

I have expatiated on the loss of my literary maidenhead, a memorable era in the life of a student when he ventures to reveal the measure of his mind. His hopes and fears are multiplied by the idea of self-importance, and he believes for a while that the eyes of mankind are fixed on his person and performance. Whatsoever may be my present reputation, it no longer rests on the merit of this first essay, and at the end of twenty-eight years I may appreciate my juvenile work with the impartiality, and almost with the indifference of a stranger. In his answer to Lady Hervey, the Count de Caylus admires, or affects to admire "les livres sans nombre que M. Gibbon a lus et très bien lus." But, alas! my stock of erudition at that time was scanty and superficial, and if I allow myself the liberty of naming the Greek masters, my genuine and personal acquaintance was confined to the Latin classics. The most serious defect of my *Essay* is a kind of obscurity and abruptness which always fatigues, and may often elude the attention of the reader. Instead of a precise and proper definition the title itself, the sense of the word *Littèrature*, is loosely and variously applied; a number of remarks and examples, historical, critical, philosophical, are heaped on each other without method or connection; and if we except some introductory pages, all the remaining chapters might indifferently be reversed or transposed. The obscurity of many passages is often affected, *brevis esse laboro, obscurus fio;* the desire of expressing perhaps a common idea with sententious and oracular brevity — alas, how fatal has been the imitation of Montesquieu! But this obscurity sometimes proceeds from a mixture of light and darkness in the author's mind; from a partial ray which strikes upon an angle, instead of spreading itself over the surface of an object. After this fair confession, I shall presume to say that the *Essay* does credit to a young writer of two and twenty years of age, who had read with taste, who thinks with freedom, and who writes in a foreign language with spirit and elegance. The defense of the early history of Rome and the new chronology of Sir Isaac Newton form a specious argument. The patriotic and political design of the *Georgics* is happily conceived, and any probable conjecture, which tends to raise the dignity of the poet and the poem, deserves to be adopted without a rigid scrutiny. Some dawning of a philosophic spirit enlightens the general remarks on the study of history and of man. I am not displeased with the inquiry into the origin and nature of the gods of polytheism. In a riper season of judgment and knowledge, I am tempted to review the curious question whether these fabulous deities were mortal men or allegorical beings. Perhaps the two systems might be blended in one, perhaps the distance between them is in a great measure verbal and apparent. In the rapid course of this narrative I have only time to scatter two or three hasty observations. That in the perusal of Homer a naturalist would pronounce his gods and men to be of the same species, since they were capable of engendering together a fruitful progeny. That before the reformation St. Francis and the virgin Mary had almost attained a similar apotheosis, and that the saints and angels, so different in their origin, were worshipped with the same rites by the same nations. That the current of superstition and science flowed from India to Egypt, from Egypt to Greece and Italy, and that the incarnations of the celestial deities, so darkly shadowed in our fragments of Egyptian theology, are copiously explained in the sacred books of the Hindoos. Fifteen centuries before Christ the great Osiris, the invisible agent of the universe, was born or manifested at Thebes in Bœotia under the name of Bacchus. The idea of Bishen is a metaphysical abstraction. The adventures of Krishen, his perfect image, are those of a man who lived and died about five thousand years ago in the neighborhood of Delhi. Upon the whole, I may apply to the first labor of my pen the speech of a far superior artist, when he surveyed the first productions of his pencil. After viewing some portraits which he had painted in his youth, my friend Sir Joshua Reynolds acknowledged to me that he was rather humbled than flattered by the comparison with his present works, and that after so much time and study, he had conceived his improvement to be much greater than he found it to have been.

At Lausanne I composed the first chapters of my *Essay* in French, the familiar language of my conversation and studies, in which it was easier for me to write than in my mother tongue. After my return to England I continued the same practice, without any affectation, or design of repudiating, as Dr. Bentley would say, my vernacular idiom. But I should have escaped some Anti-gallican clamor, had I been content with the more natural character of an English author. I should have been more consistent, had I rejected Mallet's foolish advice of prefixing an English dedication to a French book—a confusion of tongues which seemed to accuse the ignorance of my patron. The use of a foreign dialect might be excused by the hope of being employed as a negotiator, by the desire of being generally understood on the continent; but my true motive was doubtless the ambition of new and singular fame, an Englishman claiming a place among the writers of France. The Latin tongue had been consecrated by the service of the church; it was refined by the imitation of the ancients, and in the fifteenth and sixteenth centuries the scholars of Europe enjoyed the advantage, which they have gradually resigned, of conversing and writing in a common and learned idiom. As that idiom was no longer in any country the vulgar speech, they all stood on a level with each other; yet a citizen of old Rome might have smiled at the best Latinity of the Germans and Britons, and we may learn from the *Ciceronianus* of Erasmus, how difficult it was found to steer a middle course between pedantry and barbarism. The Romans themselves had sometimes attempted a more perilous task, of writing in a living language and appealing to the taste and judgment of the natives. The vanity of Tully was doubly interested in the Greek memoirs of his own consulship; and if he modestly supposes that some Latinisms might be detected in his style, he is confident of his own skill in the art of Isocrates and Aristotle, and he requests his friend Atticus to disperse the copies of his work at Athens, and in the other cities of Greece (*Ad Atticum*, i. 19. ii. 1). But it must not be forgot, that from infancy to manhood Cicero and his contemporaries had read and declaimed and composed with equal diligence in both languages, and that he was not allowed to frequent a Latin school till he had imbibed the lessons of the Greek grammarians and rhetoricians. In modern times, the language of France has been diffused by the merit of her writers, the social manners of the natives, the influence of the monarchy, and the exile of the Protestants. Several foreigners have seized the opportunity of speaking to Europe in this common dialect, and Germany may plead the authority of Leibnitz and Frederick, of the first of her philosophers and the greatest of her kings. The just pride and laudable prejudice of England has restrained the communication of idioms, and of all the nations on this side of the Alps, my countrymen are the least practiced, and least perfect in the exercise of the French tongue. By Sir William Temple and Lord Chesterfield it was only used on occasions of civility and business, and their printed letters will not be quoted as models of composition. Lord Bolingbroke may have published in French a sketch of his *Reflections on Exile*, but his reputation now reposes on the address of Voltaire, *Docte sermones utriusque linguæ;* and by his English dedication to Queen Caroline and his *Essay on Epic Poetry*, it should seem that Voltaire himself wished to deserve a return of the same compliment. The exception of Count Hamilton cannot fairly be urged; though an Irishman by birth, he was educated in France from his childhood. Yet I am surprised that a long residence in England, and the habits of domestic conversation, did not affect the ease and purity of his inimitable style, and I regret the omission of his English verses, which might have afforded an amusing object of comparison. I might therefore assume the *primus ego in patriam meam* etc., but with what success I have explored this untrodden path must be left to the decision of my French readers. Dr. Maty, who might himself be questioned as a foreigner, has secured his retreat at my expense. "Je ne crois pas que vous vous piquiez d'être moins facile à reconnoître pour un Anglois que Lucullus pour un Romain." My friends at Paris have been more indulgent, they received me as a countryman, or at least as a provincial; but they were friends and Parisians. The defects which Maty insinuates, "Ces traits saillants, ces figures hardies, ce sacrifice de la règle au sentiment, et de la cadence à la force," are the faults of the youth, rather than of the stranger, and after the long and laborious exercise of my own language, I am conscious that my French style has been ripened and improved.

[GIBBON'S MILITARY LIFE.]

I have already hinted, that the publication of my essay was delayed till I had embraced the military profession. I shall now amuse myself with the recollection of an active scene, which bears no affinity to any other period of my studious and social life. From the general idea of a militia I shall descend to the militia of England in the war before the last, to the state of the regiment in which I served, and to the influence of that service on my personal situation and character.

The defense of the state may be imposed on the body of the people, or it may be delegated to a select number of mercenaries. The exercise of arms may be an occasional duty, or a separate trade, and it is this difference which forms the distinction between a militia and a standing army. Since the union of England and Scotland the public safety has never been attacked and has seldom been threatened by a foreign invader, but the sea was long the sole safeguard of our isle. If the reign of the Tudors or the Stuarts was often signalized by the valor of our soldiers and sailors, they were dismissed at the end of the campaign or the expedition for which they had been levied. The national spirit at home had subsided in the peaceful occupations of trade, manufactures, and husbandry, and if the obsolete forms of a militia were preserved, their discipline in the last age was less the object of confidence than of ridicule.

> "The country rings around with loud alarms,
> And raw in fields the rude militia swarms:
> Mouths without hands maintained at vast expense,
> In peace a charge, in war a weak defense.
> Stout once a month they march, a blust'ring band,
> And ever but in times of need at hand.
> This was the morn when, issuing on the guard,
> Drawn up in rank and file they stood prepar'd,
> Of seeming arms to make a short essay;
> Then hastened to be drunk — the business of the day."

The impotence of such unworthy soldiers was supplied from the era of the Restoration by the establishment of a body of mercenaries. The conclusion of each war increased the numbers that were kept on foot and, although their progress was checked by the jealousy of opposition, time and necessity reconciled, or at least accustomed, a free country to the annual perpetuity of a standing army. The zeal of our patriots, both in and out of parliament (I cannot add both in and out of office), complained that the sword had been stolen from the hands of the people. They appealed to the victorious example of the Greeks and Romans, among whom every citizen was a soldier, and they applauded the happiness and independence of Switzerland which, in the midst of the great monarchies of Europe, is sufficiently defended by a constitutional and effective militia. But their enthusiasm overlooked the modern changes in the art of war, and the insuperable difference of government and manners. The liberty of the Swiss is maintained by the concurrence of political causes. The superior discipline of their militia arises from the numerous intermixture of officers and soldiers whose youth has been trained in foreign service, and the annual exercise of a few days is the sole tax which is imposed on a martial people, consisting for the most part of shepherds and husbandmen. In the primitive ages of Greece and Rome a war was determined by a battle, and a battle was decided by the personal qualities of strength, courage, and dexterity which every citizen derived from his domestic education. The public quarrel was his own. He had himself voted in the assembly of the people and the private passions of the majority had pronounced the general decree of the republic. On the event of the contest each freeman had staked his fortune and family, his liberty and life, and if the enemy prevailed he must expect to share in the common calamity of the ruin or servitude of his native city.

By such irresistible motives were the first Greeks and Romans summoned to the field, but when the art was improved, when the war was protracted, their militia was transformed into a standing army, or their freedom was oppressed by the more regular forces of an ambitious neighbor.

Two disgraceful events, the progress in the year forty-five of some naked Highlanders, the invitation of the Hessians and Hanoverians in fifty-six, had betrayed and insulted the weakness of an unarmed people. The country gentlemen of England unanimously demanded the establishment of a militia. A patriot was expected—

> "Otia qui rumpet patriæ, residesque movabit
> ——in arma viros,"

and the merit of the plan, or at least of the execution, was assumed by Mr. Pitt who was then in the full splendor of his popularity and power. In the new model the choice of the officers was founded on the most constitutional principle, since they were all obliged from the colonel to the ensign to prove a certain qualification, to give a landed security to the country which entrusted them for her defense with the use of arms. But in the first steps of this institution the legislators of the militia despaired of imitating the practice of Switzerland. Instead of summoning to the standard all the inhabitants of the kingdom who were not disabled by age, or excused by some indispensable avocation, they directed that a moderate proportion should be chosen by lot for the term of three years, at the end of which their places were to be supplied by a new and similar ballot. Every man who was drawn had the option of serving in person, of finding a substitute, or of paying ten pounds; and in a country already burthened this honorable duty was degraded into an additional tax. It is reported that the subjects of Queen Elizabeth amounted to 1,172,674 men able to bear arms (Hume's *History of England*, vol. v, p. 482 of the last octavo edition), and if in the war before the last many active and vigorous hands were employed in the fleet and army, the difference must have been amply compensated by the general increase of population, and we may smile at this mighty effort which reduced the national defense to the puny establishment of thirty-two thousand men. The Sunday afternoons had first been appointed for their exercise, but superstition clamored against the profanation of the Sabbath, and a useful day was substracted from the labor of the week. Whatever was the day, such rare and superficial practice could never have entitled them to the character of soldiers. But the king was invested with the power of calling the militia into actual service on the event or the danger of rebellion or invasion, and in the year 1759 the British islands were seriously threatened by the armaments of France. At this crisis the national spirit most gloriously disproved the charge of effeminacy which, in a popular estimate, had been imputed to the times. A martial enthusiasm seemed to have pervaded the land, and a constitutional army was formed under the command of the nobility and gentry of England. After the naval victory of Sir Edward Hawke (November 20, 1759), the danger no longer subsisted. Yet, instead of disbanding the first regiments of militia, the remainder was embodied the ensuing year, and public unanimity applauded their illegal continuance in the field till the end of the war. In this new mode of service they were subject, like the regulars, to martial law. They received the same advantages of pay and clothing and the families, at least of the principals, were maintained at the charge of the parish. At a distance from their respective counties these provincial corps were stationed and removed and encamped by the command of the secretary at war. The officers and men were trained in the habits of subordination, nor is it surprising that some regiments should have assumed the discipline and appearance of veteran troops. With the skill they soon imbibed the spirit of mercenaries, the character of a militia was lost, and under that specious name the crown had acquired a second army, more costly and less useful than the first. The most beneficial effect of this institution was to eradicate among the country gentlemen the relics of Tory, or rather of Jacobite, prejudice. The accession of a British king reconciled them to the government and even to the court, but they have been since accused of transferring their passive loyalty from the Stuarts to the family of Brunswick, and I have heard Mr. Burke exclaim in the House of Commons "they have changed the idol, but they have preserved the idolatry."

By the general ardor of the times my father, a new Cincinnatus, was drawn from the plow. His authority and advice prevailed on me to relinquish my studies. A general meeting was held at Winchester and before we knew the consequences of an irretrievable step we accepted (June 12, 1759) our respective commissions of major and captain in the South battalion of the Hampshire. The proportion of the county of Southampton had been fixed at nine hundred and sixty men who were divided into the two regiments of the North and South, each consisting of eight companies. By the special exemption of the Isle of Wight we lost a company. Our colonel resigned and we were reduced to the legal definition of an independent battalion, of a lieutenant-colonel commandant (Sir Thomas Worsley, baronet), a major, five captains, seven lieutenants, seven ensigns, twenty-one sergeants, fourteen drummers, and four hundred and twenty rank and file. I will not renew our prolix and passionate dispute with the Duke of Bolton, our lord-lieutenant, which at that time appeared to me an object of the most serious importance. By the interpretation of an act of parliament we contested his right of naming himself colonel of the two battalions. After the final decision of the attorney general and secretary at war his poor revenge was confined to the use and abuse of his power in the choice of an adjutant and the promotion of officers. In the year 1759 our ballot was slowly completed and, as the fear of an invasion passed away, we began to hope, my father and myself, that our campaigns would extend no farther than Petersfield and Alton, the seat of our particular companies. We were undeceived by the king's sign manual for our embodying, which was issued May 10, 1760. It was too late to retreat, it was too soon to repent. The battalion on the fourth of June assembled at Winchester, from whence in about a fortnight we were removed, at our own request, for the benefit of a foreign education. In a new raised militia the neighborhood of home was always found inconvenient to the officers, and mischievous to the men.

The battalion continued in actual service above two years and a half, from May 10, 1760 to December 23, 1762. In this period of a military life I have neither sieges nor battles to relate, but, like my brother Major Sturgeon, I shall describe our marches and countermarches as they are faithfully recorded in my own journal, or commentary of the times. 1. Our first and most agreeable station was at Blandford in Dorsetshire, where we enjoyed about two months (June 17–August 23) the beauty of the country, the hospitality of the neighboring gentlemen, the novelty of command and exercise, and the consciousness of our daily and rapid improvements. 2. From this school we were led against the enemy, a body of French three thousand two hundred strong who had occupied Portchester castle, near Portsmouth. It must not indeed be dissembled that our enemies were naked, unarmed prisoners, the object of pity rather than of terror. Their misery was somewhat alleviated by public and private bounty, but their sufferings exhibited the evils of war and their noisy spirits the character of the nation. During the months of September, October, and November 1760, we performed this disagreeable duty by large detachments of a captain, four subalterns, and two hundred and thirty men, at first from Hilsea Barracks and afterwards from our quarters at Titchfield and Fareham. The barracks within the Portsmouth lines are a square of low, ill-built huts in a damp and dreary situation. On this unwholesome spot we lost many men by fevers and the smallpox, and our dispute with the Duke of Bolton which produced a series of arrests, memorials, and court-martials was not less pernicious to the discipline than to the peace of the regiment. 3. Rejoicing in our escape from this sink of distemper and discord we performed with alacrity a long march (December 1–11) to Cranbrook in the Weald of Kent, where we had been sent to guard eighteen hundred French prisoners at Sissinghurst. The inconceivable dirtiness of the season, the country, and the spot aggravated the hardships of a duty too heavy for our numbers; but these hardships were of short duration and before the end of the month we were relieved by the interest of our Tory friends under the new reign. 4. At Dover in the space of five months we began to breathe (December 27, 1760–May 31, 1761). For the men the quarters were healthy and plentiful and our dull leisure was enlivened by the society of the fourteenth regiment in the castle, and some sea parties in the spring. Our persecutions were at an end. The command was settled. We smiled at our own prowess as we exercised each morning in sight of the French coast, and before we left Dover we had recovered the union and discipline which we possessed at our departure from Blandford. 5. In the summer of 1761 a camp was formed near Winchester, in which we solicited and obtained a place. Our march from Dover to Alton in Hampshire was a pleasant walk (June 1–12). I was appointed captain of the new company of grenadiers and, with proper clothing and accoutrements, we assumed somewhat of the appearance of regular troops. The four months (June 25–October 21) of this encampment were the most splendid and useful period of our military life. Our establishment amounted to near five thousand men — the thirty-fourth regiment of foot and six militia corps, the Wiltshire, Dorsetshire, South Hampshire, Berkshire, and the North and South Gloucestershire. The regulars were satisfied with their ideal preëminence. The Gloucestershire, Berkshire, and Dorsetshire approached by successive steps the superior merit of the Wiltshire, the pride and pattern of the militia — an active, steady, well-appointed regiment of eight hundred men which had been formed by the strict and skillful discipline of their colonel, Lord Bruce. At our entrance into camp we were indisputably the last and worst, but we were excited by generous shame —

"Extremos pudeat rediisse" —

and such was our indefatigable labor that in the general reviews the South Hampshire were rather a credit than a disgrace to the line. A friendly emulation, ready to teach and eager to earn, assisted our mutual progress.

But the great evolutions, the exercise of acting and moving as an army, which constitutes the best lessons of a camp never entered the thoughts of the Earl of Effingham, our drowsy general. 6. The Devises, our winter quarters during four months (October 23, 1761–February 28, 1762) are a populous town, full of disorder and disease. The men who were allowed to work earned too much money and their drunken quarrels with the townsmen and Colonel Barré's Black Muskateers were painfully repressed by the sharp sentences of one-and-twenty court-martials. The Devises afforded, however, a great number of fine young recruits whom we enlisted from the regimental stock-purse, without much regard to the forms or the spirit of the militia laws. 7. After a short march and halt at Salisbury we paid a second visit of ten weeks (March 9–May 31) to our old friends at Blandford, where, in that garden of England, we again experienced the warm and constant hospitality of the natives. The spring was favorable to our military exercise, and the Dorsetshire gentlemen who had cherished our infancy now applauded a regiment in appearance and discipline not inferior to their own. 8. The necessity of discharging a great number of men whose term of three years was expired forbade our encampment in the summer of 1762, and the colors were stationed at Southampton in the last six or seven months (June–December) of our actual service. But after so long an indulgence we could not complain that during many of the first and last weeks of this period, a detachment almost equal to the whole was required to guard the French prisoners at Forton and Fareham. The operation of the ballot was slow and tedious. In the months of August and September our life at Southampton was indeed gay and busy. The battalion had been renewed in youth and vigor and so rapid was the improvement that, had the militia lasted another year, we should not have yielded to the most perfect of our brethren. The preliminaries of peace and the suspension of arms determined our fate. We were dismissed with the thanks of the king and parliament and, on the twenty-third of December 1762, the companies were disembodied at their respective homes. The officers possessed of property rejoiced in their freedom, those who had none lamented the loss of their pay and profession; but it was found by experience that the greatest part of the men were rather civilized than corrupted by the habits of military subordination.

A young mind, unless it be of a cold and languid temper, is dazzled even by the play of arms, and in the first sallies of my enthusiasm I had seriously wished and tried to embrace the regular profession of a soldier. The military fever was cooled by the enjoyment of our mimic Bellona, who gradually unveiled her naked deformity. How often did I sigh for my true situation of a private gentleman and a man of letters. How often did I repeat the complaints of Cicero: *Clitellæ bovi sunt impositæ. Est incredibile quam me negotii tædeat. . . . Ille cursus animi et industriæ meæ præclara opera cessat. . . . Lucem, libros, urbem, domum, vos desidero. Sed feram, ut potero; sit modo annuum. Si prorogatur, actum est.* From a service without danger I might indeed have retired without disgrace; but as often as I hinted a wish of resigning, my fetters were riveted by my father's authority, the entreaties of Sir Thomas Worsley, and some regard for the welfare of a corps of which I was the principal support. My proper province was the care of my own, and afterwards of the grenadier company, but with the rank of first captain I possessed the confidence and supplied the place of the colonel and major. In their presence or in their absence

I acted as the commanding officer. Every memorial and letter relative to our disputes was the work of my pen. The detachments or court-martials of any delicacy or importance were my extraordinary duties and, to supersede the Duke of Bolton's adjutant, I always exercised the battalion in the field. Sir Thomas Worsley was an easy, good-humored man, fond of the table and of his bed. Our conferences were marked by every stroke of the midnight and morning hours, and the same drum which invited him to rest has often summoned me to the parade. His example encouraged the daily practice of hard and even excessive drinking which has sown in my constitution the seeds of the gout. The loss of so many busy and idle hours was not compensated by any elegant pleasure, and my temper was insensibly soured by the society of our rustic officers who were alike deficient in the knowledge of scholars and the manners of gentlemen. In every state there exists, however, a balance of good and evil. The habits of a sedentary life were usefully broken by the duties of an active profession. In the healthful exercise of the field I hunted with a battalion, instead of a pack, and at that time I was ready at any hour of the day or night to fly from quarters to London, from London to quarters, on the slightest call of private or regimental business. But my principal obligation to the militia was the making me an Englishman, and a soldier. After my foreign education, with my reserved temper I should long have continued a stranger in my native country, had I not been shaken in this various scene of new faces and new friends; had not experience forced me to feel the characters of our leading men, the state of parties, the forms of office, and the operation of our civil and military system. In this peaceful service I imbibed the rudiments of the language and science of tactics, which opened a new field of study and observation. I diligently read and meditated the *Mémoires Militaires* of Quintus Icilius (M. Guichard), the only writer who has united the merits of a professor and a veteran. The discipline and evolutions of a modern battalion gave me a clearer notion of the phalanx and the legions, and the captain of the Hampshire grenadiers — the reader may smile — has not been useless to the historian of the Roman empire.

When I complain of the loss of time, justice to myself and to the militia must throw the greatest part of that reproach on the first seven or eight months, while I was obliged to learn as well as to teach. The dissipation of Blandford, and the disputes of Portsmouth, consumed the hours which were not employed in the field, and amid the perpetual hurry of an inn, a barrack, or a guard-room, all literary ideas were banished from my mind. After this long fast, the longest which I have ever known, I once more tasted at Dover the pleasures of reading and thinking, and the hungry appetite with which I opened a volume of Tully's philosophical works is still present to my memory. The last review of my *Essay* before its publication, had prompted me to investigate the nature of the gods. My inquiries led me to the *Histoire Critique du Manichéisme* of Beausobre, who discusses many deep questions of pagan and Christian theology, and from this rich treasury of facts and opinions, I deduced my own consequences, beyond the holy circle of the author. After this recovery I never relapsed into indolence, and my example might prove that in the life most adverse to study some hours may be stolen, some minutes may be snatched. Amidst the tumult of Winchester camp I sometimes thought and read in my tent; in the more settled quarters of the Devizes, Blandford, and Southampton, I always secured a separate lodging and the necessary books, and in the summer of 1762, while the new militia was raising, I enjoyed at Buriton two or three months of literary repose. In forming a new plan of study, I hesitated between the mathematics and the Greek language, both of which I had neglected since my return from Lausanne. I consulted a learned and friendly mathematician, Mr. George Scott a pupil of de Moivre, and his map of a country which I have never explored, may perhaps be more serviceable to others. As soon as I had given the preference to Greek, the example of Scaliger and my own reason determined me on the choice of Homer, the father of poetry and the bible of the ancients: but Scaliger ran through the Iliad in one and twenty days, and I was not dissatisfied with my own diligence for performing the same labor in an equal number of weeks. After the first difficulties were surmounted, the language of nature and harmony soon became easy and familiar, and each day I sailed on the ocean with a brisker gale and a more steady course.

> "Ἐν δ' ἄνεμος πρῆσεν μέσον ἱστίον, ἀμφί, δὲ κῦμα
> Στείρῃ πορφύρεον μεγάλ' ἴαχε, νηὸς ἰούσης·
> Ἡ δ' ἔθεεν κατὰ κῦμα διαπρήσσουσα κέλευθον."

In the study of a poet who has since become the most intimate of my friends, I successively applied many passages and fragments of Greek writers, and among these I shall notice a life of Homer in the *Opuscula Mythologica* of Gale, several books of the geography of Strabo, and the entire treatises of Longinus, which, from the title and the style, is equally worthy of the epithet of sublime. My grammatical skill was improved, my vocabulary was enlarged; and in the militia I acquired a just and indelible knowledge of the first of languages. On every march, in every journey, Horace was always in my pocket and often in my hand; but I should not mention his two critical epistles—the amusement of a morning—had they not been accompanied by the elaborate commentary of Dr. Hurd, now Bishop of Worcester. On the interesting subjects of composition and imitation of epic and dramatic poetry, I presumed to think for myself; and thirty close-written pages in folio could scarcely comprise my full and free discussion of the sense of the master and the pedantry of the servant.

After his oracle Dr. Johnson, my friend Sir Joshua Reynolds denies all original genius, any natural propensity of the mind to one art or science rather than another. Without engaging in a metaphysical or rather verbal dispute, I know by experience that from my early youth I aspired to the character of an historian. While I served in the militia, before and after the publication of my *Essay*, this idea ripened in my mind, nor can I paint in more lively colors the feelings of the moment, than by transcribing some passages, under their respective dates, from a journal which I kept at that time.

Buriton, April 14, 1761. (In a short excursion from Dover.) — Having thought of several subjects for an historical composition, I chose the expedition of Charles VIII of France into Italy. I read two memoirs of M. de Foncemagne in the Academy of Inscriptions (tom. xvii. p. 539–607), and abstracted them. I likewise finished this day a dissertation, in which I examined the right of Charles VIII to the crown of Naples, and the rival claims of the houses of Anjou and Aragon; it consists of ten folio pages, besides large notes.

Buriton, August 4, 1761. (In a week's excursion from Winchester camp.) — After having long revolved subjects for my intended historical essay, I renounced my first thought of the expedition of Charles VIII as too remote from us, and rather an introduction to great events, than great and important in itself. I successively chose and rejected the crusade of Richard the First, the barons' wars against John and Henry III, the history of Edward the Black Prince, the lives and comparisons of Henry V and the Emperor Titus, the life of Sir Philip Sidney, or of the Marquis of Montrose. At length I have fixed on Sir Walter Raleigh for my hero. His eventful story is varied by the characters of the soldier and sailor, the courtier and historian, and it may afford such a fund of materials as I desire, which have not yet been properly manufactured. At present I cannot attempt the execution of this work. Free leisure and the opportunity of consulting many books, both printed and manuscript, are as necessary as they are impossible to be attained in my present way of life. However, to acquire a general insight into my subject and resources, I read the life of Sir Walter Raleigh by Dr. Birch, his copious article in the *General Dictionary*, by the same hand, and the reigns of Queen Elizabeth and James the First in Hume's *History of England*.

Buriton, January 1762. (In a month's absence from the Devizes.) — During this interval of repose, I again turned my thoughts to Sir Walter Raleigh, and looked more closely into my materials. I read the two volumes in quarto of the Bacon Papers, published by Dr. Birch; the *Fragmenta Regalia* of Sir Robert Naunton, Mallet's *Life of Lord Bacon*, and the political treatises of that great man in the first volume of his works, with many of his letters in the second; Sir William Monson's *Naval Tracts*, and the elaborate life of Sir Walter Raleigh, which Mr. Oldys has prefixed to the best edition of his *History of the World*. My subject opens upon me, and in general improves on a nearer prospect.

Buriton, July 26, 1762. (During my summer residence.) — I am afraid of being reduced to drop my hero; but my time has not, however, been lost in the research of his story, and of a memorable era of our English annals. The life of Sir Walter Raleigh by Oldys, is a very poor performance — a servile panegyric, or flat apology, tediously minute and composed in a dull and affected style. Yet the author was a man of diligence and learning who had read everything relative to his object, and whose ample collections are arranged with perspicuity and method. Except some anecdotes lately revealed in the Sidney and Bacon Papers, I know not what I should be able to add. My ambition, exclusive of the uncertain merit of style and sentiment, must be confined to the hope of giving a good abridgment of Oldys. I have even the disappointment of finding some parts of this copious work very dry and barren, and these parts are unluckily some of the most characteristic — Raleigh's colony of Virginia, his quarrels with Essex, the true secret of his conspiracy, and above all the detail of his private life, the most essential and important to a biographer. My best resource would be in the circumjacent history of the times, and perhaps in some digressions artfully introduced, like the fortunes of the peripatetic philosophy in the portrait of Lord Bacon. But the reigns of Elizabeth and James I are the period of English history, which has been the most variously illustrated; and what new lights could I reflect on a subject, which has exercised the accurate industry of Birch, the lively and curious acuteness of Walpole, the critical spirit of Hurd, the vigorous sense of Mallet and Robertson, and the impartial philosophy of Hume? Could I even surmount these obstacles, I should shrink with terror from the modern history of England, where every character is a problem and every reader a friend or an enemy; where a writer is supposed to hoist a flag of party, and is devoted to damnation by the adverse faction. Such would be my reception at home, and abroad the historian of Raleigh must encounter an indifference far more bitter than censure or reproach. The events of his life are interesting, but his character is ambiguous, his actions are obscure, his writings are English, and his fame is confined to the narrow limits of our language and our island. I must embrace a safer and more extensive theme.

There is one which I should prefer to all others, the history of the liberty of the Swiss, of that independence which a brave people rescued from the House of Austria, defended against a Dauphin of France, and finally sealed with the blood of Charles of Burgundy. From such a theme, so full of public spirit, of military glory, of examples of virtue, of lessons of government, the dullest stranger would catch fire. What might not I hope, whose talents whatsoever they may be, would be inflamed by the zeal of patriotism. · But the materials of this history are inaccessible to me, fast locked in the obscurity of an old barbarous German dialect of which I am totally ignorant, and which I cannot resolve to learn for this sole and peculiar purpose.

I have another subject in view, which is the contrast of the former history; the one a poor, warlike, virtuous republic which emerges into glory and freedom, the other a commonwealth, soft, opulent, and corrupt, which by just degrees is precipitated from the abuse to the loss of her liberty. Both lessons are, perhaps, equally instructive. This second subject is the history of the Republic of Florence under the house of Medicis, a period of one hundred and fifty years, which rises or descends from the dregs of the Florentine democracy to the title and dominion of Cosmo de Medicis in the Grand Duchy of Tuscany. I might deduce a chain of revolutions not unworthy of the pen of Vertot; singular men, and singular events; the Medicis four times expelled and as often recalled, and the genius of freedom reluctantly yielding to the arms of Charles V and the policy of Cosmo. The character and fate of Savonarola, and the revival of arts and letters in Italy, will be essentially connected with the elevation of the family and the fall of the republic. The Medicis — *stirps quasi fataliter nata ad instauranda vel fovenda studia* (Lipsius *Ad Germanos et Gallos, Epist.* vii.) — were illustrated by the patronage of learning; and enthusiasm was the most formidable weapon of their adversaries. On this splendid subject I shall most probably fix; but when, or where, or how will it be executed? I behold in a dark and doubtful perspective,

"Res alta terra, et caligine mersas."

[GIBBON REVISITS THE CONTINENT.]

The youthful habits of the language and manners of France had left in my mind an ardent desire of revisiting the continent on a larger and more liberal plan. According to the law of custom, and perhaps of reason, foreign travel completes the education of an English gentleman. My father had consented to my wish, but I was detained above four years by my rash engagement in the militia. I eagerly grasped the first moments of freedom; three or four weeks in Hampshire and London were employed in the preparations of my journey, and the farewell visits of friendship and civility. My last act in town was to applaud Mallet's new tragedy of *Elvira*. A post-chaise conveyed me to Dover, the packet to Boulogne, and such was my diligence that I reached Paris on the twenty-eighth of January, 1763, only thirty-six days after the disbanding of the militia. Two or three years were loosely defined for the term of my absence, and I was left at liberty to spend that time in such places and in such a manner as was most agreeable to my taste and judgment.

In this first visit I passed three months and a half (January 28–May 9), at Paris and a much longer space might have been agreeably filled without any intercourse with the natives. At home we are content to move in the daily round of pleasure and business, and a scene which is always present is supposed to be within our knowledge, or at least within our power. But in a foreign country, curiosity is our business and our pleasure; and the traveler, conscious of his ignorance and covetous of his time, is diligent in the search and the view of every object that can deserve his attention. I devoted many hours of the morning to the circuit of Paris and the neighborhood, to the visit of churches and palaces conspicuous by their architecture, to the royal manufactures, collections of books and pictures, and all the various treasures of art, of learning, and of luxury. An Englishman may hear without reluctance, that in these curious and costly articles Paris is superior to London, since the opulence of the French capital arises from the defects of the government and religion. In the absence of Louis XIV and his successors, the Louvre has been left unfinished; but the millions which have been lavished on the sands of Versailles and the morass of Marli, could not be supplied by the legal allowance of a British king. The splendor of the French nobles is confined to their town residence, that of the English is more usefully distributed in their country seats; and we should be astonished at our own riches, if the labors of architecture, the spoils of Italy and Greece, which are now scattered from Inverary to Wilton, were accumulated in a few streets between Marylebone and Westminster. All superfluous ornament is rejected by the cold frugality of the Protestants, but the Catholic superstition, which is always the enemy of reason, is often the parent of taste. The wealthy communities of priests and monks expend their revenues in stately edifices, and the parish church of St. Sulpice, one of the noblest structures in Paris, was built and adorned by the private industry of a late curate. In this outset, and still more in the sequel of my tour, my eye was amused; but the pleasing vision cannot be fixed by the pen; the particular images are darkly seen through the medium of five-and-twenty years, and the narrative of my life must not degenerate into a book of travels.

But the principal end of my journey was to enjoy the society of a polished and amiable people in whose favor I was strongly prejudiced, and to converse with some authors whose conversation, as I fondly imagined, must be far more pleasing and instructive than their writings. The moment was happlly chosen. At the close of a successful war the British name was respected on the continent —

> "Clarum et venerabile nomen
> Gentibus."

Our opinions, our fashions, even our games, were adopted in France; a ray of national glory illuminated each individual, and every Englishman was supposed to be born a patriot and a philosopher. For myself, I carried a personal recommendation; my name and my *Essay* were already known; the compliment of writing in the French language entitled me to some returns of civility and gratitude. I was considered as a man of letters, or rather as a gentleman who wrote for his amusement. My appearance, dress, and equipage distinguished me from the tribe of authors who, even at Paris, are secretly envied and despised by those who possess the advantages of birth [and] fortune. Before my departure I had obtained from the Duke de Nivernois, Lady Hervey, the Mallets, Mr. Walpole, etc., many letters of recommendation to their private or literary friends. Of these epistles the reception and success was determined by the character and situation of the persons by whom and to whom they were addressed. The seed was sometimes cast on a barren rock, and it sometimes multiplied an hundredfold in the production of new shoots, spreading branches, and exquisite fruit. But upon the whole, I had reason to praise the national urbanity, which from the court has diffused its gentle influence to the shop, the cottage, and the schools. Of the men of genius of the age, Montesquieu and Fontenelle were no more; Voltaire resided on his own estate near Geneva; Rousseau in the preceding year had been driven from his hermitage of Montmorency, and I blush at my neglecting to seek, in this journey, the acquaintance of Buffon. Among the men of letters whom I saw, d'Alembert and Diderot held the foremost rank in merit, or at least in fame. These two associates were the elements of water and fire, but the eruption was clouded with smoke and the stream, though devoid of grace, was limpid and copious. I shall content myself with enumerating the well-known names of the Count de Caylus, of the Abbés de la Bletterie, Barthélemy, Raynal, Arnaud, of Messieurs de la Condamine, du Clos, de Sainte Palaye, de Bougainville, Capperonier, de Guignes, Suard, etc., without attempting to discriminate the shades of their characters, or the degrees of our connection. Alone in a morning visit, I commonly found the wits and authors of Paris less vain, and more reasonable than in the circles of their equals, with whom they mingle in the houses of the rich. Four days in the week, I had a place without invitation at the hospitable tables of Mesdames Geoffrin and du Bocage, of the celebrated Helvetius, and of the Baron d'Holbach. In these symposia the pleasures of the table were improved by lively and liberal conversation; the company was select, though various and voluntary, and each unbidden guest might mutter a proud and ungrateful sentence,

"'Αυτόματοι δ' ἀγαθοὶ δειλῶν ἐπὶ δαῖτας ἴασι."

Yet I was often disgusted with the capricious tyranny of Madame Geoffrin, nor could I approve the intolerant zeal of the philosophers and encyclopædists, the friends of d'Holbach and Helvetius. They laughed at the skepticism of Hume, preached the tenets of atheism with the bigotry of dogmatists, and damned all believers with ridicule and contempt. The society of Madame du Bocage was more soft and moderate than that of her rivals, and the evening conversations of M. de Foncemagne were supported by the good sense and learning of the principal members of the Academy of Inscriptions. The opera and the Italians I occasionally visited, but the French theatre, both in tragedy and comedy, was my daily and favorite amusement. Two famous actresses then divided the public applause. For my own part, I preferred the consummate art of the Clairon, to the intemperate sallies of the Dumesnil, which were extolled by her admirers as the genuine voice of nature and passion. I have reserved for the last the most pleasing connection which I formed at Paris, the acquisition of a female friend by whom I was sure of being received every evening with a smile of confidence and joy. I delivered a letter from Mrs. Mallet to Madame Bontemps who had distinguished herself by a translation of Thompson's

Seasons into French prose. At our first interview we felt a sympathy which banished all reserve and opened our bosoms to each other. In every light, in every attitude, Madame B[ontemps] was a sensible, and amiable companion, an author careless of literary honors, a devotee untainted with religious gall. She managed a small income with elegant economy. Her apartment on the Quai des Theatins commanded the river, the bridges, and the Louvre. Her familiar suppers were adorned with freedom and taste and I attended her in my carriage to the houses of her acquaintance, to the sermons of the most popular preachers, and in pleasant excursions to St. Denys, St. Germain, and Versailles. In the middle season of life her beauty was still an object of desire. The Marquis de Mirabeau, a celebrated name, was neither her first nor her last lover. But if her heart was tender, if her passions were warm, a veil of decency was cast over her frailties. Fourteen weeks insensibly stole away, but had I been rich and independent, I should have prolonged and perhaps have fixed my residence at Paris.

Between the expensive style of Paris and of Italy it was prudent to interpose some months of tranquil simplicity, and at the thoughts of Lausanne I again lived in the pleasures and studies of my early youth. Shaping my course through Dijon and Besançon, in the last of which places I was kindly entertained by my cousin Acton, I arrived in the month of May, 1763, on the banks of the Leman Lake. It had been my intention to pass the Alps in the autumn, but such are the simple attractions of the place, that the annual circle was almost revolved before my departure from Lausanne in the ensuing spring. An absence of five years had not made much alteration in manners, or even in persons. My old friends, of both sexes, hailed my voluntary return, the most genuine proof of my attachment. They had been flattered by the present of my book, the produce of their soil, and the good Pavilliard shed tears of joy as he embraced a pupil with whose success his vanity as well as friendship might be delighted. To my old list I added some new acquaintance, who in my former residence had not been on the spot or in my way, and among the strangers I shall distinguish Prince Lewis of Würtemberg, the brother of the reigning Duke, at whose country-house near Lausanne I frequently dined; a wandering meteor, and at length a falling star, his light and ambitious spirit had successively dropped from the firmament of Prussia, of France, and of Austria, and his faults, which he styled his misfortunes, had driven him into philosophic exile in the Pays de Vaud. He could now moralize on the vanity of the world, the equality of mankind, and the happiness of a private station. His address was affable and polite, and as he had shone in courts and armies, his memory could supply, and his eloquence could adorn, a copious fund of interesting anecdotes. His first enthusiasm was that of charity and agriculture; but the sage gradually lapsed in the saint, and Prince Lewis of Würtemberg is now buried in an hermitage near Mayence, in the last stage of mystic devotion. By some ecclesiastical quarrel, Voltaire had been provoked to withdraw himself from Lausanne; but the theatre which he had founded, the actors whom he had formed survived the loss of their master, and recent from Paris, I assisted with pleasure at the representation of several tragedies and comedies. I shall not descend to specify particular names and characters, but I cannot forget a private institution, which will display the innocent freedom of Swiss manners. My favorite society had assumed, from the age of its members, the proud denomination of the spring — *La Société du Printemps.* It consisted of fifteen or twenty young unmarried ladies, of genteel though not of the very first families, the eldest perhaps about twenty; all agreeable, several handsome, and two or three of exquisite beauty. At each other's houses they assembled almost every day, without the control or even the presence of a mother or an aunt; they were trusted to their own prudence among a crowd of young men of every nation in Europe. They laughed, they sung, they danced, they played at cards, they acted comedies; but in the midst of this careless gaiety, they respected themselves, and were respected by the men. The invisible line between liberty and licentiousness was never transgressed by a gesture, a word, or a look, and their virgin chastity was never sullied by the breath of scandal or suspicion. After tasting the luxury of England and Paris, I could not have returned with patience to the table and table-cloth of Madame Pavilliard; nor was her husband offended that I now entered myself as a *pensionnaire*, or boarder, in the more elegant house of M. de Mésery, which may be entitled to a short remembrance, as it has stood above twenty years, perhaps without a parallel in Europe. The house in which we lodged was spacious and convenient, in the best street, and commanding from behind a noble prospect over the country and the Lake. Our table was served with neatness and plenty; the boarders were numerous; we had the liberty of inviting any guests at a stated price, and in the summer the scene was occasionally transferred to a pleasant villa, about a league from Lausanne. The characters of the master and mistress were happily suited to each other, and to their situation. At the age of seventy-five Madame de Mésery, who has survived her husband, is still a graceful, I had almost said a handsome woman. She was alike qualified to preside in her kitchen and her drawing-room;

and such was the equal propriety of her conduct, that of two or three hundred foreigners, none ever failed in respect, none could complain of her neglect, and none could ever boast of her favor. Mésery himself, of the noble family of de Crousaz, was a man of the world, a jovial companion whose easy manners and natural sallies maintained the cheerfulness of his house. His wit could laugh at his own ignorance; he disguised, by an air of profusion, a strict attention to his interest, and in the exercise of a mean trade he appeared like a nobleman who spent his fortune and entertained his friends. In this agreeable family I resided near eleven months (May 1763–April 1764); but the habits of the militia and the example of my countrymen betrayed me into some riotous acts of intemperance, and before my departure I had deservedly forfeited the public opinion which had been acquired by the virtues of my better days. Yet in this second visit to Lausanne, among a crowd of my English companions, I knew and esteemed Mr. Holroyd, late captain in the Royal Foresters, and our mutual attachment was renewed and fortified in the subsequent stages of our Italian journey. Our lives are in the power of chance, and a slight variation on either side in time or place, might have deprived me of a friend whose activity in the ardor of youth was always prompted by a benevolent heart, and directed by a strong understanding.

If my studies at Paris had been confined to the study of the world, three or four months would not have been unprofitably spent. My visits, however superficial, to the Cabinet of Medals and the public libraries opened a new field of inquiry, and the view of so many manuscripts of different ages and characters induced me to consult the two great Benedictine works, the *Diplomatica* of Mabillon, and the *Palæographia* of Montfaucon. I studied the theory without attaining the practice of the art; nor should I complain of the intricacy of Greek abbreviations and Gothic alphabets, since every day, in a familiar language, I am at a loss to decipher the hieroglyphics of a female note. In a tranquil scene, which revived the memory of my first studies, idleness would have been less pardonable; the public libraries of Lausanne and Geneva liberally supplied me with books, and if many hours were lost in dissipation, many more were employed in literary labor. In the country, Horace and Virgil, Juvenal and Ovid, were my assiduous companions; but in town I formed and executed a plan of study for the use of my transalpine expedition — the topography of old Rome, the ancient geography of Italy, and the science of medals. 1. I diligently read, almost always with my pen in my hand, the elaborate treatises of Nardini, Donatus, etc., which fill the fourth volume of the *Roman Antiquities* of Grævius. 2. I next undertook and finished the *Italia Antiqua* of Cluverius, a learned native of Prussia who had measured on foot every spot, and has compiled and digested every passage of the ancient writers. These passages in Greek or Latin I perused in the text of Cluverius, in two folio volumes. But I separately read the descriptions of Italy by Strabo, Pliny, and Pomponius Mela, the catalogues of the epic poets, the itineraries of Wesseling's Antoninus, and the coasting voyage of Rutilius Numatianus; and I studied two kindred subjects in the *Mesures Itinéraires* of d'Anville, and the copious work of Bergier, *Histoire des grands Chemins de l'Empire Romain.* From these materials I formed a table of roads and distances reduced to our English measure, filled a folio common-place book with my collections and remarks on the geography of Italy, and inserted in my journal many long and learned notes on the *insulæ* and populousness of Rome, the social war, the passage of the Alps by Hannibal, etc. 3. After glancing my eye over Addison's agreeable dialogues, I more seriously read the great work of Ezechiel Spanheim *De Præstantia et Usu Numismatum*, and applied with him the medals of the kings and emperors, the families and colonies, to the illustration of ancient history. And thus was I armed for my Italian journey. Perhaps I might boast that few travelers more completely armed and instructed have ever followed the footsteps of Hannibal. As soon as the return of spring had unlocked the mountains, I departed from Lausanne (April 18, 1764) with an English companion (Mr., afterwards Sir William, Guise) whose partnership divided and alleviated the expenses of the journey.

I shall advance with rapid brevity in the narrative of my Italian tour, in which somewhat more than a year (April 1764–May 1765) was agreeably employed. Content with tracing my line of march, and slightly touching on my personal feelings, I shall waive the minute investigation of the scenes which have been viewed by thousands, and described by hundreds of our modern travelers. Rome is the great object of our pilgrimage; and (1) the journey, (2) the residence, and (3) the return, will form the most proper and perspicuous division. 1. I climbed Mount Cenis and descended into the plain of Piedmont, not on the back of an elephant, but on a light osier seat in the hands of the dexterous and intrepid chairmen of the Alps. The architecture and government of Turin presented the same aspect of tame and tiresome uniformity; but the court was regulated with decent and splendid economy, and I was introduced to his Sardinian majesty Charles Emanuel, who after the incomparable Frederick held the second rank—*proximus longo tamen intervallo*—among the kings of Europe. The size and populousness of Milan could not surprise an inhabitant of London; the dome or cathedral is an unfinished monument of Gothic superstition and wealth, but the fancy is amused by a visit to the Borromean Islands, an enchanted palace, a work of the fairies in the midst of a lake encompassed with mountains and far removed from the haunts of men. I was less amused by the marble palaces of Genoa, than by the recent memorials of her deliverance (in December 1746) from the Austrian tyranny, and I took a military survey of every scene of action within the inclosure of her double walls. My steps were detained at Parma and Modena, by the precious relics of the Farnese and Este collections; but, alas! the far greater part had been already transported, by inheritance or purchase, to Naples and Dresden. By the road of Bologna and the Apennine I at last reached Florence, where I reposed from June to September, during the heat of the summer months. In the gallery, and especially in the Tribune, I first acknowledged at the feet of the Venus of Medicis that the chisel may dispute the pre-eminence with the pencil, a truth in the fine arts which cannot on this side of the Alps be felt or understood. At home I had taken some lessons of Italian; on the spot I read with a learned native the classics of the Tuscan idiom. But the shortness of my time, and the use of the French language, prevented my acquiring any facility of speaking, and I was a silent spectator in the conversations of our envoy, Sir Horace Mann, whose most serious business was that of entertaining the English at his hospitable table. After leaving Florence, I compared the solitude of Pisa with the industry of Lucca and Leghorn, and continued my journey through Sienna to Rome, where I arrived in the beginning of October.

2. My temper is not very susceptible of enthusiasm, and

the enthusiasm which I do not feel, I have ever scorned to affect. But, at the distance of twenty-five years, I can neither forget nor express the strong emotions which agitated my mind as I first approached and entered the eternal city. After a sleepless night, I trod with a lofty step the ruins of the Forum. Each memorable spot, where Romulus stood, or Tully spoke, or Cæsar fell, was at once present to my eye, and several days of intoxication were lost or enjoyed before I could descend to a cool and minute investigation. My guide was Mr. Byers, a Scotch antiquary of experience and taste; but in the daily labor of eighteen weeks the powers of attention were sometimes fatigued, till I was myself qualified in a last review to select and study the capital works of ancient and modern art. Six weeks were borrowed for my tour of Naples, the most populous of cities relative to its size, whose luxurious inhabitants seem to dwell on the confines of paradise and hell-fire. I was presented to the boy king by our new envoy, Sir William Hamilton, who, wisely diverting his correspondence from the secretary of state to the Royal Society and British Museum, has elucidated a country of such inestimable value to the naturalist and antiquarian. On my return, I fondly embraced for the last time the miracles of Rome; but I departed without kissing the feet of Rezzonico (Clement XIII), who neither possessed the wit of his predecessor Lambertini, nor the virtues of his successor Ganganelli. 3. In my pilgrimage from Rome to Loretto I again crossed the Apennine. From the coast of the Adriatic I traversed a fruitful and populous country, which would alone disprove the paradox of Montesquieu, that modern Italy is a desert. Without adopting the exclusive prejudice of the natives, I sincerely admired the paintings of the Bologna school. I hastened to escape from the sad solitude of Ferrara, which in the age of Cæsar was still more desolate. The spectacle of Venice afforded some hours of astonishment and some days of disgust; the University of Padua is a dying taper; but Verona still boasts her amphitheatre, and his native Vicenza is adorned by the classic architecture of Palladio. The road of Lombardy and Piedmont (did Montesquieu find them without inhabitants?) led me back to Milan, Turin, and the passage of Mount Cenis, where I again crossed the Alps in my way to Lyons.

The use of foreign travel has been often debated as a general question, but the conclusion must be finally applied to the character and circumstances of each individual. With the education of boys, where or how they may pass over some juvenile years with the least mischief to themselves or others, I have no concern. But after supposing the previous and indispensable requisites of age, judgment, a competent knowledge of men and books, and a freedom from domestic prejudices, I will briefly describe the qualifications which I deem most essential to a traveler. He should be endowed with an active, indefatigable vigor of mind and body, which can seize every mode of conveyance, and support with a careless smile every hardship of the road, the weather, or the inn. It must stimulate him with a restless curiosity, impatient of ease, covetous of time and fearless of danger, which drives him forth at any hour of the day or night to brave the flood, to climb the mountain, or to fathom the mine, on the most doubtful promise of entertainment or instruction. The arts of common life are not studied in the closet. With a copious stock of classical and historical learning my traveler must blend the practical knowledge of husbandry and manufactures. He should be a chemist, a botanist, and a master of mechanics. A musical ear will multiply the pleasures of his Italian tour, but a correct and exquisite eye which commands the landscape of a country, discerns the merit of a picture and measures the proportions of a building, is more closely connected with the finer feelings of the mind, and the fleeting image shall be fixed and realized by the dexterity of the pencil. I have reserved for the last a virtue which borders on a vice, the flexible temper which can assimilate itself to every tone of society from the court to the cottage, the happy flow of spirits which can amuse and be amused in every company and situation. With the advantage of an independent fortune and the ready use of national and provincial idioms, the traveler should unite the pleasing aspect and decent familiarity which makes every stranger an acquaintance, and the art of conversing with ignorance and dullness on some topic of local or professional information. The benefits of foreign travel will correspond with the degrees of these various qualifications; but, in this sketch of ideal perfection, those to whom I am known will not accuse me of framing my own panegyric. Yet the historian of the *Decline and Fall* must not regret his time or expense, since it was the view of Italy and Rome which determined the choice of the subject. In my journal the place and moment of conception are recorded, the fifteenth of October 1764, in the close of evening, as I sat musing in the church of the Zoccolanti or Franciscan friars, while they were singing vespers in the temple of Jupiter on the ruins of the capital. But my original plan was circumscribed to the decay of the city rather than of the empire, and though my reading and reflections began to point towards that object, some years elapsed and several avocations intervened, before I was seriously engaged in the execution of that laborious work.

[GIBBON RETURNS TO ENGLAND.]

I had not totally renounced the southern provinces of France, but the letters which I found at Lyons were expressive of some impatience; the measure of absence and expense was filled; Rome and Italy had satiated my curious appetite, and the excessive heat of the weather decided the sage resolution of turning my face to the north and seeking the peaceful retreat of my family and books. After an happy fortnight I tore myself from the embraces of Paris, embarked at Calais, again landed at Dover after an interval of two years and five months, and hastily drove through the summer dust and solitude of London. On the 25th of June, 1765, I reached the rural mansion of my parents to whom I was endeared by my long absence and cheerful submission.

After my first (1758) and my second return to England (1765), the forms of the pictures were nearly the same, but the colors had been darkened by time, and the five years and a half between my travels and my father's death (1770) are the portion of my life which I passed with the least enjoyment, and which I remember with the least satisfaction. I have nothing to change — for there was not any change — in the annual distribution of my summers and winters, between my domestic residence in Hampshire and a casual lodging at the west end of the town; though once from the trial of some months I was tempted to substitute the tranquil dissipation of Bath instead of the smoke, the expense, and the tumult of the metropolis, —*fumum et opes strepitumque Romæ.* Every spring I attended the monthly meeting and exercise of the militia at Southampton, and by the resignation of my father and the death of Sir Thomas Worsley, I was successively promoted to the rank of major and lieutenant-colonel commandant. Under the care (may I presume to say of a veteran officer?) the South battalion of the Hampshire militia acquired the degree of skill and discipline which was compatible with the brevity of time and the looseness of peaceful subordination; but I was each year more disgusted with the inn, the wine, the company, and the tiresome repetition of annual attendance and daily exercise. At home the economy of the family and farm still maintained the same creditable appearance. I was received, entertained and dismissed with similar kindness and indulgence. My connection with Mrs. Gibbon was mellowed into a warm and solid attachment; my growing years abolished the distance that might yet remain between a parent and a son, and my behavior satisfied my father, who was proud of the success, however imperfect in his own lifetime, of my literary talents. Our solitude was soon and often enlivened by the visit of the friend of my youth, of M. Deyverdun, whose absence from Lausanne I had sincerely lamented. About three years after my first departure, he had migrated from his native lake to the banks of the Oder in Germany. The *res angusta domi*, the waste of a decent patrimony by an improvident father, obliged him, like many of his countrymen, to confide in his own industry, and he was entrusted with the education of a young prince, the grandson of the Margrave of Schwedt, of the royal family of Prussia. Our friendship was never cooled, our correspondence was sometimes interrupted; but I rather wished than hoped to obtain M. Deyverdun for the companion of my Italian tour. An unhappy, though honorable passion, drove him from his German court, and the attractions of hope and curiosity were fortified by the expectation of my speedy return to England. I was allowed to offer him the hospitality of the house. During four successive summers he passed several weeks or months at Buriton, and our free conversations on every topic that could interest the heart or understanding, would have reconciled me to a desert or a prison. In the winter months of London, my sphere of knowledge and action was somewhat enlarged by the many new acquaintance which I had contracted in the militia and abroad, and I must regret, as more than an acquaintance, Mr. Godfrey Clark of Derbyshire, an amiable and worthy young man who was snatched away by an untimely death. A weekly convivial meeting was instituted by myself and my fellow travelers, under the name of the Roman Club, and I was soon balloted into Boodle's, the school of virtue as the Earl of Shelburne had first named it, where I found the daily resource of excellent dinners, mixed company, and moderate play. I must own, however, with a blush that my virtues of temperance and sobriety had not completely recovered themselves from the wounds of the militia, that my connections were much less among women than men, and that these men, though far from contemptible in rank and fortune, were not of the first eminence in the literary or political world.

The renewal, or perhaps the improvement, of my English life was embittered by the alteration of my own feelings. At the age of twenty-one I was, in my proper station of a youth, delivered from the yoke of education, and delighted with the comparative state of liberty and affluence. My filial obedience was natural and easy, and in the gay prospect of futurity, my ambition did not extend beyond the enjoyment of my books, my leisure, and my patrimonial estate, undisturbed by the cares of a family and the duties of a profession. But in the militia I was armed with power, in my travels I was exempt from control; and as I approached, as I gradually transcended my thirtieth year, I began to feel the desire of being master in my own house. The most gentle authority will sometimes frown without reason, the most cheerful submission will sometimes murmur without cause, and such is the law of our imperfect nature, that we must either command or obey; that our personal liberty is supported by the obsequiousness of our own dependants. While so many of my acquaintance were married or in parliament, or advancing with a rapid step in the various roads of honors and fortune, I stood alone immovable and insignificant; for after the monthly meeting of 1770, I had even withdrawn myself from the militia by the resignation of an empty and barren commission. My temper is not susceptible of envy, and the view of successful merit has always excited my warmest applause. A matrimonial alliance has ever been the object of my terror rather than of my wishes. I was not very strongly pressed by my family or my passions to propagate the name and race of the Gibbons and, if some reasonable temptations occurred in the neighborhood, the vague idea never proceeded to the length of a serious negotiation. The miseries of a vacant life were never known to a man whose hours were insufficient for the inexhaustible pleasures of study. But I lamented that at the proper age I had not embraced the lucrative pursuits of the law or of trade, the chances of civil office or India adventure, or even the fat slumbers of the church, and my repentance became more lively as the loss of time was more irretrievable. Experience showed me the use of grafting my private consequence on the importance of a great professional body; the benefits of those firm connections which are cemented by hope and interest, by gratitude and emulation, by the mutual exchange of services and favors. From the emoluments of a profession I might have derived an ample fortune, or a competent income, instead of being stinted to the same narrow allowance, to be increased only by an event which I sincerely deprecated. The progress and the knowledge of our domestic disorders aggravated my anxiety, and I began to apprehend that I might be left in my old age without the fruits either of industry or inheritance.

In the first summer after my return, whilst I enjoyed at Buriton the society of my friend Deyverdun, our daily conversations expatiated over the field of ancient and modern literature, and we freely discussed my studies, my first *Essay*, and my future projects. The decline and fall of Rome I still contemplated at an awful distance. But the two historical designs which had balanced my choice were submitted to his taste, and in the parallel between the revolutions of Florence and Switzerland, our common partiality for a country which was his by birth, and mine by adoption, inclined the scale in favor of the latter. According to the plan which was soon conceived and digested, I embraced a period of two hundred years, from the association of the three peasants of the Alps to the plenitude and prosperity of the Helvetic body in the sixteenth century. I should have described the deliverance and victory of the Swiss, who have never shed the blood of their tyrants but in a field of battle; the laws and manners of the confederate states; the splendid trophies of the Austrian, Burgundian, and Italian wars, and the wisdom of a nation, who after some sallies of martial adventure has been content to guard the blessings of peace with the sword of freedom.

> "Manus hæc inimica tyrannis
> Ense petit placidam sub libertate quietem."

My judgment, as well as my enthusiasm, was satisfied with the glorious theme, and the assistance of Deyverdun seemed to remove an insuperable obstacle. The French or Latin memorials, of which I was not ignorant, are inconsiderable in number and weight, but in the perfect acquaintance of my friend with the German language I found the key of a more valuable collection. The most necessary books were procured; he translated for my use the folio volume of Schilling, a copious and contemporary relation of the war of Burgundy; we read and marked the most interesting parts of the great chronicle of Tschudi, and by his labor, or that of an inferior assistant, large extracts were made from the *History* of Lauffer and the *Dictionary* of Lew. Yet such was the distance and delay, that two years elapsed in these preparatory steps, and it was late in the third summer (1767) before I entered with these slender materials on the more agreeable task of composition. A specimen of my history, the first book, was read the following winter in a literary society of foreigners in London, and as the author was unknown, I listened without observation to the free strictures and unfavorable sentence of my judges. The momentary sensation was painful, but their condemnation was ratified by my cooler thoughts. I delivered my imperfect sheets to the flames, and forever renounced a design on which some expense, much labor, and more time had been so vainly consumed. I cannot regret the loss of a slight and superficial essay, for such the work must have been in the hands of a stranger, uninformed by the scholars and statesmen, remote from the libraries and archives of the Swiss republics. My ancient habits, and the presence of Deyverdun, encouraged me to write in French for the continent of Europe, but I was conscious myself that my style, above prose and below poetry, degenerated into a verbose and turgid declamation. Perhaps I may impute the failure to the injudicious choice of a foreign language.

Perhaps I may suspect that the language itself is ill adapted to sustain the vigor and dignity of an important narrative. But if France, so rich in literary merit, had produced a great original historian, his genius would have formed and fixed the idiom to the proper tone, the peculiar mode of historical eloquence.

It was in search of some liberal and lucrative employment that my friend Deyverdun had visited England. His remittances from home were scanty and precarious. My purse was always open, but it was often empty, and I bitterly felt the want of riches and power, which might have enabled me to correct the errors of his fortune. His wishes and qualifications solicited the station of the travelling governor of some wealthy pupil; but every vacancy provoked so many eager candidates, that for a long time I struggled without success, nor was it till after much application that I could even place him as a clerk in the office of the secretary of state. In a residence of several years he never acquired the just pronunciation and familiar use of the English tongue, but he read our most difficult authors with ease and taste. His critical knowledge of our language and poetry was such as few foreigners have possessed, and few of our countrymen could enjoy the theatre of Shakespeare and Garrick with more exquisite feeling and discernment. The consciousness of his own strength and the assurance of my aid, emboldened him to imitate the example of Dr. Maty whose *Journal Britannique* was esteemed and regretted, and to improve his model, by uniting with the transactions of literature a philosophic view of the arts and manners of the British nation. Our Journal for the year 1767, under the title of *Mémoires Littéraires de la Grand Bretagne*, was soon finished, and sent to the press. For the first article, Lord Lyttelton's *History of Henry II*, I must own myself responsible; but the public has ratified my judgment of that voluminous work, in which sense and learning are not illuminated by a ray of genius. The next specimen was the choice of my friend, *The Bath Guide*, a light and whimsical performance of local and even verbal pleasantry. I started at the attempt; he smiled at my fears; his courage was justified by success, and a master of both languages will applaud the curious felicity with which he has transfused into French prose the spirit, and even the humor, of the English verse. It is not my wish to deny how deeply I was interested in these Memoirs, of which I need not surely be ashamed; but at the distance of more than twenty years, it would be impossible for me to ascertain the respective shares of the two associates. A long and intimate communication of ideas had cast our sentiments and style in the same mould. In our social labors we composed and corrected by turns, and the praise which I might honestly bestow, would fall perhaps on some article or passage most properly my own. A second volume (for the year 1768) was published of these Memoirs. I will presume to say, that their merit was superior to their reputation, but it is not less true that they were productive of more reputation than emolument. They introduced my friend to the protection, and myself to the acquaintance, of the Earl of Chesterfield, whose age and infirmities secluded him from the world, and of Mr. David Hume, who was under-secretary to the office in which Deyverdun was more humbly employed. The former accepted a dedication (April 12, 1769), and reserved the author for the future education of his successor; the latter enriched the Journal with a reply to Mr. Walpole's *Historical Doubts*, which he afterwards shaped into the form of a note. The materials of the third volume were almost completed, when I recommended Deyverdun as governor to Sir Richard Worsley, a youth, the son of my old Lieutenant-colonel who was lately deceased. They set forwards on their travels, nor did they return to England till some time after my father's death.

My next publication was an accidental sally of love and resentment, of my reverence for modest genius and my aversion to insolent pedantry. The sixth book of the *Æneid* is the most pleasing and perfect composition of Latin poetry. The descent of Æneas and the Sibyl to the infernal regions, to the world of spirits, expands an awful and boundless prospect from the nocturnal gloom of the Cumæan grot,

> "Ibant obscuri sola sub nocte per umbram,"

to the meridian brightness of the Elysian fields,

> "Largior hic campos æther et lumine vestit
> Purpureo;—"

from the dreams of simple nature to the dreams, alas! of Egyptian theology and the philosophy of the Greeks. But the final dismission of the hero through the ivory gate, from whence

> "Falsa ad cælum mittunt insomnia manes,"

seems to dissolve the whole enchantment, and leaves the reader in a state of cold and anxious skepticism. This most lame and impotent conclusion has been variously imputed to the haste or irreligion of Virgil; but according to the more elaborate interpretation of Bishop Warburton, the descent to hell is not a false, but a mimic scene, which represents the initiation of Æneas in the character of a lawgiver to the Eleusinian mysteries. This hypothesis, a singular chapter in the *Divine Legation of Moses*, had been admitted by many as true; it was praised by all as ingenious, nor had it been exposed in a space of thirty years to a fair and critical discussion. The learning and abilities of the author had raised him to a just eminence, but he reigned the dictator and tyrant of the world of literature. The real merit of Warburton was degraded by the pride and presumption with which he pronounced his infallible decrees. In his polemic writings he lashed his antagonists without mercy or moderation, and his servile flatterers (see the base and malignant *Delicacy of Friendship*), exalting the master critic far above Aristotle and Longinus, assaulted every modest dissenter who refused to consult the oracle and to adore the idol. In a land of liberty, such despotism must provoke a general opposition, and the zeal of opposition is seldom candid or impartial. A late professor of Oxford (Dr. Lowth), in a pointed and polished epistle (Aug. 31, 1765) defended himself and attacked the Bishop; and whatsoever might be the merits of an insignificant controversy, his victory was clearly established by the silent confusion of Warburton and his slaves. I too, without any private offense, was ambitious of breaking a lance against the giant's shield, and in the beginning of the year 1770 my *Critical Observations on the Sixth Book of the Æneid* were sent, without my name, to the press. In this short essay, my first English publication, I aimed my strokes against the person and the hypothesis of Bishop Warburton. I proved at least to my own satisfaction, that the ancient lawgivers did not invent the mysteries, and that Æneas was never invested with the office of lawgiver; that there is not any argument, any circumstance, which can melt a fable into allegory, or remove the scene from the Lake Avernus to the temple of Ceres; that such a wild supposition is equally injurious to the poet and the man; that if Virgil was not initiated he could not, if he were, he would not reveal the secrets of the initiation; that the anathema of Horace (*vetabo qui Cereris sacrum vulgarit*, etc.) at once attests his own ignorance and the innocence of his friend. As the Bishop of Gloucester and his party maintained a discreet silence, my critical disquisition was soon lost among the pamphlets of the day; but the public coldness was overbalanced to my feelings by the weighty approbation of the last and best editor of Virgil, Professor Heyne of Göttingen, who acquiesces in my confutation, and styles the unknown author *doctus . . . et elegantissimus Britannus*. But I cannot resist the temptation of transcribing the favorable judgment of Mr. Hayley, himself a poet and a scholar: "An intricate hypothesis, twisted into a long and labored chain of quotation and argument, the *Dissertation on the Sixth book of Virgil*, remained some time unrefuted. . . . At length a superior, but anonymous critic arose, who, in one of the most judicious and spirited essays that our nation has produced on a point of classical literature, completely overturned this ill-founded edifice, and exposed the arrogance and futility of its assuming architect." He even condescends to justify an acrimony of style, which had been gently blamed by the more unbiased German; *Paulo acrius quam velis . . . perstrinxit*. But I cannot forgive myself the contemptuous treatment of a man who, with all his faults, was entitled to my esteem, and I can less forgive in a personal attack the cowardly concealment of my name and character.

[GIBBON BEGINS HIS HISTORY OF THE ROMAN EMPIRE.]

In the fifteen years between my *Essay on the Study of Literature* and the first volume of the *Decline and Fall* (1761–1776), this criticism on Warburton and some articles in the Journal were my sole publications. It is more especially incumbent on me to mark the employment, or to confess the waste of time from my travels to my father's death, an interval in which I was not diverted by any professional duties from the labors and pleasures of a studious life. 1. As soon as I was released from the fruitless task of the Swiss revolutions I more seriously undertook (1768) to methodize the form and to collect the substance of my Roman decay, of whose limits and extent I had yet a very inadequate notion. The classics, as low as Tacitus, the younger Pliny, and Juvenal, were my old and familiar companions. I insensibly plunged into the ocean of the *Augustan History*, and in the descending series I investigated, with my pen almost always in my hand, the original records both Greek and Latin from Dion Cassius to Ammianus Marcellinus, from the reign of Trajan to the last age of the Western Cæsars. The subsidiary rays of medals, and inscriptions of geography and chronology, were thrown on their proper objects, and I applied the collections of Tillemont, whose inimitable accuracy almost assumes the character of genius, to fix and arrange within my reach the loose and scattered atoms of historical information. Through the darkness of the middle ages I explored my way in the *Annals* and *Antiquities* of Italy of the learned Muratori, and diligently compared them with the parallel or transverse lines of Sigonius and Maffei, Baronius and Pagi, till I almost grasped the ruins of Rome in the fourteenth century, without suspecting that this final chapter must be attained by the labor of six quartos and twenty years. Among the books which I purchased, the *Theodosian Code* with the commentary of James Godefroy must be gratefully remembered. I used it (and much I used it) as a work of history rather than of jurisprudence, but in every light it may be considered as a full and capacious repository of the political state of the empire in the fourth and fifth centuries. As I believed, and as I still believe, that the propagation of the gospel and the triumph of the church are inseparably connected with the decline of the Roman monarchy, I weighed the causes and effects of the revolution, and contrasted the narratives and apologies of the Christians themselves, with the glances of candor or enmity which the pagans have cast on the rising sect. The *Jewish and Heathen Testimonies*, as they are collected and illustrated by Dr. Lardner, directed without superseding my search of the originals, and in an ample dissertation on the miraculous darkness of the passion, I privately drew my conclusions from the silence of an unbelieving age. I have assembled the preparatory studies, directly or indirectly relative to my history; but in strict equity they must be spread beyond this period of my life, over the two summers (1771 and 1772) that elapsed between my father's death and my settlement in London. 2. In a free conversation with books and men, it would be endless to enumerate the names and characters of all who are introduced to our acquaintance; but in this general acquaintance we may select the degrees of friendship and esteem. According to the wise maxim, *multum legere potius quam multa*, I reviewed again and again the immortal works of the French and English, the Latin and Italian classics. My Greek studies, though less assiduous than I designed, maintained and extended my knowledge of that incomparable idiom. Homer and Xenophon were still my favorite authors, and I had almost prepared for the press an essay on the *Cyropædia*, which in my own judgment is not unhappily labored. After a certain age, the new publications of merit are the sole food of the many, and the most austere student will be often tempted to break the line, for the sake of indulging his own curiosity, and of providing the topics of fashionable currency. A more respectable motive may be assigned for the triple perusal of Blackstone's *Commentaries*, and a copious and critical abstract of that English work was my first serious production in my native language. 3. My literary leisure was much less complete and independent than it might appear to the eye of a stranger. In the hurry of London I was destitute of books; in the solitude of Hampshire I was not master of my time.[1] My quiet was gradually disturbed by our domestic anxiety, and I should be ashamed of my unfeeling philosophy, had I found much time or taste for study in the last fatal summer (1770) of my father's decay and dissolution.

The disembodying of the militia at the close of the war (1762) had restored the Major, a new Cincinnatus, to a life of agriculture. His labors were useful, his pleasures innocent, his wishes moderate, and my father seemed to enjoy the state of happiness which is celebrated by poets and philosophers, as the most agreeable to nature and the least accessible to fortune;

> "Beatus ille, qui procul negotiis,
> Ut prisca gens mortalium,
> Paterna rura bobus exercet suis,
> Solutus omni fœnore."

[1] Here occurs a sentence which is found also in Memoir B. though in a slightly different form; see p. 99. It here reads as follows:

By the habit of early rising I always secured a sacred portion of the day, and many precious moments were stolen and saved by my rational avarice. But the family hours of breakfast and dinner, of tea and supper, were regular and tedious. After breakfast Mrs. Gibbon expected my company in her dressing room; after tea my father claimed my conversation and the perusal of the newspapers. In the heat of some interesting pursuit I was called down to receive

But the last indispensable condition, the freedom from debt, was wanting to my father's felicity, and the vanities of his youth were severely punished by the solicitude and sorrow of his declining age. The first mortgage, on my return from Lausanne (1758), had afforded him a partial and transient relief. The annual demand of interest and allowance was an heavy deduction from his income; the militia was a source of expense, the farm in his hands was not a profitable adventure; he was loaded with the costs and damages of an obsolete law-suit, and each year multiplied the number, and exhausted the patience, of his creditors. Under these painful circumstances, my own behavior was not only guiltless but meritorious. Without stipulating any personal advantages I consented, at a mature and well informed age, to an additional mortgage, to the sale of Putney, and to every sacrifice that could alleviate his distress. But he was no longer capable of a rational effort, and his reluctant delays postponed not the evils themselves, but the remedies of those evils — *remedia malorum potius quam mala differebat.* The pangs of shame, tenderness, and self-reproach, incessantly preyed on his vitals; his constitution was broken; he lost his strength and his sight; the rapid progress of a dropsy admonished him of his end, and he sunk into the grave on the 10th of November, 1770, in the sixty-fourth year of his age. A family tradition insinuates that Mr. William Law has drawn his pupil in the light and inconstant character of *Flatus,* who is ever confident and ever disappointed in the chase of happiness. But these constitutional failings were amply compensated by the virtues of the head and heart, by the warmest sentiments of honor and humanity.

the visits of our idle neighbors. Their civilities required a suitable return, and I dreaded the period of the full moon which was usually reserved for our more distant excursions.

His graceful person, polite address, gentle manners, and unaffected cheerfulness, recommended him to the favor of every company, and in the change of times and opinions, his liberal spirit had long since delivered him from the zeal and prejudice of a Tory education. The tears of a son are seldom lasting. I submitted to the order of nature, and my grief was soothed by the conscious satisfaction that I had discharged all the duties of filial piety. Few perhaps are the children who, after the expiration of some months or years, would sincerely rejoice in the resurrection of their parents, and it is a melancholy truth that my father's death, not unhappy for himself, was the only event that could save me from an hopeless life of obscurity and indigence.

As soon as I had paid the last solemn duties to my father, and obtained from time and reason a tolerable composure of mind, I began to form the plan of an independent life most adapted to my circumstances and inclination. Yet so intricate was the net, my efforts were so awkward and feeble, that near two years (November 1770–October 1772) were suffered to elapse before I could disentangle myself from the management of the farm, and transfer my residence from Buriton to an house in London. During this interval I continued to divide my year between town and the country; but my new freedom was brightened by hope, nor could I refuse the advantages of a change which had never — I have scrutinized my conscience — which had never been the object of my secret wishes. Without indulging the vanity and extravagance of a thoughtless heir, I assumed some additional latitude of lodging, attendance, and equipage. I no longer numbered with the same anxious parsimony my dinners at the club or tavern. My stay in London was prolonged into the summer, and the uniformity of the summer was occasionally broken by visits and excursions at a distance from home. That home, the house and estate at Buriton, were now my own. I could invite without control the persons most agreeable to my taste; the horses and servants were at my disposal, and in all their operations my rustic ministers solicited the commands and smiled at the ignorance of their master. I will not deny that my pride was flattered by the local importance of a country gentleman. The busy scene of the farm, productive of seeming plenty, was embellished in my eyes by the partial sentiment of property and, still adhering to my original plan, I expected the adequate offers of a tenant and postponed without much impatience the moment of my departure. My friendship for Mrs. Gibbon long resisted the idea of our final separation. After my father's decease she preserved the tenderness without the authority of a parent. The family and even the farm were intrusted to her care and, as the habits of fifteen years had attached her to the spot, she was herself persuaded, and she tried to persuade me, of the pleasures and benefits of a country life. But, as I could not afford to maintain a double establishment, my favorite project of an house in London was incompatible with the farm at Buriton and it was soon apparent that a woman and a philosopher could not direct, with any prospect of advantage, such a complex and costly machine. In the second summer my resolution was declared and effected. The advertisement of the farm attracted many competitors, the fairest terms were preferred, the proper leases were executed, I abandoned the mansion to the principal tenant and Mrs. G[ibbon], with some reluctance, departed for Bath, the most fashionable asylum for the sober singleness of widowhood. But the produce of the effects and stock was barely sufficient to clear my accounts in the country and my first settlement in town. From the mischievous extravagance of the tenant I sustained many subsequent injuries, and a change of ministry could not be accomplished without much trouble and expense.

Besides the debts for which my honor and piety were engaged, my father had left a weighty mortgage of seventeen thousand pounds. It could only be discharged by a landed sacrifice and my estate at Lenborough, near Buckingham, was the devoted victim. At first the appearances were favorable, but my hopes were too sanguine, my demands were too high. After slighting some offers by no means contemptible, I rashly signed an agreement with a worthless fellow — half knave and half madman — who, in three years of vexatious chicanery refused either to consummate or to relinquish his bargain. After I had broken my fetters the opportunity was lost. The public distress had reduced the value of land. I waited the return of peace and prosperity and my last secession to Lausanne preceded the sale of my Buckinghamshire estate. The delay of fifteen years, which I may impute to myself, my friends, and the times, was accompanied with the loss of many thousand pounds. A delicious morsel, a share in the New River Company, was cast with many a sigh into the gulf of principle, interest, and annual expense, and the far greater part of the inadequate price of poor Lenborough was finally devoured by the insatiate monster. Such remembrance is bitter, but the temper of a mind exempt from avarice suggests some reasonable topics of consolation. My patrimony has been diminished in the enjoyment of life. The gratification of my desires (they were not immoderate) has been seldom disappointed by the want of money or credit. My pride was never insulted by the visit of an importunate tradesman, and any transient anxiety for the past or future was soon dispelled by the studious or social occupation of the present hour. My conscience does not accuse me of any act of extravagance or injustice. The remnant of my estate affords an ample and honorable provision for my declining age, and my spontaneous bounty must be received with implicit gratitude by the heirs of my choice. I shall not expatiate more minutely on my economical affairs, which cannot be instructive or amusing to the reader. It is a rule of prudence, as well as of politeness, to reserve such confidence for the ear of a private friend, without exposing our situation to the envy or pity of strangers; for envy is productive of hatred, and pity borders too nearly on contempt. Yet I may believe, and even assert, that in circumstances more indigent or more wealthy, I should never have accomplished the task, or acquired the fame of an historian; that my spirit would have been broken by poverty and contempt, and that my industry might have been relaxed in the labor and luxury of a superfluous fortune. Few works of merit and importance have been executed either in a garret or a palace. A gentleman possessed of leisure and independence, of books and talents, may be encouraged to write by the distant prospect of honor and reward, but wretched is the author and wretched will be the work where daily diligence is stimulated by daily hunger.

I had now attained the solid comforts of life — a convenient well furnished house, a domestic table, half a dozen chosen servants, my own carriage, and all those decent luxuries whose value is the more sensibly felt the longer they are enjoyed. These advantages were crowned by the first of earthly blessings, independence. I was the absolute master of my hours and actions, nor was I deceived in the hope that the establishment of my library in town would allow me to divide the day between study and society. Each year the circle of my acquaintance, the number of my dead and living companions, was enlarged. To a lover of books, the shops and sales in London present irresistible temptations, and the manufacture of my history required a various and growing stock of materials. The militia, my travels, the House of Commons, the fame of an author contributed to multiply my connections. I was chosen a member of the fashionable clubs, and before I left England there were few persons of any eminence in the literary or political world to whom I was a stranger. By my own choice I passed in town the greatest part of the year; but whenever I was desirous of breathing the air of the country, I possessed an hospitable retreat at Sheffield Place in Sussex, in the family of Mr. Holroyd, a valuable friend whose character, under the name of Lord Sheffield, has since been more conspicuous to the public.

No sooner was I settled in my house and library, than I undertook the composition of the first volume of my history. At the outset all was dark and doubtful — even the title of the work, the true era of the decline and fall of the empire, the limits of the introduction, the division of the chapters, and the order of the narrative; and I was often tempted to cast away the labor of seven years. The style of an author should be the image of his mind, but the choice and command of language is the fruit of exercise. Many experiments were made before I could hit the middle tone between a dull chronicle and a rhetorical declamation. Three times did I compose the first chapter, and twice the second and third, before I was tolerably satisfied with their effect. In the remainder of the way I advanced with a more equal and easy pace; but the fifteenth and sixteenth chapters have been reduced by three successive revisals, from a large volume to their present size, and they might still be compressed, without any loss of facts or sentiments. An opposite fault may be imputed to the concise and superficial narrative of the first reigns from Commodus to Alexander — a fault of which I have never heard, except from Mr. Hume in his last journey to London. Such an oracle might have been consulted and obeyed with rational devotion, but I was soon disgusted with the modest practice of reading the manuscript to my friends. Of such friends some will praise from politeness, and some will criticise from vanity. The author himself is the best judge of his own performances. None has so deeply meditated on the subject, none is so sincerely interested in the event.

By the friendship of Mr. (now Lord) Eliot, who had married my first cousin, I was returned at the general election for the borough of Liskeard. I took my seat at the beginning of the memorable contest between Great Britain and America, and supported with many a sincere and silent vote the rights, though not perhaps the interests, of the mother country. After a fleeting illusive hope, prudence condemned me to acquiesce in the humble station of a mute. I was not armed by nature or education with the intrepid energy of mind and voice, —

> "Vincentem strepitus, et natum rebus agendis."

Timidity was fortified by pride, and even the success of my pen discouraged the trial of my voice. But I assisted at the debates of a free assembly which agitated the most important questions of peace and war, of justice and policy. I listened to the attack and defense of eloquence and reason; I had a near prospect of the characters, views, and passions of the first men of the age. The eight sessions that I sat in parliament were a school of civil prudence, the first and most essential virtue of an historian.

The volume of my history which had been somewhat delayed by the novelty and tumult of a first session, was now ready for the press. After the perilous adventure had been declined by my timid friend Mr. Elmsley, I agreed on very easy terms with Mr. Thomas Cadell, a respectable bookseller, and Mr. William Strahan, an eminent printer; and they undertook the care and risk of the publication, which derived more credit from the name of the shop than from that of the author. The last revisal of the proofs was submitted to my vigilance, and many blemishes of style which had been invisible in the manuscript, were discovered and corrected in the printed sheet. So moderate were our hopes, that the original impression had been stinted to five hundred, till the number was doubled by the prophetic taste of Mr. Strahan. During this awful interval I was neither elated by the ambition of fame, nor depressed by the apprehension of contempt. My diligence and accuracy were attested by my own conscience. History is the most popular species of writing, since it can adapt itself to the highest or the lowest capacity. I had chosen an illustrious subject. Rome is familiar to the schoolboy and the statesman, and my narrative was deduced from the last period of classical reading. I had likewise flattered myself, that an age of light and liberty would receive without scandal an inquiry into the human causes of the progress and establishment of Christianity.

[RECEPTION OF THE DECLINE AND FALL.]

I am at a loss how to describe the success of the work, without betraying the vanity of the writer. The first impression was exhausted in a few days; a second and third edition were scarcely adequate to the demand, and the bookseller's property was twice invaded by the pirates of Dublin. My book was on every table, and almost on every toilette; the historian was crowned by the taste or fashion of the day, nor was the general voice disturbed by the barking of any profane critic. The favor of mankind is most freely bestowed on a new acquaintance of any original merit, and the mutual surprise of the public and their favorite is productive of those warm sensibilities, which at a second meeting can no longer be rekindled. If I listened to the music of praise, I was more seriously satisfied with the approbation of my judges. The candor of Dr. Robertson embraced his disciple. A letter from Mr. Hume overpaid the labor of ten years, but I have never presumed to accept a place in the triumvirate of British historians.

My second excursion to Paris was determined by the pressing invitation of M. and Mme. Necker, who had visited England in the preceding summer. On my arrival I found M. Necker director-general of the finances, in the first bloom of power and popularity. His private fortune enabled him to support a liberal establishment, and his wife, whose talents and virtues I had long admired, was admirably qualified to preside in the conversation of her table and drawing-room. As their friend, I was introduced to the best company of both sexes, to the foreign ministers of all nations, and to the first names and characters of France, who distinguished me by such marks of civility and kindness as gratitude will not suffer me to forget, and modesty will not allow me to enumerate. The fashionable suppers often broke into the morning hours; yet I occasionally consulted the Royal Library, and that of the Abbey of St. Germain, and in the free use of their books at home I had always reason to praise the liberality of those institutions. The society of men of letters I neither courted nor declined, but I was happy in the acquaintance of M. de Buffon, who united with a sublime genius the most amiable simplicity of mind and manners. At the table of my old friend, M. de Foncemagne, I was involved in a dispute with the Abbé de Mably, and his jealous, irascible spirit revenged itself on a work which he was incapable of reading in the original.

Near two years had elapsed between the publication of my first and the commencement of my second volume, and the causes must be assigned of this long delay. 1. After a short holiday, I indulged my curiosity in some studies of a very different nature, a course of anatomy which was demonstrated by Dr. Hunter, and some lessons of chemistry, which were delivered by Mr. Higgins. The principles of these sciences, and a taste for books of natural history, contributed to multiply my ideas and images, and the anatomist or chemist may sometimes track me in their own snow. 2. I dived, perhaps too deeply, into the mud of the Arian controversy, and many days of reading, thinking, and writing were consumed in the pursuit of a phantom. 3. It is difficult to arrange with order and perspicuity the various transactions of the age of Constantine, and so much was I displeased with the first essay, that I committed to the flames above fifty sheets. 4. The six months of Paris and pleasure must be deducted from the account. But when I resumed my task I felt my improvement; I was now master of my style and subject, and while the measure of my daily performance was enlarged, I discovered less reason to cancel or correct. It has always been my practice to cast a long paragraph in a single mould, to try it by my ear, to deposit it in my memory, but to suspend the action of the pen till I had given the last polish to my work. Shall I add, that I never found my mind more vigorous, or my composition more happy than in the winter hurry of society and parliament?

Had I believed that the majority of English readers were so fondly attached even to the name and shadow of Christianity; had I foreseen that the pious, the timid, and the prudent would feel or affect to feel with such exquisite sensibility, I might perhaps have softened the two invidious chapters, which would create many enemies and conciliate few friends. But the shaft was shot, the alarm was sounded, and I could only rejoice, that if the voice of our priests was clamorous and bitter, their hands were disarmed of the powers of persecution. I adhered to the wise resolution of trusting myself and my writings to the candor of the public, till Mr. Davies of Oxford presumed to attack, not the faith, but the good faith of the historian. My *Vindication*, expressive of less anger than contempt, amused for a moment the busy and idle metropolis, and the most rational part of the laity, and even of the clergy, appears to have been satisfied of my innocence and accuracy. My antagonists, however, were rewarded in this world. Poor Chelsum was indeed neglected, and I dare not boast the making Dr. Watson a bishop; but I enjoyed the pleasure of giving a Royal pension to Mr. Davies, and of collating Dr. Apthorpe to an archiepiscopal living. Their success encouraged the zeal of Taylor the Arian, and Milner the Methodist, with many others whom it would be difficult to remember and tedious to rehearse. The list of my adversaries was graced with the more respectable names of Dr. Priestley, Sir David Dalrymple, and Dr. White, and every polemic of either university discharged his sermon or pamphlet against the impenetrable silence of the Roman historian. Let me frankly own that I was startled at the first volleys of this ecclesiastical ordnance; but as soon as I found that this empty noise was mischievous only in the intention, my fear was converted to indignation, and every feeling of indignation or curiosity has long since subsided in pure and placid indifference.

The prosecution of my history was soon afterwards checked by another controversy of a very different kind. At the request of the Chancellor, and of Lord Weymouth then secretary of state, I vindicated against the French manifesto the justice of the British arms. The whole correspondence of Lord Stormont, our late ambassador at Paris, was submitted to my inspection, and the *Mémoire Justificatif* which I composed in French was first approved by the Cabinet Ministers, and then delivered as a State paper to the courts of Europe. The style and manner are praised by Beaumarchais himself, who in his private quarrel attempted a reply; but he flatters me by ascribing the memoir to Lord Stormont, and the grossness of his invective betrays the loss of temper and of wit.

Among the honorable connections which I had formed, I may justly be proud of the friendship of Mr. Wedderburne, at that time attorney-general, who now illustrates the title of Lord Loughborough, and the office of Chief Justice of the Common Pleas. By his strong recommendation, and the favorable disposition of Lord North, I was appointed one of the Lords Commissioners of Trade and Plantations, and my private income was enlarged by a clear addition of between seven and eight hundred pounds a year. The fancy of an hostile orator may paint in the strong colors of ridicule, "the perpetual virtual adjournment, and the unbroken sitting vacation of the Board of Trade." But it must be allowed that our duty was not intolerably severe, and that I enjoyed many days and weeks of repose without being called away from my library to the office. My acceptance of a place provoked some of the leaders of opposition, with whom I lived in habits of intimacy, and I was most unjustly accused of deserting a party in which I had never been enlisted.

The aspect of the next session of parliament was stormy and perilous; county meetings, petitions, and committees of correspondence announced the public discontent, and instead of voting with a triumphant majority, the friends of government were often exposed to a struggle, and sometimes to a defeat. The House of Commons adopted Mr. Dunning's motion, "That the influence of the crown had increased, was increasing, and ought to be diminished"; and Mr. Burke's bill of reform was framed with skill, introduced with eloquence, and supported by numbers. Our late president, the American secretary of state, very narrowly escaped the sentence of proscription; but the unfortunate Board of Trade was abolished in the committee by a small majority (207 to 199) of eight votes. The storm, however, blew over for a time; a large defection of country gentlemen eluded the sanguine hopes of the patriots; the Lords of Trade were revived; administration recovered their strength and spirit, and the flames of London, which were kindled by a mischievous madman, admonished all thinking men of the danger of an appeal to the people. In the premature dissolution which followed this session of parliament I lost my seat. Mr. Eliot was now deeply engaged in the measures of opposition, and the electors of Liskeard are commonly of the same opinion as Mr. Eliot.

In this interval of my senatorial life, I published the second and third volumes of the *Decline and Fall*. My ecclesiastical history still breathed the same spirit of freedom, but Protestant zeal is more indifferent to the characters and controversies of the fourth and fifth centuries.

My obstinate silence had damped the ardor of the polemics. Dr. Watson, the most candid of my adversaries, assured me that he had no thoughts of renewing the attack, and my impartial balance of the virtues and vices of Julian was generally praised. This truce was interrupted only by some animadversions of the Catholics of Italy, and by some angry letters from Mr. Travis, who made me personally responsible for condemning with the best critics the spurious text of the three heavenly witnesses. The bigoted advocate of popes and monks may be turned over even to the bigots of Oxford, and the wretched Travis still howls under the lash of the merciless Porson. But I perceived, and without surprise, the coldness and even prejudice of the town, nor could a whisper escape my ear, that in the judgment of many readers my continuation was much inferior to the original attempt. An author who cannot ascend will always appear to sink; envy was now prepared for my reception and the zeal of my religious, was fortified by the malice of my political, enemies. I was, however, encouraged by some domestic and foreign testimonies of applause, and the second and third volumes insensibly rose in sale and reputation to a level with the first. But the public is seldom wrong, and I am inclined to believe that, especially in the beginning, they are more prolix and less entertaining than the first. My efforts had not been relaxed by success, and I had rather deviated into the opposite fault of minute and superfluous diligence. On the continent my name and writings were slowly diffused; a French translation of the first volume had disappointed the booksellers of Paris, and a passage in the third was construed as a personal reflection on the reigning monarch.

Before I could apply for a seat at the general election the list was already full; but Lord North's promise was sincere, his recommendation was effectual, and I was soon chosen on a vacancy for the borough of Lymington, in Hampshire. In the first session of the new parliament, administration stood their ground; their final overthrow was reserved for the second. The American war had once been the favorite of the country; the pride of England was irritated by the resistance of her colonies, and the executive power was driven by national clamor into the most vigorous and coercive measures. But the length of a fruitless contest, the loss of armies, the accumulation of debt and taxes, and the hostile confederacy of France, Spain, and Holland, indisposed the public to the American war and the persons by whom it was conducted. The representatives of the people followed at a slow distance the changes of their opinion, and the ministers who refused to bend were broken by the tempest. As soon as Lord North had lost, or was about to lose, a majority in the House of Commons, he surrendered his office, and retired to a private station with the tranquil assurance of a clear conscience and a cheerful temper; the old fabric was dissolved, and the posts of government were occupied by the victorious and veteran troops of opposition. The Lords of Trade were not immediately dismissed, but the board itself was abolished by Mr. Burke's bill, which decency compelled the patriots to revive, and I was stripped of a convenient salary after I had enjoyed it about three years.

So flexible is the title of my history, that the final era might be fixed at my own choice, and I long hesitated whether I should be content with the three volumes, the fall of the Western empire, which fulfilled my first engagement with the public. In this interval of suspense, near a twelvemonth, I returned by a natural impulse to the Greek authors of antiquity. In my library in Bentinck street, at my summer lodgings at Brighthelmstone, at a country house which I hired at Hampton Court, I read with new pleasure the Iliad and Odyssey, the histories of Herodotus, Thucydides, and Xenophon, a large portion of the tragic and comic theatre of Athens, and many interesting dialogues of the Socratic school. Yet in the luxury of freedom I began to wish for the daily task, the active pursuit which gave a value to every book, and an object to every inquiry; the preface of a new edition announced my design, and I dropped without reluctance from the age of Plato to that of Justinian. The original texts of Procopius and Agathias supplied the events and even the characters of his reign; but a laborious winter was devoted to the codes, the pandects, and the modern interpreters, before I presumed to form an abstract of the civil law. My skill was improved by practice, my diligence perhaps was quickened by the loss of office, and, except the last chapter, I had finished my fourth volume before I sought a retreat on the banks of the Leman Lake.

It is not the purpose of this narrative to expatiate on the public or secret history of the times, the schism which followed the death of the Marquis of Rockingham, the appointment of the Earl of Shelburne, the resignation of Mr. Fox, and his famous coalition with Lord North. But I may affirm, with some degree of assurance, that in their political conflict those great antagonists had never felt any personal animosity to each other, that their reconciliation was easy and sincere, and that their friendship has never been clouded by the shadow of suspicion or jealousy. The most violent or venal of their respective followers embraced this fair occasion of revolt, but their alliance still commanded a majority in the House of Commons; the peace was censured, Lord Shelburne resigned, and the two friends knelt on the same cushion to take the oath of secretary of state. From a principle of gratitude I adhered to the coalition; my vote was counted in the day of battle, but I was overlooked in the division of the spoil. There were many claimants more deserving and importunate than myself; the Board of Trade could not be restored, and while the list of places was curtailed, the number of candidates was doubled. An easy dismission to a secure seat at the board of customs or excise was promised on the first vacancy; but the chance was distant and doubtful, nor could I solicit with much ardor an ignoble servitude, which would have robbed me of the most valuable of my studious hours. At the same time the tumult of London and the attendance on parliament were grown more irksome, and, without some additional income, I could not long or prudently maintain the style of expense to which I was accustomed.

[GIBBON SETTLES AT LAUSANNE.]

From my early acquaintance with Lausanne I had always cherished a secret wish, that the school of my youth might become the retreat of my declining age. A moderate fortune would secure the blessings of ease, leisure, and independence. The country, the people, the manners, the language were congenial to my taste, and I might indulge the hope of passing some years in the domestic society of a friend. After traveling with several English, M. Deyverdun was now settled at home in a pleasant habitation, the gift of his deceased aunt. We had long been separated, we had long been silent, yet in my first letter I exposed with the most perfect confidence my situation, my sentiments, and my designs. His immediate answer was a warm and joyful acceptance; the picture of our future life provoked my impatience, and the terms of arrangement were short and simple, as he possessed the property, and I undertook the expense of our common house. Before I could break my English chain, it was incumbent on me to struggle with the feelings of my heart, the indolence of my temper, and the opinion of the world, which unanimously condemned this voluntary banishment. In the disposal of my effects, the library, a sacred deposit, was alone excepted; as my post-chaise moved over Westminster bridge I bid a long farewell to the *fumum et opes strepitumque Romæ.* My journey by the direct road through France was not attended with any accident, and I arrived at Lausanne near twenty years after my second departure. Within less than three months the coalition struck on some hidden rocks; had I remained aboard, I should have perished in the general shipwreck.

Since my establishment at Lausanne, more than seven years have elapsed, and if every day has not been equally soft and serene, not a day, not a moment has occurred in which I have repented of my choice. During my absence, a long portion of human life, many changes had happened. My elder acquaintance had left the stage; virgins were ripened into matrons, and children were grown to the age of manhood. But the same manners were transmitted from one generation to another. My friend alone was an inestimable treasure; my name was not totally forgotten, and all were ambitious to welcome the arrival of a stranger and the return of a fellow-citizen. The first winter was given to a general embrace, without any nice discrimination of persons and characters. After a more regular settlement, a more accurate survey, I discovered three solid and permanent benefits of my new situation. 1. My personal freedom had been somewhat impaired by the House of Commons and the Board of Trade, but I was now delivered from the chain of duty and dependence, from the hopes and fears of political adventure. My sober mind was no longer intoxicated by the fumes of party, and I rejoiced in my escape as often as I read of the midnight debates which preceded the dissolution of parliament. 2. My English economy had been that of a solitary bachelor who might afford some occasional dinners. In Switzerland I enjoyed at every meal, at every hour, the free and pleasant conversation of the friend of my youth, and my daily table was always provided for the reception of one or two extraordinary guests. Our importance in society is less a positive than a relative weight. In London I was lost in the crowd; I ranked with the first families of Lausanne, and my style of prudent expense enabled me to maintain a fair balance of reciprocal civilities. 3. Instead of a small house between a street and a stable-yard, I began to occupy a spacious and convenient mansion, connected on the north side with the city and open on the south to a beautiful and boundless horizon. A garden of four acres had been laid out by the taste of M. Deyverdun. From the garden a rich scenery of meadows and vineyards descends to the Leman Lake, and the prospect far beyond the Lake is crowned by the stupendous mountains of Savoy. My books and my acquaintance had been first united in London, but this happy position of my library in town and country was finally reserved for Lausanne. Possessed of every comfort in this triple alliance, I could not be tempted to change my habitation with the changes of the seasons.

My friends had been kindly apprehensive that I should not be able to exist in a Swiss town at the foot of the Alps, after so long conversing with the first men of the first cities of the world. Such lofty connections may attract the curious, and gratify the vain; but I am too modest, or too proud to rate my own value by that of my associates, and whatsoever may be the fame of learning or genius, experience has shown me that the cheaper qualifications of politeness and good sense are of more useful currency in the commerce of life. By many, conversation is esteemed as a theatre or a school; but after the morning has been occupied by the labors of the library, I wish to unbend rather than to exercise my mind, and in the interval between tea and supper I am far from disdaining the innocent amusement of a game at cards. Lausanne is peopled by a numerous gentry, whose companionable idleness is seldom disturbed by the pursuits of avarice or ambition. The women, though confined to a domestic education, are endowed for the most part with more taste and knowledge than their husbands or brothers; but the decent freedom of both sexes is equally remote from the extremes of simplicity and refinement. I shall add, as a misfortune rather than a merit, that the situation and beauty of the Pays de Vaud, the long habits of the English, the medical reputation of Dr. Tissot, and the fashion of viewing the mountains and glaciers, have opened us on all sides to the incursions of foreigners. The visits of M. and Mme. Necker, of Prince Henry of Prussia, and of Mr. Fox may form some pleasing exceptions; but in general Lausanne has appeared most agreeable in my eyes, when we have been abandoned to our own society.

My transmigration from London to Lausanne could not be effected without interrupting the course of my historical labors. The hurry of my departure, the joy of my arrival, the delay of my tools, suspended their progress, and a full twelvemonth was lost before I could resume the thread of regular and daily industry. A number of books most requisite and least common had been previously selected. The academical library of Lausanne, which I could use as my own, contains at least the fathers and councils, and I have derived some occasional succor from the public collections of Berne and Geneva. The fourth volume was soon terminated by an abstract of the controversies of the incarnation, which the learned Dr. Prideaux was apprehensive of exposing to profane eyes. In the fifth and sixth volumes the revolutions of the empire and the world are most rapid, various, and instructive, and the Greek or Roman historians are checked by the hostile narratives of the barbarians of the east and west. It was not till after many designs, and many trials, that I preferred, as I still prefer the method of grouping my picture by nations, and the seeming neglect of chronological order is surely compensated by the superior merits of interest and perspicuity. The style of the first volume is in my opinion somewhat crude and elaborate, in the second and third it is ripened into ease, correctness, and numbers ; but in the three last I may have been seduced by the facility of my pen, and the constant habit of speaking one language and writing another may have infused some mixture of Gallic idioms. Happily for my eyes, I have always closed my studies with the day, and commonly with the morning, and a long but temperate labor has been accomplished without fatiguing either the mind or body. But when I computed the remainder of my time and my task, it was apparent that, according to the season of publication, the delay of a month would be productive of that of a year. I was now straining for the goal, and in the last winter many evenings were borrowed from the social pleasures of Lausanne. I could now wish that a pause, an interval, had been allowed for a serious revisal.

[GIBBON COMPLETES THE DECLINE AND FALL.]

I have presumed to mark the moment of conception; I shall now commemorate the hour of my final deliverance. It was on the day, or rather the night of the 27th of June 1787, between the hours of eleven and twelve, that I wrote the last lines of the last page, in a summer-house in my garden. After laying down my pen, I took several turns in a *berceau*, or covered walk of acacias, which commands a prospect of the country, the lake, and the mountains. The air was temperate, the sky was serene, the silver orb of the moon was reflected from the waters, and all nature was silent. I will not dissemble the first emotions of joy on the recovery of my freedom and, perhaps, the establishment of my fame. But my pride was soon humbled, and a sober melancholy was spread over my mind, by the idea that I had taken my everlasting leave of an old and agreeable companion, and that whatsoever might be the future date of my history, the life of the historian must be short and precarious. I will add two facts, which have seldom occurred in the composition of six, or at least of five, quartos. 1. My first rough manuscript, without any intermediate copy, has been sent to the press. 2. Not a sheet has been seen by any human eyes, except those of the author and the printer; the faults and the merits are exclusively my own.

After a quiet residence of four years during which I had never moved ten miles from Lausanne, it was not without some reluctance and terror that I undertook, in a journey of two hundred leagues, to cross the mountains and the sea. Yet this formidable adventure was achieved without danger or fatigue, and at the end of a fortnight I found myself in Lord Sheffield's house and library, safe, happy, and at home. The character of my friend Mr. Holroyd had recommended him to a seat in parliament for Coventry, the command of a regiment of light dragoons, and an Irish peerage. The sense and spirit of his political writings have decided the public opinion on the great questions of our commercial intercourse with America and Ireland. He fell (in 1784) with the unpopular coalition, but his merit has been acknowledged at the last general election (1790) by the honorable invitation and free choice of the city of Bristol. During the whole time of my residence in England I was entertained at Sheffield Place and in Downing street by his hospitable kindness, and the most pleasant period was that which I passed in the domestic society of the family. In the larger circle of the metropolis I observed the country and the inhabitants with the knowledge, and without the prejudices of an Englishman; but I rejoiced in the apparent increase of wealth and prosperity, which might be fairly divided between the spirit of the nation and the wisdom of the minister. All party resentment was now lost in oblivion; since I was no man's rival, no man was my enemy. I felt the dignity of independence, and as I asked no more, I was satisfied with the general civilities of the world. The house in London which I frequented with the most pleasure and assiduity was that of Lord North. After the loss of power and of sight, he was still happy in himself and his friends, and my public tribute of gratitude and esteem could no longer be suspected of any interested motive. Before my departure from England, I assisted at the august spectacle of Mr. Hastings's trial in Westminster Hall. I shall not absolve or condemn the Governor of India; but Mr. Sheridan's eloquence demanded my applause, nor could I hear without emotion the personal compliment which he paid me in the presence of the British nation.

As the publication of my three last volumes was the principal object, so it was the first care of my English journey. The previous arrangements with the bookseller and the printer were settled in my passage through London, and the proofs, which I returned more correct, were transmitted every post from the press to Sheffield Place. The length of the operation, and the leisure of the country allowed some time to review my manuscript. Several rare and useful books, the *Assises de Jérusalem*, Ramusius *De Bello Constantinopolitano*, the Greek *Acts of the Synod of Florence*, the *Statuta Urbis Romæ*, etc., were procured, and I introduced in their proper places the supplements which they afforded. The impression of the fourth volume had consumed three months. Our common interest required that we should move with a quicker pace, and Mr. Strahan fulfilled his engagement, which few printers could sustain, of delivering every week three thousand copies of nine sheets. The day of publication was however delayed, that it might coincide with the fifty-first anniversary of my own birthday. The double festival was celebrated by a cheerful literary dinner at Cadell's house, and I seemed to blush while they read an elegant compliment from Mr. Hayley, whose poetical talent had more than once been employed in the praise of his friend. As most of the former purchasers were naturally desirous of completing their sets, the sale of the quarto edition was quick and easy, and an octavo size was printed, to satisfy at a cheaper rate the public demand. The conclusion of my work appears to have diffused a strong sensation. It was generally read, and variously judged. The style has been exposed to much academical criticism. A religious clamor was revived, and the reproach of indecency has been loudly echoed by the rigid censors of morals. Yet upon the whole, the *History of the Decline and Fall* seems to have struck a root both at home and abroad, and may perhaps an hundred years hence still continue to be abused. The French, Italian, and German translations have been executed with various success; but instead of patronizing I should willingly suppress such imperfect copies, which injure the character while they propagate the name of the author. The Irish pirates are at once my friends and my enemies. But I cannot be displeased with the two numerous and correct impressions of the English original which have been published for the use of the continent at Basel in Switzerland. The conquests of our language and literature are not confined to Europe alone, and the writer who succeeds in London is speedily read on the banks of the Delaware and the Ganges.

In the preface of the fourth volume, while I gloried in the name of an Englishman, I announced my approaching return to the neighborhood of the Lake of Lausanne. This last trial confirmed my assurance that I had wisely chosen for my own happiness, nor did I once, in a year's visit, entertain a wish of settling in my native country. Britain is the free and fortunate island; but where is the spot in which I could unite the comforts and beauties of my establishment at Lausanne? The tumult of London astonished my eyes and ears; the amusements of public places were no longer adequate to the trouble; the clubs and assemblies were filled with new faces and young men, and our best society, our long and late dinners, would soon have been prejudicial to my health. Without any share in the political wheel, I must be idle and insignificant; yet the most splendid temptations would not have enlisted me a second time in the servitude of parliament or office. At Tunbridge, some weeks after the publication of my history, I tore myself from the embraces of Lord and Lady Sheffield, and with a young Swiss friend, whom I had introduced to the English world, I pursued the road of Dover and Lausanne. My habitation was embellished in my absence, and the last division of books, which followed my steps, increased my chosen library to the number of six or seven thousand volumes. My seraglio was ample, my choice was free, my appetite was keen. After a full repast on Homer and Aristophanes, I involved myself in the philosophic maze of the writings of Plato, of which the dramatic is perhaps more interesting than the argumentative part; but I stepped aside into every path of inquiry which reading or reflection accidentally opened.

Alas! the joy of my return and my studious ardor were soon damped by the melancholy state of my friend M. Deyverdun. His health and spirits had long suffered a gradual decline, a succession of apoplectic fits announced his dissolution, and before he expired, those who loved him could not wish for the continuance of his life. The voice of reason might congratulate his deliverance, but the feelings of nature and friendship could be subdued only by time. His amiable character was still alive in my remembrance; each room, each walk, was imprinted with our common footsteps, and I should blush at my own philosophy, if a long interval of study had not preceded and followed the death of my friend. By his last will he left me the option of purchasing his house and garden, or of possessing them during my life on the payment either of a stipulated price, or of an easy retribution to his kinsman and heir. I should probably have been tempted by the demon of property, if some legal difficulties had not been started against my title. A contest would have been vexatious, doubtful, and invidious, and the heir most gratefully subscribed an agreement which rendered my life-possession more perfect, and his future condition more advantageous. The certainty of my tenure has allowed me to lay out a considerable sum in improvements and alterations. They have been executed with skill and taste, and few men of letters, perhaps, in Europe are so desirably lodged as myself. But I feel, and with the decline of years I shall more painfully feel, that I am alone in paradise. Among the circle of my acquaintance at Lausanne, I have gradually acquired the solid and tender friendship of a respectable family. The four persons of whom it is composed are all endowed with the virtues best adapted to their age and situation, and I am encouraged to love the parents as a brother, and the children as a father. Every day we seek and find the opportunities of meeting; yet even this valuable connection cannot supply the loss of domestic society.

Within the last two or three years our tranquillity has been clouded by the disorders of France. Many families of Lausanne were alarmed and affected by the terrors of an impending bankruptcy; but the revolution, or rather the dissolution of the kingdom has been heard and felt in the adjacent lands. A swarm of emigrants of both sexes, who escaped from the public ruin, has been attracted by the vicinity, the manners, and the language of Lausanne, and our narrow habitations in town and country are now occupied by the first names and titles of the departed monarchy. These noble fugitives are entitled to our pity; they may claim our esteem, but they cannot in the present state of their mind and fortune much contribute to our amusement. Instead of looking down as calm and idle spectators on the theatre of Europe, our domestic harmony is somewhat embittered by the infusion of party spirit. Our ladies and gentlemen assume the character of self-taught politicians, and the sober dictates of wisdom and experience are silenced by the clamors of the triumphant *démocrates.* The fanatic missionaries of sedition have scattered the seeds of discontent in our cities and villages, which had flourished above two hundred and fifty years without fearing the approach of war, or feeling the weight of government. Many individuals and some communities appear to be infected with the French disease, the wild theories of equal and boundless freedom; but I trust that the body of the people will be faithful to their sovereign and themselves, and I am satisfied that the failure or success of a revolt would equally terminate in the ruin of the country. While the aristocracy of Berne protects the happiness, it is superfluous to inquire whether it is founded in the rights of man; the economy of the state is liberally supplied without the aid of taxes, and the magistrates must reign with prudence and equity, since they are unarmed in the midst of an armed nation. For myself (may the omen be averted) I can only declare, that the first stroke of a rebel drum would be the signal of my immediate departure.

When I contemplate the common lot of mortality, I must acknowledge that I have drawn a high prize in the lottery of life. The far greater part of the globe is overspread with barbarism or slavery. In the civilized world the most numerous class is condemned to ignorance and poverty, and the double fortune of my birth in a free and enlightened country, in an honorable and wealthy family, is the lucky chance of an unit against millions. The general probability is about three to one, that a new-born infant will not live to complete his fiftieth year. I have now passed that age, and may fairly estimate the present value of my existence in the threefold division of mind, body, and estate.

1. The first indispensable requisite of happiness is a clear conscience, unsullied by the reproach or remembrance of an unworthy action;

> "HIC murus aheneus esto,
> Nil conscire sibi, nulla pallescere culpa."

I am endowed with a cheerful temper, a moderate sensibility, and a natural disposition to repose rather than to action; some mischievous appetites and habits have perhaps been corrected by philosophy or time. The love of study, a passion which derives fresh vigor from enjoyment, supplies each day, each hour with a perpetual source of independent and rational pleasure, and I am not sensible of any decay of the mental faculties. The original soil has been highly improved by labor and manure, but it may be questioned, whether some flowers of fancy, some grateful errors, have not been eradicated with the weeds of prejudice. 2. Since I have escaped from the long perils of my childhood, the serious advice of a physician has seldom been requisite. "The madness of superfluous health" I have never known; but my tender constitution has been fortified by time, the play of the animal machine still continues to be easy and regular, and the inestimable gift of the sound and peaceful slumbers of infancy may be imputed both to the mind and body. About the age of forty I was first afflicted with the gout which, in the space of fourteen years, has made seven or eight different attacks. Their duration, though not their intensity, appears to increase and after each fit I rise and walk with less strength and agility than before. But the gout has hitherto been confined to my feet and knees, the pain is never intolerable; I am surrounded by all the comforts that art and attendance can bestow; my sedentary life is amused with books and company, and in each step of my convalescence I pass through a progress of agreeable sensations. 3. I have already described the merits of my society and situation, but these enjoyments would be tasteless and bitter if their possession were not assured by an annual and adequate supply. By the painful method of amputation my father's debts have been completely discharged. The labor of my pen, the sale of lands, the inheritance of a maiden aunt Miss Hester Gibbon, have improved my property and it will be exonerated on some melancholy day from the payment of Mrs. Gibbon's jointure. According to the scale of Switzerland I am a rich man, and I am indeed rich, since my income is superior to my expense, and my expense is equal to my wishes. My friends, more especially Lord Sheffield, kindly relieve me from the cares to which my taste and temper are most adverse. The economy of my house is settled without avarice or profusion. At stated periods all my bills are regularly paid and in the course of my life I have never been reduced to appear either as plaintiff or defendant in a court of justice. Shall I add, that since the failure of my first wishes, I have never entertained any serious thoughts of a matrimonial connection?

I am disgusted with the affectation of men of letters, who complain that they have renounced a substance for a shadow, and that their fame — which sometimes is no insupportable weight — affords a poor compensation for envy, censure, and persecution. My own experience, at least, has taught me a very different lesson. Twenty happy years have been animated by the labor of my history, and its success has given me a name, a rank, a character in the world, to which I should not otherwise have been entitled. The freedom of my writings has indeed provoked an implacable tribe, but as I was safe from the stings, I was soon accustomed to the buzzing of the hornets. My nerves are not tremblingly alive, and my literary temper is so happily framed, that I am less sensible of pain than pleasure. The rational pride of an author may be offended, rather than flattered by vague indiscriminate praise; but he cannot, he should not, be indifferent to the fair testimonies of private and public esteem. Even his social sympathy may be gratified by the idea, that now in the present hour, he is imparting some degree of amusement or knowledge to his friends in a distant land; that one day his mind will be familiar to the grandchildren of those who are yet unborn. I cannot boast of the friendship or favor of princes. The patronage of English literature has long since been devolved on our booksellers, and the measure of their liberality is the least ambiguous test of our common success. Perhaps the golden mediocrity of my fortune has contributed to fortify my application.[1]

The present is a fleeting moment, the past is no more, and our prospect of futurity is dark and doubtful. This day may possibly be my last; but the laws of probability, so true in general so fallacious in particular, still allow me about fifteen years, and I shall soon enter into the period which, as the most agreeable of his long life, was selected by the judgment and experience of the sage Fontenelle. His choice is approved by the eloquent historian of nature, who fixes our moral happiness to the

[1] A sentence is here omitted since it occurs, in a slightly different form, in Memoir C., see p. 163. It reads, Few books of merit and importance have been composed either in a garret or a palace. A gentleman possessed of leisure and competency may be encouraged by the assurance of an honorable reward, but wretched is the writer and wretched will be the work where daily diligence is stimulated by daily hunger.

mature season in which our passions are supposed to be calmed, our duties fulfilled, our ambition satisfied, our fame and fortune established on a solid basis. I am far more inclined to embrace than to dispute this comfortable doctrine. I will not suppose any premature decay of the mind or body; but I must reluctantly observe that two causes, the abbreviation of time, and the failure of hope, will always tinge with a browner shade the evening of life. 1. The proportion of a part to the whole is the only standard by which we can measure the length of our existence. At the age of twenty, one year is a tenth, perhaps, of the time which has elapsed within our consciousness and memory; at the age of fifty it is no more than a fortieth, and this relative value continues to decrease till the last sands are shaken by the hand of death. This reasoning may seem metaphysical but on a trial it will be found satisfactory and just. 2. The warm desires, the long expectations of youth, are founded on the ignorance of themselves and of the world. They are gradually damped by time and experience, by disappointment or possession, and after the middle season the crowd must be content to remain at the foot of the mountain, while the few who have climbed the summit aspire to descend or expect to fall. In old age the consolation of hope is reserved for the tenderness of parents who commence a new life in their children, the faith of enthusiasts who sing hallelujahs above the clouds, and the vanity of authors who presume the immortality of their name and writings.

NOTES.

In the following notes a reference to Murray means the *Autobiographies of Edward Gibbon*, edited by John Murray, London, 1896. The *Private Letters of Edward Gibbon*, edited by Rowland E. Prothero, London, 1896, are referred to as *Letters*, with the volume and page. References to the *Miscellaneous Works of Gibbon* are in all cases to the second edition, published by Lord Sheffield in 1814.

1 1. **My family.** Gibbon says in a note to Memoir E, "I have obtained much domestic information from an English treatise of Heraldry (with a Latin title) composed by John Gibbon, Bluemantle Pursuivant, and the brother as I believe of my great-grandfather Matthew, — *Introductio ad Latinam Blazoniam*, London, 1682." See the Introduction, in which the origin and connections of Gibbon's family are discussed.

1 2. **earliest antiquity.** On this Gibbon has the following jottings which he no doubt intended to enlarge: "From Cæsar, William of Malmesbury, John of Salisbury — Provincial marks lost — Progress of society — Isle of Sky superior to old Kent."

1 8. **Rolvenden.** In Memoir A Gibbon says, "The adjacent hundreds of Rolvenden and Tenterden form one of the most southern districts of Kent, with Sussex to the west, the Isle of Oxney to the south, and Romney Marsh to the east."

1 15. **Queenborough.** Gibbon says (Memoir A), "It is more than supposed that John Gibbon was the principal architect in the building Queenborough castle. At a time when the English coast was infested by the French and Flemings this strong and stately fortress was erected on the west side of the Isle of Sheppey, to guard the entrance of the river Medway. It was denominated from the heroic Queen Philippa of Hainault, and it is praised by the royal founder as a castle in a pleasant situation, a terror to his enemies and a comfort to his subjects."

2 3. **Benenden.** In 1602 Edmund Gibbon of Benenden gave a house for the free school and eighty acres of land for the maintenance of the master. In 1677 Edmund Gibbon of Hole added seventy acres

for the maintenance of an usher, and John Gibbon of Hole in 1713 gave an annuity of fourteen pounds 'for a further augmentation of the schoolmaster provided he be neither vicar, curate, or reader; and if he be, then for the use of poor girls.' The school is still in existence.

2 10. **Go, search, etc.** The quotation is from Pope's *Moral Essays*, III, 287.

2 12. **so recent.** "By order of Thomas Cromwell, Earl of Essex, vicar general of Henry VIII, upon the dissolution of the monasteries every incumbent minister in all the parishes in England was compelled to keep a register of all the weddings, christenings, and burials." — Adam Anderson's *Origin of Commerce*, I, 367. This order was given in 1538 but was little obeyed, so that few registers are as old as the time of Cromwell.

2 24. **Livery and Companies.** The reference is to the Guilds or great companies of the city of London, relics of institutions of great commercial and political importance in earlier times. The livery of the companies was adopted in the reign of Edward III. One of these companies, the Clothworkers mentioned at 5 3, was founded in 1480.

3 8. **ogresses.** A writer in *Notes and Queries* (Third Series, VII, 417) points out that Gibbon has mistaken the heraldic term ogress 'a pellet,' represented by a black disk, for ogress 'a female cannibal.' The change from a scallop to an ogress (pellet) would be slight. Of it John Gibbon in his *Introductio ad Latinam Blazoniam* says, "He [Edmund Gibbon] assumed this new coat out of distaste against three ladies, his kinswomen. . . . The falling out was about the will of Edmund Gibbon, founder of the free school at Benenden." As to the disappearance of the ogresses, Gibbon had himself doubtless seen the monument in Temple Church, London, and had found no female cannibals.

3 17. **Bluemantle.** One of the four pursuivants of the English college of arms, so called from the color of his official robe. A pursuivant is an attendant of a herald.

3 24. **nam genus.** The quotation (Ovid, *Metamorphoses*, XIII, 140, is extended and slightly changed in Memoir A:

> "Et genus et proavos et quæ non fecimus ipsi
> Vix ea nostro voco."

3 29. **Memoirs.** They were written by Antony, or Antoine, Hamilton (1646–1740), brother-in-law of the Count de Gramont, and give a faithful, though by no means pleasing picture of court life in England

at the period of the restoration. It is Antony's brother George who is referred to in line 34.

4 5. **James Fiennes,** Lord Say and Sele died in 1450. In Cade's memorial preserved by Stow, William Cromer is named among 'great extortioners and false traitors.' In Memoir A Gibbon says: "Lord Say and Sele was governor of Dover, Warden of the Cinque Ports, Constable of the Tower, Lord Chamberlain and Lord High Treasurer of England. After the marriage of Queen Margaret he was accused by the Commons of delivering Maine and Anjou to the French and, to appease the popular discontent, this favorite and perhaps innocent minister was sequestered from his office and then committed to the Tower. But neither his dignity nor his disgrace could save him from the blind rage of the Kentish insurgents and their leader Jack Cade. Lord Say was dragged from the asylum of his prison and, after a mock trial at Guildhall, more illegal than any act of which he was accused, his head was struck off and borne in triumph about the street." There seems to be no evidence that Lord Say and Sele was a patron of learning, as mentioned in line 34.

4 9. **eleventh degree.** In Memoir A Gibbon says: "Elizabeth, his daughter, married William Cromer, twice sheriff of Kent and the son of a Lord Mayor of London. Their son, Sir James Cromer, was the father of Anne the wife of William Whetnall of Peckham; George their son was the father of the above mentioned Rose, the mother of Margaret Phillips, the wife of Robert Gibbon of Rolvenden."

4 19. **Thou hast.** The quotation is from the second part of *Henry VI*, IV, vii, 41. The accusation in regard to printing (l. 23) is, as Gibbon suggests, an anachronism. It is based on a story that, in the reign of Henry VI, Frederic Corsellis a workman from Harlem had introduced printing into England.

5 1. **Robert Gibbon.** In Memoir A Gibbon adds, "My lineal ancestor in the fifth degree, Robert Gibbon of Rolvenden, Esquire, was captain of the Kentish militia and, as he died in the year 1618, it may be presumed that he had appeared in arms at the time of the Spanish invasion."

5 10. **Matthew.** In the Introduction it is shown how at this point in his family history Gibbon made a mistake, not unnatural under the circumstances, as to other ancestors. Of Matthew Gibbon he himself admits that he knew no more than that he was a linen merchant of Leadenhall street.

5 12. **John.** A somewhat longer account of this John is given in Memoir A, but all essentials are here summarized. For the manner in

which Gibbon learned of the herald see Introduction. John Gibbon died August 2, 1718.

5 20. **Mr. Hobbes.** Thomas Hobbes the philosopher (1588–1679), after leaving Magdalen College, Oxford, became companion and tutor to the son of William Cavendish, Baron Hardwick and afterwards Earl of Devonshire. The position resulted in a close friendship which continued through life. Hobbes says (*Vita, carmine expressa*, 1679) that the twenty years which he spent with the young earl were the happiest of his life.

6 12. **Sir William Dugdale** (1605–1686) was an antiquary and author of several works, the most important of which is the *Monasticon Anglicanum* (1655–1673), reprinted in 1817–1830. Elias Ashmole (1617–1692) was also an antiquary whose principal work is *Institutions, Laws and Ceremonies of the Order of the Garter* (1672). The Ashmolean Museum is named for him, although he did not begin the collection. John Betts (d. 1695) was a famous physician and author of various medical works. Nehemiah Grew (1641–1671) was a natural philosopher, best known by his *Anatomy of Plants* (1682).

6 20. **cause of the Duke of York.** Reference is to the attempt to exclude the Duke, afterwards James II, from the succession because he was a Roman Catholic. John Gibbon showed his sympathy with the Duke in various 'moral verses' scattered through his works, especially *Day Fatality* (1678) and *Dux bonis omnibus appellens or the Swan's Welcome* (1679). In 1688 he published *Edvardus Confessor redivivus . . . in the sacred majesty of James II.*

6 24. **diabolical escutcheon.** It is thus blazoned: "Bellua multorum capitum, coloris diabolici (viz. nigri) in campo sanguineo."

6 34. **Gothic.** This word was commonly used for the northern nations in general, to imply their lower culture. It thus became the opposite of 'classical' in literature and art.

7 18. **Zoilus.** A Greek grammarian of the time of Philip of Macedon, who assailed the writings of Homer with such bitterness that his name has since been a synonym for a captious and malignant critic.

7 19. **Clypearis.** Evidently a word for 'heraldic,' coined from *clipeus* (*clypeus*) 'shield.'

7 22. **last of his name.** Gibbon adds in a note, "Oblivion — from Wolfenbüttel to Lausanne," referring to his own possible loss of fame.

8 8. **second husband.** In Memoir A Gibbon says: "After his [Matthew Gibbon's] decease, Hester, his relict, remarried with Richard Acton, third son of Sir Walter Acton baronet, who exercised the same trade in the same street. . . . This lady, who survived both her hus-

bands and lived to a great age, was of an active and notable spirit. While her son, my grandfather Edward Gibbon, was in Flanders, his mother managed all his mercantile affairs at home." It is this Edward Gibbon's marriage which is referred to in line 10.

8 22. **Prior.** Matthew Prior, the poet (1664–1721), who succeeded Locke as Commissioner of Trade.

8 27. **South Sea Company.** In a note Gibbon refers to Anderson's *Origin of Commerce*, and Rapin de Thoyras's *History of England* continued by N. Tindal (1747), IV, ii, 630–649.

9 2. **equity of modern times.** In Memoir A Gibbon discusses the subject at some length, but he no doubt later concluded that a long argument was unnecessary to support his position.

9 10. **Lord Molesworth.** Robert, first Viscount Molesworth (1656–1725), was made envoy extraordinary to Denmark in 1692. His *Account of Denmark as it was in the year 1692* was published two years later. An abstract of his speech in regard to the South Sea directors may be found in Hansard's *Parliamentary History*, VII, 682.

9 28. **previous.** That is, before being actually brought to trial, they were deprived of certain civil rights, as if they had been already found guilty.

10 20. **One man.** "On the motion for allowing Grigsby £10,000, whose estate was valued at £31,687, a member observed that since that upstart had once been so prodigally vain as to bid his coachman feed his horses with gold, no doubt he could feed on it himself; and therefore he moved that he might be allowed as much gold as he could eat, and that the rest of the estate might go to the relief of the sufferers." —Chandler's *Political State of Great Britain*, June, 1721.

10 31. **first parliament.** The Septennial bill was passed in 1716 and was made to take effect immediately, that is, to be retroactive, a proceeding which a Tory like Gibbon might rightly criticise.

11 3. **il serrar.** Gibbon adds a note referring to Daru, *Histoire de Venise*, I, 515, 520, where the following passage occurs: "C'est cette révolution qu'on a désignée à Venise par le nom de *serrar del consiglio*, que je ne puis traduire qu'imparfaitement par clôture de grand conseil." By this event the government of Venice became a pure aristocracy.

11 16. **suspicious secret.** This perhaps refers to a supposed connection with the disposal of fictitious stock to ministers of the crown in order to promote the company's interest, and with the flight of the cashier Knight, who took important records with him. Many believed that this last step was taken with the connivance of the government.

However, it may mean no more than that Gibbon's father was suspected of being a Jacobite.

11 25. **antecedent settlements.** Property which had been legally set aside for relatives before the proceedings against the directors began. Such sums, of course, could not be touched by process of law.

12 1. **Francis Acton.** Probably son of the Sir Walter who died at the home of Gibbon's grandfather. See note to 13 29.

12 20. **Putney.** Gibbon in a note refers to Mallet's *Cupid and Hymen, or The Wedding Day*, in which Putney is somewhat inadequately described. It is now a suburb of London about eight miles by river above London bridge, and four and a half from Hyde Park. Thomas Cromwell, Earl of Essex and minister under Henry VIII was also born at Putney.

12 31. **king for whom.** The Jacobites still adhered to the Stuarts, represented at this time by James Edward Frederic (1688–1766), called by his followers James III of England, and known at the French court as the Chevalier St. George.

13 3. **disinherited.** That is, by the act which in 1720 took away his father's property.

13 14. **William Law.** For an interesting account of this eighteenth-century mystic see the *Dictionary of National Biography*, XXXII, 236.

13 29. **kinsman.** According to Memoir A he was son of Edward, of Walter, of Sir Walter.

14 1. **General Acton.** Sir John Francis Edward Acton (1736–1811) became prime minister through the influence of Queen Caroline, whose favor he had gained. In 1803 he was for a short time deprived of power, and in 1806 fled with the royal family on the entry of the French into Naples, and died in exile.

14 10. **burgage tenure.** "A tenure by which houses or lands are held of the king or other lord of a borough or city at a certain yearly rental, or by services relating to trade or handicraft."

14 17. **great opposition.** This was a coalition of Whigs — "Patriots" and "Boys" — and Tories, the 'strange coalitions' of 21 33. Walpole was made Lord Orford at the close of his long term of power; see 22 7.

14 23. **James Porten.** In Memoir B Gibbon says that "he was a merchant of doubtful credit which soon ended in bankruptcy." He failed in business in 1748 and absconded. See p. 35.

15 9. **Notitiam.** The quotation is from Ovid's *Metamorphoses*, iv, 59.

16 17. **only daughter.** In Memoir B Gibbon says: "their daughter and heiress Catherine was married in the year 1756 to Edward Eliot,

Esq., now Lord Eliot of Port Eliot in the county of Cornwall, and their three sons are my nearest male relations on the father's side." Lord Eliot (1727–1804) was a politician of some influence, sending seven members to parliament from Cornwall. Gibbon was one of these for a time; see 165 14 and note.

16 19. **Flavia and Miranda.** The first is described in chapter vii, the second in chapters viii and ix of the *Serious Call*. A writer in the *Dictionary of National Biography* (XXXII, 237) suggests that these identifications and that of Flatus (159 28) are probably not well founded, as the *Serious Call* was published in 1728 when the Gibbon children were too young to be so portrayed. Gibbon perceived this, and, in speaking of Flatus, says in Memoir A, "All these features cannot indeed be applied to the same person; and as the second edition of the *Serious Call to a Devout and Holy Life* was published in the year 1732, the prophetic eye of the tutor must have discerned the butterfly in the caterpillar. But our family tradition attests his laudable or malicious design, and from my own observation I can acknowledge the skill and the likeness of the portrait."

16 30. **Miss Hester Gibbon.** Miss Hester Gibbon died in 1790 at the age of eighty-six, leaving her estate to the historian. Her devotion to Law is shown by her being buried at the foot of his grave in King's Cliffe churchyard. According to eighteenth century custom, Gibbon regularly uses Mrs. instead of Miss for an unmarried woman. Miss was then a term of reproach except as applied to very young girls.

17 10. **Her fortune.** The quotations are from different parts of the same chapter; second edition, pp. 92–189.

18 8. **personal acquaintance.** Gibbon mentions her but once afterwards, in speaking of her estate (p. 188), but several references to her occur in his *Letters*.

18 15. **non-juror.** An adherent of James II, who refused to take the oath of allegiance to William and Mary after the Revolution of 1688, or to their successors; a Jacobite. The clergy of England remained particularly attached to the deposed Stuarts, owing to their belief in the doctrine of "divine right."

18 23. **Jacob Behmen,** or Boehme (1575–1624), was a German mystic, whose works were popular in England during the Commonwealth. The Behmenists later united with the Friends or Quakers. Law seems to have attempted a revival of Behmenism but was unsuccessful.

18 26. **The actors.** The quotation seems to have been from memory, as it does not follow the text exactly. The full title of the book is

The Absolute Unlawfulness of the Stage Entertainment fully demonstrated (1726).

19 4. **Bangorian controversy.** This takes its name from the little borough and market town of Bangor in North Wales, the bishopric of which was held by Benjamin Hoadley when he published a *Preservative against the Principles and Practices of the Non-Jurors in Church and State* (1716), and the following year when he preached before the King on the *Kingdom of Christ.* In these Hoadley attacked the divine authority of king and clergy, the power of the church over conscience, and its authority to determine man's condition in respect to the favor of God. These positions resulted in a storm of controversy. Hoadley, though not a great controversialist, was a champion of civil and religious liberty, and a not unimportant factor in changing the course of church history in England. His doctrines, in so far as they related to the "divine right" of kings, naturally had political significance, and this accounts for Gibbon's characterization of him as 'the object of Whig idolatry and Tory abhorrence.'

19 13. **Fable of the Bees.** The name of the *Miscellaneous Works* of Bernard de Mandeville (1670–1733), a physician from Rotterdam who settled in London about 1691. The work consists of the fable proper, *The Grumbling Hive or Knaves turned Honest*, which appeared in 1705; *Remarks on the Fable*, and the *Origin of Moral Virtue*, added in 1714; an *Essay on Charity Schools*, and *Origin of Society*, added in 1723. It was this last edition which Law attacked in *Remarks on a late book entitled the Fable of the Bees* (1724).

19 16. **Mr. Law's master work.** In a note Gibbon mentions that "Dr. Johnson styles it 'the finest piece of hortatory theology in any language.'" — Boswell's *Life* (Hill), II, 141. See also index to *Johnson's Letters* edited by Hill.

19 21. **La Bruyère.** Jean de la Bruyère (1645–1696), essayist and moralist, whose best-known work is his *Caractères*, published in 1688.

20 5. **From my birth.** In Memoir B Gibbon adds a sentence which has usually been printed here: "My lot might have been that of a slave, a savage, or a peasant; nor can I reflect without pleasure on the bounty of nature, which cast my birth in a free and civilized country, in an age of science and philosophy, in a family of honourable rank, and decently endowed with the gifts of fortune."

21 12. **Catholic kings.** Philip V had left enormous debts and Ferdinand VI, desiring to be relieved of paying them, called a council of bishops, ministers, and lawyers to consider the question whether a king was bound to pay the debts of his predecessors. The council

conveniently decided the question in the negative, and the king repudiated all debts contracted by kings of Spain before his time.

21 23. **successful contest.** It was for the privilege of representing Southampton.

21 27. **creation of freemen.** A common method of turning the scale in the eighteenth century. Freemen alone had the right of suffrage.

21 33. **strange coalitions.** Gibbon adds a note to this, "Of P[rince] of W[ales] and Jac[obites]," implying the strange character of the combination against Walpole. A Hanoverian prince and the supporters of the Pretender were indeed strange bed-fellows.

22 6. **Some courtiers . . . some patriots.** The first were the Tories, the second the more violent Whigs of the coalition; see note to 14 17. As Pelham, who became prime minister in 1743, was the choice of Walpole, neither part of the coalition gained much by the change.

22 11. **a rebellion.** In 1745 the young Pretender, Charles Edward grandson of James II, landed with seven friends on one of the Hebrides. He was soon joined by many Highlanders, entered Edinborough in triumph and was proclaimed as James VIII. Marching into Lancashire, the supposed stronghold of the Jacobites, he received no reënforcements from his English friends and was forced to retreat into Scotland. The next year the battle of Culloden was fought and the cause of the Pretender lost forever.

22 23. **prematurely dissolved.** The parliament, elected in 1741, should have lasted according to the Septennial act until 1748. Gibbon's father seems to have had some hopes of again entering parliament, although he did not think it best to stand for Southampton again at this time; see *Notes and Queries*, First Series, IX, 511.

23 8. **White's.** A fashionable coffee-house for the court end of the town in the early eighteenth century, and later (1736) changed into a club, as were many of the coffee-houses. Steele mentions it in the first number of the *Tatler*: "All accounts of gallantry shall be under the article of White's Chocolate-house."

23 32. **As new waked.** Milton, *Paradise Lost*, viii, 253.

25 2. **fortieth day.** Gibbon refers in a note to Buffon, *Histoire Naturelle*, tomes II, III, Supplement IV. The passage in vol. III, p. 363 is apparently intended. It describes at length the gradual development of the child mind.

26 10. **uno avulso.** *Æneid* vi, 143, where 'primo' takes the place of 'uno.'

27 1. **inoculation.** This means of preventing the disease had been long practiced in the east but was almost unknown in England till the beginning of the eighteenth century. In 1717 Lady Mary Wortley Montague, wife of the English ambassador at Constantinople, had her son inoculated and wrote accounts of the practice in Turkey. The result was the introduction of the new method into England. The process of inoculation, however, was long and dangerous and it was later superseded by vaccination, discovered by Dr. Jenner in the last part of the eighteenth century.

27 10. **Sir Hans Sloane, etc.** Sir Hans Sloane (1660–1753) was a celebrated physician and naturalist. He succeeded Newton as President of the Royal Society and on his death left immense collections in natural history, especially botany, which were purchased by the British Museum. Richard Mead (1673–1754) was also a celebrated physician and writer, physician in ordinary to George II at his accession, and friend of Pope and Newton. He published various treatises on medicine, and his life was written by the Dr. Maty mentioned at 104 10. Joshua Ward was a practitioner of the reign of George II. A contemporary wrote of him,

> "Of late, without the least pretense to skill,
> Ward's grown a famed physician by a pill,"

referring to his practice of giving no medicine except pills, one blue, one red, and one purple. Ward is also satirized in Pope's *Imitations of Horace*, first epistle of second book, 180; Fielding, however, refers to him with approbation in *Tom Jones* and the *Voyage to Lisbon*. Ward's presumption was such that he desired, in his will, to be buried in front of the altar in Westminster Abbey, or 'as near the altar as might be.' There was much rivalry between Mead and Ward, as indicated by the following anecdote. Queen Caroline one day asked General Charles Churchill, the patron of Ward, whether it were true, as reported, that Ward's medicine had made a man mad. "Yes, madam, very true," answered the General. "And do *you* own it?" said the Queen. "Yes, madam." "And who is it?" "Dr. Mead, madam." See Walpole's note in Chesterfield's *Miscellaneous Works*. The 'Chevalier' Taylor was a quack oculist, says Milman, on whom Walpole wrote the following epigram:

> "Why Taylor the Quack calls himself Chevalier
> 'T is not easy a reason to render,
> Unless he would own what his practice makes clear,
> That at best he is but a Pretender."

The Pretender (see note on 12 31) went by the name of Chevalier St. George.

27 20. **Cardinal Querini.** Giralamo (in religion Angelo Maria) Querini (1680–1759), an eminent Italian, who wrote various works especially connected with church history. He was librarian of the Vatican and to him Voltaire dedicated his *Semiramis*. His autobiography or memoirs, called by him *Commentarius de rebus pertinentibus ad A. M. Quirinum*, was published in 1749.

27 22. **Montaigne.** Gibbon says in a note, "Not in *Essays* but in *Voyage en Italie*, performed in 1580–1581, found in the old castle, printed in 1774." He adds that the book is 'the body rather than soul of Montaigne.'

28 27. **deciphering them.** In a note Gibbon says that the handwriting of Englishmen is better than that of foreigners, and that of his age better than that of the preceding. He refers to specimens of handwriting of the reformers in Jortin's *Life of Erasmus* (1758) as compared with the Round Robin on Johnson's epitaph for the monument of Goldsmith; see the facsimile in Boswell's *Life of Johnson* (Hill), III, 95–97.

29 3. **Bernoulli.** The name, sometimes written Bernouilli, belongs to a famous family of mathematicians. Originally of Antwerp, they were driven from their country on account of their religion, and settled first in Frankfort, afterwards in Basel. Eight members of the family attained distinction, the more celebrated being James, John, and Daniel, the first born in 1654, the last in 1700. Gibbon probably refers to Daniel Bernoulli (1700–1782), a physician, and professor at Basel from 1733 to 1782.

29 11. **Mr. John Kirkby** (1705–1754), divine, and author of several works of religious controversy besides those mentioned on page 30. In 1743 he published *A Demonstration . . . that the present Regulation of Ecclesiastical Revenues in the Church of England is contrary to the Design of Christianity*. This is said to have destroyed his hopes of preferment, and he was compelled to become a tutor in order to maintain himself.

30 3. **One day reading prayers.** In Memoir B Gibbon says Kirkby was a non-juror (see note to 18 15), "and it was on his omission of the prayer for the royal family that loyalty or prudence obliged my father to dismiss him from the house." In Memoir C the historian is even more explicit as to the offense. He says, "but his public refusal to name King George in the prayers of the church obliged my father to dismiss him."

30 8. **Life of Automathes.** The fuller title of the work is *The Capacity and Extent of the Human Understanding exemplified in the extraordinary case of Automathes, a Young Gentleman . . . accidentally left in his infancy upon a desert island.* It is said to be largely borrowed from the *History of Autonoüs* (1736). It was a favorite tale of Sir Walter Scott when a boy, and was reprinted in Weber's *Popular Romances* in 1812. Gibbon adds in a note, "A self-taught youth who discovers religion and science in a desert island is indeed a romance. The characters of a philosopher and a bigot are blended in my old tutor; but the story of Automathes is agreeably told."

30 32. **Pocock.** This is Edward Pocock (1604–1691) an eminent oriental scholar. One of Pocock's chief works is a Latin translation of the Arabic *History of the World* by Abulfaragius (1226–1286), to which Gibbon refers at 43 4. The 'Arabian romance of Hai Ebn Yokhdan,' written by Abn Jasper Ibn Tophail, a Mohammedan philosopher, was translated into Latin in 1671. The design of the work was to show how human reason, by observation and experience, may arrive at a knowledge of both natural and supernatural things, especially of God and a future life. This appealed to the Quakers who made a translation of the work.

31 13. **Kingston.** A borough and market town on the right bank of the Thames in Surrey, twelve miles from London.

31 14. **Dr. Wooddeson.** Richard Wooddeson (1704–1774) was clerk and afterwards chaplain of Magdalen College. Among his pupils at Kingston were Stevens, the editor of Shakespeare, and Hayley the poet. Murray prints the name Wooddesdon, but incorrectly according to Gibbon and to the *Memoirs of Gilbert Wakefield*, a book which frequently mentions the schoolmaster.

31 18. **must learn.** Murray prints "[had] much [to learn]," supplying the bracketed words; but 'must,' the reading of all the early editions, seems so much more likely to be right that it is here adopted as the correct reading.

31 25. **insolent.** Murray reads 'insont,' either a misprint or a slip for insolent.

31 32. **year forty-six.** The year of the defeat of the Pretender, with whom the Tories were supposed to be in sympathy.

31 34. **many tears and some blood.** "No man who has gone through what they call a great school . . . but must have seen an ingenuous creature expiring with shame, — with pale looks, beseeching sorrow and silent tears, — throw up its honest eyes, and kneel on its tender knees to an inexorable blockhead, to be forgiven the false quan-

tity of a word in making a Latin verse. The child is punished, and the next day he commits a like crime, and so a third with the same consequence." — Steele on *Flogging at Schools* in *Spectator*, 157.

32 16. **Scruples of Rousseau.** In *Émile*, Book II, the French philosopher reasons at length against the use of fables in teaching children.

32 26. **Peter Pithou.** Pierre Pithou (1539–1596), scholar, sage, friend of Thuanus, as Gibbon calls him, was a French lawyer who wrote a great many legal and historical books, besides preparing editions of ancient authors. He is best known for the part which he took in writing the famous *Satire Menappée* (1593).

32 30. **Bentley.** Richard Bentley (1662–1742), one of the greatest scholars of his time. His most celebrated work, *The Dissertation upon the Epistles of Phalaris*, was but slightly appreciated in England, and on account of it Bentley became one of the objects of Swift's satire in *Battle of the Books.*

32 31. **Burmann.** Pieter Burmann (1668–1741), a famous Dutch classicist, was professor of eloquence and history, later also of Greek and politics, in the University of Utrecht. In 1715 he was appointed to a similar position at Leyden. He was editor of numerous classical works, among them a *Phædrus* (1698).

33 10. **inconsolable.** In Memoir A Gibbon says, "That interesting romance of the Abbé Prévôt d'Exiles, the *Mémoires d'un homme de qualité*, had lately been translated into English; and as soon as I had read them, the grief of the Marquis on the death of his beloved Selima most forcibly brought to my mind the situation and behavior of my poor father."

33 23. **Mr. Mallet.** David Mallet (1705?–1765), a Scotchman who changed his name from Malloch because Englishmen, as he said, could not pronounce the latter. Gibbon refers to him in a note to Memoir E as, "The author of a life of Bacon, which has been rated above its value; of some forgotten poems and plays; and of the pathetic ballad of *William and Margaret*." He also claimed to be the author of *Rule Britannia*, now known to have been written by Thomson. In his *Lives of the Poets* Johnson praised Mallet for his conversation, but predicted that his reputation would scarcely outlive his life; see 97 4 and note. As to religious views, Mallet was a deist. The full title of the poem quoted at l. 30 is *Cupid and Hymen, or The Wedding Day*. The poem may be found in Chalmers' *English Poets*, vol. XIV.

34 14. **Buriton.** The little village is in Hampshire near the Sussex line, and almost directly east from Southampton. The brick manor

house where Gibbon passed many of his early years may still be seen. At Buriton, also, Bishop Lowth (see 46 26 and note) was born in 1710.

34 28. **Putney bridge.** A picturesque old timber bridge built in 1729, and connecting Putney with Fulham on the left bank of the Thames. It has since been replaced by a more permanent structure.

35 24. **favorite tale.** Gibbon refers to *Histoire d'Hypolite, Comte de Douglas* (1699), by Mme. Catherine Jumelle de Bernville, Countess D'Aulnoy—"a foolish novel of love and honor."

35 30. **Pope's Homer.** In Memoir B the historian has the fuller statement: "I soon tasted the *Arabian Nights Entertainments*—a book of all ages, since in my present maturity I can revolve without contempt that pleasing medley of oriental manners and supernatural fictions. But it is in rude ages and to youthful minds that the marvelous is most attractive. . . . From these tales I rose to the father of poetry but I could only embrace the phantom of Homer; nor was I then capable of discerning that Pope's translation is a portrait endowed with every merit except likeness to the original." The *Arabian Nights* had been introduced to European readers through Antoine Galland (1646–1715), of whom Gibbon says in a note, "He chose the best . . . he found the medium between Arab tongue and French ear."

36 27. **she preferred.** Lord Sheffield says, "It is said in the family that she was principally induced to this undertaking by her affection for her nephew, whose weak constitution required her constant attention."

36 28. **Westminster School.** St. Peter's School, Westminster, one of the great schools of London, was reëndowed in 1560 by Queen Elizabeth. There attend about forty scholars on the queen's foundation, and one hundred and eighty day scholars.

37 1. **Dr. John Nicoll,** or Nichols (1685–1765), was head-master from 1733 to 1753 in the school over which the famous Richard Busby (1616–1695) had presided in the seventeenth century.

37 22. **that the child.** In a note Gibbon refers to Plutarch's *Apothegms* (Agesilaus, lxvii), which reads as follows: *'Επιζητοῦντος δέ τινος, τίνα δεῖ μανθάνειν τοὺς παῖδας, Ταῦτ', εἶπεν, οἷς καὶ ἄνδρες γενόμενοι χρήσονται.*

37 27. **these schools.** Gibbon refers in a note to Adam Smith (*Wealth of Nations*, II, 348), who says: "In England the public schools are much less corrupted than the universities. [See his arraignment of the universities at 50 26.] "In the schools the youth are taught, or at least may be taught Greek and Latin, that is everything which the masters pretend to teach, or which it is expected they should teach."

38 7. **well-flogged critic.** Gibbon refers in a note to an incident in connection with one of Burke's speeches. It is given in Harford's *Recollections of Wilberforce* as follows: "Mr. Burke in the course of some very severe animadversions which he made on Lord North for want of due economy in his management of the public purse, introduced the well-known aphorism *magnum vectigal est parsimonia*, but was guilty of a false quantity by saying *vectĭgal*. Lord North while this philippic went on had been half asleep, and sat heaving backwards and forwards like a great turtle; but the sound of a false quantity instantly aroused him and, opening his eyes, he exclaimed in a very marked and distinct manner *vectīgal*. 'I thank the noble Lord,' said Burke with happy adroitness, 'for the correction, the more particularly as it affords me the opportunity of repeating a maxim which he greatly needs to have reiterated upon him.' He then thundered out *magnum vectīgal est parsimonia*." In the same note Gibbon has the jotting, "Sir Grey, Montague, tutti quanti, his superior knowledge." This Murray supposes a reference to Sir Grey Cooper (1726–1801) and Frederic Montagu (1733–1800), but does not indicate in what the allusion consists, though Sir Grey Cooper, he says, does not seem to have been at any public school.

38 25. **Lord Huntingtower.** Lionel, Lord Huntingtower, became first Earl Dysart in 1799.

38 31. **Michaelmas vacation.** That is the long, or summer vacation, ending about Michaelmas or the 29th September. The same title is also applied to the school term beginning soon after the latter date.

39 4. **pumping.** The term was used in the eighteenth century as equivalent to drinking the waters of a mineral spring; so also pump room for the place where the waters were taken.

39 34. **Mr. Philip Francis** (1708?–1773), a clergyman and miscellaneous writer, is best known for a translation of Horace (1743) which was highly praised by Johnson. His other attempts in literature were less successful, but his political pamphlets included a famous lampoon, *Mr. Pitt's Letter Versified*. The latter was inspired by Lord Holland, through whom Francis became rector of Barrow in Suffolk and chaplain to Chelsea Hospital. The father's more famous son, Sir Philip Francis, was the antagonist of Hastings and long supposed to be the author of the *Junius Letters*.

40 27. **gentleman commoner.** One of the aristocratic distinctions still preserved at an English University. The gentleman commoner has, however, no special privileges in compensation for the extra fees which he pays.

41 15. **Universal History.** This was published in twenty-six volumes folio (1736–1765) and was frequently reprinted. Goldsmith wrote the preface for the work, on which many writers had been employed.

41 17. **Hearne.** Thomas Hearne the antiquary (1678–1735). After graduating at Oxford he became assistant keeper of the Bodleian Library (1701) and second keeper and janitor in 1702. The latter office was at his own suggestion, since it enabled him to get at the books at any time. He was a voluminous writer, diligent and accurate, though somewhat lacking in discrimination. Among his most important works is the *Ductor Historicus, or a Short System of Universal History* (1704), to which Gibbon here refers.

41 33. **Speed, . . . Bower.** John Speed (1542–1629) was an English antiquary who published several works bearing on the history of Great Britain. Paul de Rapin (1661–1725) accompanied the Prince of Orange to England in 1688 and wrote *L'Histoire d'Angleterre* (1624). Francois Eudes de Mézerai (1610–1683) was a celebrated historian whose *Histoire de France* is his most famous work. Henrico Caterino Davila (1576–1631), a Spanish historian, lived in France most of his life, fought in the civil wars, and finally wrote *Istoria delle Guerre Civili di Francia* (1630), a standard work which has been translated into most modern languages, and at least twice into English (1647, 1666). Niccolo Machiavelli (1469–1527) is too well known to need any special notice here. He is by far the most famous of the modern historians whom Gibbon enumerates. Father Paul is Pietro Sarpi (1552–1623), who, from the name he assumed as a monk, is known as Fra Paulo Sarpi, or Father Paul. One of the most learned men of his time, his chief fame rests upon his *History of the Council of Trent* which was printed in London under an assumed name in 1619. He was also a vigorous supporter of the rights of the Venetians against the encroachments of the Pope. Dr. Johnson published a brief sketch of Father Paul in the *Gentleman's Magazine* for 1738. Archibald Bower (1686–1766), a Scotchman, was educated at the Jesuit College of St. Omer, became a Protestant, and settled in England. He was one of the contributors to the *Universal History* mentioned above and wrote besides a *History of the Popes*.

42 2. **descriptions of India.** The eighteenth century witnessed a new interest in travel and geographical knowledge, and this resulted in many descriptions of foreign lands. The particular books to which Gibbon refers cannot, perhaps, be determined.

42 15. **Mr. Hoare.** Probably Henry Hoare, father of Sir Richard Colt Hoare (1758–1838), historian of Wiltshire.

42 18. **Echard.** Laurent Echard (1671–1730), whose *Histoire Romaine*, to the establishment of the empire, was continued by the Abbé Guyon to the taking of Constantinople. He also wrote a *Histoire d'Angleterre*, as well as other historical works.

42 27. **Howell's History.** William Howell (1638?–1683), author of an *An Institution of General History . . . from the Beginning of the World till the Monarchy of Constantine the Great.*

42 30. **Simon Ockley.** This famous Orientalist (1678–1720) was made Professor of Arabic in Cambridge University in 1711. His most celebrated work, *The History of the Saracens* (1708–1718), was long regarded as of great authority, but was founded upon what is now known to be more historical romance than actual fact.

43 3. **d'Herbelot.** Barthelemy d'Herbelot (1625–1695) was a French orientalist whose chief work, still important in many respects, is the *Bibliothèque Orientale, or universal dictionary concerning the peoples of the orient* (1697). See also a note on 55 20.

43 4. **Pocock's Abulfaragius.** For the first see note to 24 29. Abulfaragius is the Latinized form of the name Gregor Abulfarag (1226–1286) — also called Barhebræus from his Jewish parentage — who wrote a Syriac *History of the World* from the creation to his own day. It is valuable for those parts which treat of the Eastern nations, the Saracens, Tartars, etc.

43 8–12. **Cellarius . . . Prideaux.** The first reference is doubtless to the *Harmonia Macrocosmia seu Atlas Universalis* of André Cellarius (d. 1562). Edward Wells (1664–1727) was an English scholar who published several works on geography, especially an *Historical Geography of the Old and New Testament.* Ægidius Strauch, or Strauchius (1632–1682), a professor of theology at Dantzic, published numerous works on chronology. The *Breviarum Chronologicum*, recommended by Locke, was translated into English in 1720. Christopher Helvicus (1581–1617) published his *Theatrum Chronologicum* in 1609. The work of James Anderson (1680?–1739) to which reference is made is the *Royal Genealogies* (1732), an important book in its time. The next reference is to James Usher's (1580–1656) *Annales Veteri et Novi Testamenti.* Until recently his scheme of Scripture chronology was generally accepted. Humphrey Prideaux (1648–1724), an English churchman, is best known by the work here referred to, *The Old and New Testament connected in the History of the Jews.* See another reference to him at 179 8 and note.

43 17–18. **Scaliger . . . Newton.** Joseph Justus Scaliger (1540–1608), called the younger, to distinguish him from his famous father

Julius Cæsar Scaliger, was one of the greatest scholars of modern times. The book referred to is his *De Emendatione Temporum* (1583) which revolutionized modern conceptions of chronology, and first emphasized its importance as an adjunct to historical narration. Denys Petau (1583–1652), or Dionysius Petavius in Latin form, was a distinguished Roman Catholic theologian of France. He wrote, among other scholarly works, *Opus de Doctrina Temporum* (1627), an abridgment of which, *Rationarium Temporum*, passed through many editions and was translated into French and English. Sir John Marsham (1602–1685) published in 1629 the *Doctrina Chronologica* in which he examines the chronology of the Old Testament. Another of his works, the *Chronicus Canon Ægypticus, Ebraicus, Græcus* (1672) is referred to at 56 18. The work of Sir Isaac Newton (1642–1727) which Gibbon had in mind is the *Chronology of Ancient Kingdoms Amended*, published in 1728 after Newton's death.

43 28. **happiness of our boyish years.** Gibbon adds in a note to Memoir E, "A similar opinion is ascribed by d'Alembert (*Éloges des Académiciens*, vol. III, p. 24) to Boileau, who had suffered indeed many hardships in his childhood and youth. The life of a schoolboy is by no means exempt from care or passion, and he is yet unripe for the highest enjoyments of the mind and body."

44 6. **Who, etc.** The images are from Gray's *Ode on a Distant Prospect of Eton College.* The stanza is as follows:

" Say, Father Thames, for thou hast seen
Full many a sprightly race
Disporting on the margent green
The paths of pleasure trace,
Who foremost now delight to cleave
With pliant arm the glassy wave?
The captive linnet which enthral?
What idle progeny succeed
To chase the rolling circle's speed,
Or urge the flying ball?"

Gibbon adds, "Father Thames at Westminster [his own school], instead of margent green has trading barges and carpenters' yards."

44 24. **parva leves.** Ovid, *Ars Amatoria*, i, 159.

44 32. **Under the scourge.** The reference is to Herodotus vii 56, the description of Xerxes' army crossing the Hellespont. Gibbon adds these jottings: "I do not absolutely condemn the rod . . . had almost extinguished Erasmus (*Works* vol. I, p. 504) — Horrid cruelty of Dean Colet, founder of St. Paul's (*Life* p. 173) — Busby would give 30, 40,

60 lashes to poor little boys for trivial offenses (*Biographia Britannica*, 1784, vol. III, p. 53)."

45 9. **order and tranquillity.** Gibbon had in mind, as he tells us in a note, two different books. The first is the *Voyage Littéraire* of Charles Étienne Jordan (1700–1745) who traveled in England and France in 1733 and in Holland in 1735, as a correspondent of Frederick the Great. In this he describes the quiet of Oxford as compared with the German universities. The second is *Travels through France, Italy, Germany, and Switzerland* (1752) by Bishop Gilbert Burnet (1643–1715), especially his description of Padua (p. 101). The book consists of letters originally written to Robert Boyle.

46 18. **adjacent walks.** Gibbon refers in a note to *Moral and Political Dialogues* by Richard Hurd (1720–1806). In Dialogue VII Hurd represents Mr. Locke as defending the English mode of education against Lord Shaftesbury who contends for foreign travel.

46 26. **Bishop Lowth.** Robert Lowth (1710–1787), bishop of London after 1777, but holding the see of Oxford for the eleven years preceding. The quotation is from a letter (see 154 16 and note) to Warburton, author of the *Divine Legation of Moses* (see note on 153 31), who had attacked Lowth's theories as to the book of Job in an appendix to the above mentioned work. The controversy was by no means to the credit of Warburton.

47 16. **Hooker, Chillingworth, Locke.** The first, Richard Hooker (1553–1600) a famous English divine, is best known for his *Ecclesiastical Polity*, a book important for its style as for its theological and political views. William Chillingworth (1602–1644) was a celebrated English churchman and controversialist ; see note on 63 28. The philosopher John Locke (1632–1704) was expelled from Christ Church Oxford, not directly by the University but "by a special order of Charles II, as visitor of the college. His majesty, at the instigation of Charles, Earl of Middleton, secretary of state, applied to Dr. Fell then dean of Christ Church, and enforced his expulsion by expressing his astonishment that Locke should be suffered to retain any place of profit in that society. . . . The college afterwards offered to admit him again as a supernumerary student, the vacancy occasioned by his dismission having been filled up." — *A Word or two in Vindication* by James Hurdis (see note on 58 19). Milman adds, " The subject of the expulsion of Locke has been set at rest by the publication of the late Chancellor [*Oxford and Locke* (1829) by George Grenville, Lord Nugent]. . . . The disgraceful act was not that of the University, but of the servile head of a college in obedience to an arbitrary court."

Gibbon's own comment in Memoir B is, "It may indeed be observed that the atmosphere of Oxford did not agree with Mr. Locke's constitution, and that the philosopher justly despised the academical bigots who expelled his person and despised his principles."

48 18. **real and fabulous antiquities.** It was customary for both Oxford and Cambridge to claim great antiquity, Oxford, for example, naming Alfred the Great as her founder. It is now known that the English universities are at best not older than the twelfth century, while the earliest colleges were not founded till the thirteenth century. In Gibbon's Commonplace Book (*Miscellaneous Works*, V, 522) will be found some notes on this subject.

48 20. **In the meanwhile.** This arraignment of the English universities in the eighteenth century, while perhaps partly due to the attacks made upon the historian, is fully justified by what is known of their condition at the time. Compare, for example, the chapter on a similar subject in Goldsmith's *Enquiry into the Present State of Polite Learning in Europe* (1759), and Adam Smith's *Wealth of Nations*, Book V, chap. I.

49 6. **any reformation.** Gibbon refers in a note to the wish of Lord Townshend (1674–1738) to reform the universities, and to the preparation of schemes for Oxford by Dean Prideaux (see note to 43 13), and for Cambridge by William Whiston. Nothing was really done especially as the scheme of Prideaux was found highly impracticable.

49 17. **licentiate.** A university degree intermediate between those of bachelor and doctor. The term is still common in Europe, but in America is mainly confined to theology.

49 31. **budge doctors.** The reference is to *Comus*, 707–709:

"O foolishness of men! that lend their ears
To these budge doctors of the Stoick fur,
And fetch their precepts from the cynic tub,
Praising the lean and sallow abstinence."

Budge is a kind of fur made of lambskin, and was formerly used as an ornament on the scholastic habit. From this the word came to imply 'austere, stiff,' perhaps 'surly.' Gibbon adds, "I do not apply 'lean and sallow.'"

50 4. **Royal College.** The Royal College of Physicians founded by Thomas Linacre (1460–1524), physician to Henry VII and Henry VIII, is an examining board for diplomas in medicine. It first gave the medical profession a recognized standing in England.

50 7. **bachelor's.** The MS., according to Murray, reads *bachelor*. Gibbon had merely extended the use of the group genitive.

50 11. **general contempt.** Gibbon says in a note, "Here Vicesimus Knox must be used." The allusion is to *A Liberal Education* published by Knox (1752–1821), a miscellaneous writer, in 1781, and very popular in its time.

50 17. **assiduously employed.** Gibbon has a jotting, "Information from Göttingen — Professors — Lectures, etc.," apparently showing what he intended to do, in comparing the English with the German universities.

50 26. **"that in the university."** The quotation is from Adam Smith's *Wealth of Nations*, Book V, chap. 1. Adam Smith (1723–1790), after three years at the University of Glasgow, studied seven years (1740–1747) at Balliol College Oxford. He thus had foundation in experience for his harsh criticism of the University.

51 3. **control.** Gibbon, in a note, cites the case of the poet Gray who was Professor of Modern History and Languages at Cambridge on a salary of £400 a year, and never lectured once during three years, though he did provide a French and Italian teacher for the languages. The only valid excuse for Gray is that other Oxford professors were equally negligent.

It has indeed been observed. Gibbon evidently refers to Boswell's *Life of Johnson* (Hill), II, 8, a reference which helps to date the writing of Memoir F, since the famous *Life* was published in 1791. The passage reads as follows: "People have now-a-days (said he) got a strange opinion that everything should be taught by lectures. Now I cannot see that lectures can do so much good as reading the books from which the lectures are taken. I know nothing that can be best taught by lectures, except where experiments are to be shown. You may teach chemistry by lectures; you might teach making of shoes by lectures!" In the same (IV, 106) Johnson, with unusual consistency, expresses a similar view: "Lectures were once useful, but now, when all can read and books are so numerous, lectures are unnecessary. If your attention fails and you miss part of a lecture, it is lost; you cannot go back, as you do upon a book."

51 11. **ought to be abolished.** In a note Gibbon refers to Dodwell who, as professor at Oxford on the Camden foundation, thought his salary of £400 earned when he had read twenty-five lectures on Roman history.

51 30. **Prælectiones.** For Dr. Lowth see note on 46 26. The work referred to is *Prælectiones Academicæ de Sacra Poesi Hebræorum*,

one of the earliest attempts to examine sacred poetry by the standards applied to secular literature. The book was of great influence both in England and on the continent, though later largely supplanted by the more natural æsthetic criticism of Herder.

51 34. **a bishop.** This was William Patton of Wainfleet (d. 1486) who was successively bishop of Winchester and Lord Chancellor, as well as founder of Magdalen.

52 19. **St. Germain de Prés.** The early importance of this abbey, founded in the sixth century, is shown by the fact that its abbots were cardinals and sometimes kings, as in the case of Hugh Capet.

53 2. **young fellow.** The reference is to George Horne (1730–1792), who was fellow and afterwards President of Magdalen College. Later he was successively Dean of Canterbury and Bishop of Norwich. His best-known work is his *Commentary on the Psalms* (1771).

53 5. **Ballard.** George Ballard (1706–1755) was choral clerk, not chaplain, according to Bloxam's *Magdalen College Register*. He had been a stay-maker but showed scholarly tendencies especially in the study of Old English, a knowledge of which he had acquired while working at his trade. The book referred to is *Memoirs of Several Ladies of Great Britain who have been celebrated for their Writings, or Skill in the Learned Languages, Arts, and Sciences* (1752), and Gibbon was himself a subscriber.

53 15. **loyalty for the House of Hanover.** Gibbon refers in a note to The Journal of a Senior Fellow or Genuine Idler, just transmitted from Cambridge by a Facetious Correspondent, *Idler* No. 33.

53 16. **great Oxfordshire contest.** This contest, in 1754 after the death of Pelham, was exceedingly bitter on both sides. Lord Parker and Sir Edward Turner were declared elected, defeating Lord Wenman and Sir James Dashwood who represented the old, or court interest. See *Three Oxford Parishes* (Oxford Historical Society).

53 26. **ascribi.** The quotation is from Horace, *Odes*, iii, 3, 35.

54 18. **Dr. Waldegrave.** Thomas Waldegrave (1721–1784) was dean and bursar of the college until July 1752 when he accepted the living in Sussex, as mentioned on page 55. He published *Annotationes in Platonis Opera*. When Gibbon again became a Protestant he wrote his old tutor of the change, and the reply, dated Dec. 7, 1758, is as follows:

Dear Sir,—I have read nothing for some time (and I keep reading on still) that has given me so much pleasure as your letter, which I received by the last post. I rejoice at your return to your country, to your father, and to the good principles of truth and reason. Had I in the least suspected your design of leaving us, I should immediately have put you upon reading Mr. Chillingworth's *Religion of Protestants*, any one page of which is worth a library of Swiss divinity. It will give me great pleasure to see you at Washington; where I am, I thank God, very well and very happy. I desire my respects to Mr. Gibbon; and am, with very great regard, dear Sir,

Your most affectionate humble servant,

THO. WALDEGRAVE.

55 20. **younger students.** In a letter to the *Gentleman's Magazine* (LXIV, 119) Daniel Parker, bookseller at Oxford, said of Gibbon, "I knew him personally. He was a singular character and but little connected with the young gentlemen of his college. They admit at Magdalen only men of fortune, no commoners. One uncommon book for a young man I remember selling him — *La Bibliothèque Orientale d'Herbelot* — which he seems to have used for authorities in his eastern Roman history." Milman reports from Dr. Routh, formerly president of Magdalen, the following: "Mr. Finden, an ancient fellow and contemporary of Gibbon, told me that his superior abilities were known to many but that the gentlemen commoners, of which number Gibbon was one, were disposed to laugh at his peculiarities; and were once informed by Finden, rather coarsely but with some humor, that if their heads were entirely scooped out Gibbon had brains sufficient to supply them all."

55 23. **Pocock and Hyde.** For the first see note on 24 29. Thomas Hyde (1636–1703) was a celebrated Orientalist and successor of Pocock as Laud professor of Arabic at Oxford. His chief work is *Historia Religionis Veterum Persarum* (1700), the first attempt to correct the errors of classical historians by the use of oriental authorities.

55 25. **inclination to study Arabic.** Milman reports Dr. Waldegrave to have said, when he heard of Gibbon's becoming a Roman Catholic, "he should rather have thought that he would have turned Mahometan," alluding to his fondness for reading the Arabic historians in the Latin translations. This probably accounts for the conversation in Boswell's *Johnson* (Hill), II, 448, quoted in a note to 63 11.

56 1. **Trinity, etc.** The four terms of the English university year are somewhat variously named. De Quincey in the *English Mail Coach* speaks of them in order as Michaelmas, Lent, Easter, and Act, the last from the thesis originally maintained by the student at graduation. The name Trinity, like the others, rests on an ecclesiastical foundation.

56 6. **alteration of the style.** The Gregorian calendar, as it is called, was established by Pope Gregory XIII in 1582, Italy, Spain, Portugal, and France adopting it in that year. Catholic Germany fol-

lowed the next year, but the Protestant countries, from motives of prejudice, held out against the change for some time. Scotland adopted the new calendar in 1600, Germany, Denmark, and Sweden in 1700. In 1751 an act of parliament ordered the change to be made in England by reckoning the third of September, 1752, as the fourteenth of that month. At the same time the legal year was made to begin on January 1 instead of on March 25. Russia still adheres to the Julian calendar, so that all Russian dates are now twelve days behind those of other countries.

56 14. **Age of Louis XIV.** This work had been published in 1752, while Voltaire was at the court of Frederick the Great.

56 17. **Sir John Marsham.** See note on 35 16.

56 26. **Manetho.** A celebrated Egyptian priest and historian who lived in the third century B.C.

56 28. **Parian Marble.** The reference is to an ancient marble chronicle of the city of Athens, found on the island of Paros. It was purchased for the Earl of Arundel and is the most remarkable part of a collection known as the Arundelian Marbles, which was presented in 1667 to the University of Oxford by Henry Howard, grandson of the earl. The Parian chronicle consisted of a series of events in Greek history from Cecrops (1582 B.C.) to the archonship of Liognetus, 264 B.C.

57 16. **symptom.** The MS., according to Murray, reads *symptoms*, unless indeed this is one of the occasional misprints in Murray's volume.

57 24. **Dr. Winchester.** Thomas Winchester (1713–1780) was successively rector of Horsington, Lincolnshire, and Appleton, Buckinghamshire. He took part in religious controversies of the time as a stanch supporter of the Church of England.

58 3. **Bath.** In the eighteenth century the most fashionable watering place in England.

58 9. **manly Oxonian.** Gibbon refers in a note to the *Connoisseur* No. 11, worked up in Coleman's farce.

58 19. **restraint and discipline.** In answer to this attack upon the University of Oxford, the Rev. James Hurdis (1763–1801) wrote *A Word or Two in Vindication of the University of Oxford, and of Magdalen College in particular, from the posthumous aspersions of Mr. Gibbon* (1800), reprinted in *Reminiscences of Oxford* (Oxford Historical Society) p. 130. Hurdis heaps considerable abuse on the historian, but admits most of the charges. He was known as the Sussex poet and was a friend and correspondent of Cowper.

58 27. **every student.** This remained true until 1871 when "subscription to the articles of the church of England, all declarations and

oaths respecting religious belief, and all compulsory attendance at public worship in the universities of Oxford, Cambridge, and Durham" were abolished except in the case of divinity students.

59 14. **worst mischiefs.** In a note Gibbon speaks of the religious ignorance of undergraduates who are soon ordained, refers to a similar complaint of Dr. Prideaux (*Life of Dr. Prideaux*, 1748, p. 91), and the refusal of the universities to accept from Dr. Busby the endowment of two catechetical lectures, on condition of compulsory attendance and examination of the undergraduates (*Ibid.*, p. 92).

59 25. **Middleton.** The famous Conyers Middleton (1683–1750), divine and controversialist. He wrote numerous works, especially a *Life of Cicero*, referred to at 77 4, and *A Free Inquiry into the Miraculous Powers which are supposed to have subsisted in the Christian Church* (1749), in which he attacked ecclesiastical miracles. Answers were written by Dr. William Dodwell and Dr. Thomas Church, the 'two dullest of their champions' (l. 28), to whom Middleton replied in a '*Vindication*' published in 1751 after his death.

60 3. **Via Prima.** *Æneid*, vi, 96, 97. The prediction was verified in the case of Æneas in that Evander, his faithful ally, was from Arcadia. Gibbon means that his first decided impulse to Catholicism was from Middleton, an opponent of that form of Christianity. In the quotation Gibbon has *minimum* for *minime*, due, no doubt, to his quoting from memory.

60 19. **Basils, etc.** The first is Basil the Great, a famous ecclesiastic of the fourth century (c. 330–379). St. John Chrysostom also belongs to the fourth century (c. 347–406). Austin, or Augustine (354–430), was one of the four great Fathers of the Christian church. Eusebius Sophronius Hieronymus, St. Jerome, was born about 340 and died in 420.

60 30. **Mr. ——.** In Lord Sheffield's second edition of Gibbon's *Memoirs* the name Molesworth is here inserted, although it does not occur in any of the texts.

60 34. **Bossuet.** Jacques Benigne Bossuet (1627–1704), the celebrated French pulpit orator and author. The first work mentioned, *L'Exposition de la Doctrine Catholique* written in 1669, is his most famous book and that which has been most widely translated. *L'Histoire des Variations des Églises Protestantes* in fifteen books was published in 1688. The work, though praised by Gibbon, is lacking in fairness, especially to the early reformers.

61 3. **fell by a noble hand.** Lord Sheffield adds the following note: "Mr. Gibbon never talked with me on the subject of his conver-

sion to popery but once, and then he imputed his change to the works of Parsons the Jesuit, who lived in the reign of Elizabeth, and who, he said, had urged all the best arguments in favor of the Roman Catholic religion."

61 8. **ten horned monster . . . milk white hind.** The first refers to the beast in *Revelations* 13, 1, interpreted by Protestants as the Church of Rome. The second is a reference to Dryden's poem, *The Hind and Panther*, in which the Church of Rome is represented as a milk white hind. The next line is a reminiscence of Dryden's verse (i, 34) referring indirectly to the hind,

"As to be loved needs only to be seen."

61 18. **transubstantiation.** Regularly spelled transubstantion in the MSS., according to Murray.

61 20. **Hoc est.** The Latin version of Christ's words as he broke the bread (*Luke* 22, 19) quoted in the mass. 'My conqueror' of the preceding line is of course Bossuet, according to the account above.

61 23. **Athanasian creed.** The last of the creeds of the early and medieval church. Its name implies a connection with Athanasius, the great opponent of Arianism in the fourth century, but it is now believed to have been produced not before the eighth century. For Arianism see note on 64 34.

61 25. **To take up.** The lines are from Dryden's *Hind and Panther*, i, 141.

62 15. **Roman Catholic bookseller.** In Memoir C Gibbon says, "But no sooner had I resolved to save my soul at the expense of my fortune than I eloped to London, and addressed myself to Mr. Lewis, a popish bookseller in Russell street, who introduced me to a priest, perhaps a Jesuit, of his acquaintance." In a note to the second edition Lord Sheffield says, "His name [the priest's] was Baker, a Jesuit and one of the chaplains of the Sardinian ambassador. Mr. Gibbon's conversion made some noise and Mr. Lewis, the Roman Catholic bookseller of Russel street, Covent Garden, was summoned before the Privy Council and interrogated upon the subject. This was communicated by Mr. Lewis's son."

62 33. **elaborate controversial epistle.** Gibbon afterwards described this letter to Lord Sheffield as written with all the pomp, dignity, and self-satisfaction of the martyr.

63 8. **many years afterwards.** After Gibbon had published the first volume of his *History* which raised a storm of controversy in England.

63 11. **turned papist.** Gibbon here refers to a conversation concerning his *History* recorded in Boswell's *Life of Johnson* (Hill), II, 447. "We talked of a work much in vogue at that time, written in a very mellifluous style but which, under pretext of another subject, contained much artful infidelity. . . . The author had been an Oxonian and was remembered there for having 'turned papist.' I observed that, as he had changed several times — from the Church of England to the Church of Rome, from the Church of Rome to infidelity — I did not despair yet of seeing him a Methodist preacher. Johnson (laughing): 'It is said that his range has been more extensive, and that he has once been Mahometan. However, now that he has published his infidelity, he will probably persist in it.'" See note to 55 25.

63 19. **Chillingworth and Bayle.** Gibbon adds, in a note to Memoir E, "When these masters of argument were seduced by Popery, the Frenchman was near twenty-two, the Englishman about twenty-eight years of age. In their retrograde motion the logic of Chillingworth paused on the last verge of Christianity, the genius of Bayle pervaded the boundless regions of skepticism."

63 26. **Whom the grim wolf.** *Lycidas*, 128–129. The passage is one of the most striking of the whole poem. The exact reading of the line is "Besides what the grim wolf."

63 28. **William Chillingworth.** See note on 47 16. As Gibbon says on the preceding page, Romish priests were busy workers in England during the reign of Charles I, and it is also known that they made the universities special points of attack. Chillingworth, like Gibbon, was converted to Catholicism while a student at Oxford, and was persuaded to go to the Catholic university of Douay. While there, Laud, Bishop of London and godfather to Chillingworth, attempted to bring him back to the Church of England and persuaded him to return to Oxford, of which Laud was chancellor. There Chillingworth began an impartial inquiry into the claims of the two churches, finally deciding in favor of Protestantism. Soon after he wrote *The Religion of Protestants a Safe Way to Salvation* (1637). Meanwhile, in 1635, he had refused preferment because, as he informed Dr. Sheldon in the letter mentioned by Gibbon (64 18), to subscribe the thirty-nine articles would be to 'subscribe his own damnation.' He also added that he was resolved upon two points, that the fourth commandment was not binding upon Christians, and that the damning clauses of the Athanasian creed, directed against the Arians, were most false and in a high degree presumptuous. In his book, however, Chillingworth took the ground that subscription to the thirty-nine articles meant no more than general acceptance of the

Scriptures as the word of God, and the obligation to try to find their true sense and to live thereby. He was thus able in the following year to become chancellor of the church of Sarum (Salisbury) and prebend of Brixworth, annexed to it. The charge of Socinianism (65 4) was frequently made against Chillingworth, but he has long been regarded as a champion of liberal orthodoxy. In his implication of insincerity, (64 23; 65 6) Gibbon followed the *Biographia Britannica* (1784) which somewhat misstates the facts in regard to the letter quoted and the subscription in the Salisbury register (64 28). Gibbon did not know that the letter was written before, the subscription to the Salisbury register after, the publication of Chillingworth's *Religion of Protestants*.

64 34. **doctrine of Arius.** Called the first great heresy of the Christian church. Arius asserted a form of Unitarianism, but his doctrine was condemned by the Council of Nicæa (A.D. 325), the great opponent of Arius being Athanasius, afterwards bishop of Alexandria.

65 3. **firmer ground of the Socinians.** The name is from that of two Italian theologians, Laelius (1525–1562) and Faustus (1539–1562) Socinus, or Sozzini. They held in the main the belief of modern Unitarians, but rejected every doctrine not supported by human reason, and were thus the forerunners of modern rationalism.

65 17. **Bayle.** Little need be said of Pierre Bayle (1647–1706) beyond what Gibbon here tells. As to the 'private state' at Rotterdam (66 9), it may be explained that he was professor of philosophy and rhetoric from 1681 to 1693, when he was deprived of his chair. His greatest work is the *Historical and Critical Dictionary* (1697) of which Gibbon says in his *Essai sur l'Étude de la Littérature*, "Le Dictionnaire de Bayle sera un monument éternal de la force, et de la fécondité de l'érudition combinée avec le génie." The reference to his balancing false religions may be appreciated from his article on the Greek philosophers.

66 19. **persecution of Louis the Fourteenth.** The persecution of the Huguenots which followed the revocation of the Edict of Nantes in 1685. At this time the persecuted Protestants left France in great numbers, many going to England and the colonies.

66 20. **republican maxims of the Calvinists.** Gibbon probably refers in this passage to Bayle's *Critique Générale de l'Histoire du Calvinisme de Maimbourg*.

66 29. **ancient paradox of Plutarch.** "Is he that holds there is no God guilty of impiety and is not he that describes him as the superstitious do much more guilty?" Plutarch's *Morals*, Of Superstition, § 10. In Bacon's essay on the same subject Plutarch's sentiment appears in

this form: "It were better to have no opinion of God at all, than such an opinion as is unworthy of him."

67 8. **Pyrrhonism.** Pyrrho of Elis (about 360–270 B.C.), an early Greek philosopher whose name has long been a synonym for skepticism. His teaching, although he himself left no writings, is summed up by Zeller in three statements: "We know nothing about the nature of things; hence the right attitude towards them is to withhold judgment; the necessary result of withholding judgment is imperturbability." It will thus be seen that Pyrrhonism has its most modern type in agnosticism.

68 1. **Sir William Scott.** William Scott (1745–1836), a famous English judge especially known for his decisions in cases of international law, rose from comparative obscurity to recognized eminence in his profession. He succeeded William, afterwards Sir William, Jones as tutor of University College, retaining the position from about 1767 to 1776. At the coronation of George IV (1821) he was made Baron Stowell.

68 8. **Dr. Markham.** William Markham (1719–1807) was Dean of Christ Church, Oxford, from 1767 until made Archbishop of York in 1777.

68 9. **a more regular discipline.** Upon this Lord Sheffield added a note as follows: "This was written on the information Mr. Gibbon had received, and the observation he had made, previous to his late residence at Lausanne. During his last visit to England, he had an opportunity of seeing at Sheffield Place some young men of the college above alluded to; he had great satisfaction in conversing with them, made many inquiries respecting their course of study, applauded the discipline of Christ Church, and the liberal attention shown by the Dean, to those whose only recommendation was their merit." This was followed in the second edition by the following note of the same editor: "I have to observe that I have not met with any person who lived at the time to which Mr. Gibbon alludes, who was not of opinion that his representation, at least of his own college, was just."

68 14. **young gentlemen do honor.** The MS., according to Murray, reads 'who do honor,' but this makes no sense unless we are to suppose some omission as 'I have seen several, etc.,' or 'there are several, etc.' The note preceding would seem to imply the former.

68 17. **Lord Clarendon's History.** By the will of Clarendon's great-grandson Henry, Lord Cornbury, the Chancellor's manuscripts were left to the University with directions that the proceeds of publication should be used to establish an academy for riding and other exercises.

On the failure to establish the riding school see Boswell's *Life of Johnson* (Hill), II, 424. With the profits from the sale of Clarendon's *History* the well-known Clarendon Press had been established.

68 19. **Vinerian professorship.** Founded by Charles Viner (1680–1756), a compiler of a *General Abridgment of the Laws of England.*

69 10. **highest . . . authority.** The allusion is probably to the foreign education of the sons of George III.* In 1780 Frederick Augustus was sent to Hanover to study French, German, and military tactics, and in 1786 Ernest Augustus and his younger brothers were sent to the University of Göttingen.

69 18. **After conveying me.** Memoir F ends with the preceding sentence, and Memoir B is taken up at this point. In the MS. this is the last sentence of a paragraph, the new one beginning "The gates of Oxford" (l. 22). With this slight variation no change is necessary in joining Memoirs F and B. Lord Sheffield took up Memoir B at the same place and in early editions indicated this by a space on the page. In other respects, however, the first editor made many changes in the text.

69 26. **Mr. Eliot.** This was Edward, afterwards Lord Eliot, mentioned in note to 16 17. See also note to 165 14.

69 28. **M. Frey.** This may possibly have been Jean Louis Frey (1682–1759) who was professor of theology at Berne. Here, as in other references to Frenchmen, Gibbon uses Mr. for Monsieur, according to eighteenth century custom. For this older abbreviation M. has been regularly substituted in the text.

71 11. **small chamber.** On taking up his residence at Lausanne Gibbon wrote to his aunt, Miss Porten, Dec. 27, 1783, "I am no longer at Pavilliard's house where I was almost starved with cold and hunger." *Miscellaneous Works,* II, 343.

72 13. **some irregularities.** One of these is recorded in *Letters* I, 2. The young Gibbon was led into play, lost one hundred and ten guineas, and undertook to go to London and raise money on his prospects. Pavilliard overtook him in Geneva and persuaded him to return.

73 9. **Lesueur.** Jean Lesueur (d. 1681) published the work referred to in 1672. Milman says, "The work was not of very high pretensions, nor of merit exceeding its pretensions. It was, I believe, the common history of the French Protestant clergy in Switzerland."

73 19. **M. Deyverdun.** George Deyverdun (1735–1789), the friend of Gibbon, afterwards published anonymously many articles in *Étrennes Helvétiques,* and they were later reproduced in *Mémoires Helvétiques.*

He also translated Goethe's *Werther* into French in 1784. Other facts in regard to his life are given by Gibbon.

74 20. **M. de Crousaz.** Jean Pierre de Crousaz (1663–1748) was born at Lausanne, and for some years held a professorship of philosophy and mathematics in that place. His works are numerous but not of great value. He attacked Bayle in *Examen du Pyrrhonisme l'ancien et moderne*, and also the optimism of Pope in *Examen de l'Essay de Monsieur Pope sur l'homme.*

74 25. **Limborch and Le Clerc.** Philip van Limborch (1633–1712) was a prominent Remonstrant theologian of Holland. His most important work was *Institutiones Theologiæ Christianæ* (1686) which was translated into English in 1702. Jean Le Clerc (1657–1736) was a Swiss theologian and man of letters. He was appointed to a professorship in the Remonstrant seminary at Amsterdam in 1684, through the influence of Limborch whose friend he was. Le Clerc was remarkable for his liberal views of inspiration and for his inquiry into the origin of the books of the Bible. He also exerted a great influence on his contemporaries through various serials which he edited. His *Logica* (74 31) was published in 1792.

75 9. **some of his letters.** These are printed in *Miscellaneous Works*, I, 78 ff. With the statement here should be compared Gibbon's letter to his Aunt Porten, announcing his reconversion (*Letters*, I, 2). The latter is a curious example of how quickly Gibbon had lost his English idiom.

75 11. **well managed defense.** Lord Sheffield says in a note, "M. Pavilliard has described to me the astonishment with which he gazed on Mr. Gibbon standing before him — a thin little figure, with a large head — disputing and urging, with the greatest ability, all the best arguments that had ever been used in favour of popery. Mr. Gibbon many years ago became very fat and corpulent, but he had uncommonly small bones, and was very slight made."

75 31. **But in the life.** In Memoir C Gibbon puts this idea somewhat more sententiously: "Every man who rises above the common level has received two educations, the first from his teachers, the second more personal and important from himself. He will not, like the fanatics of the last age, define the moment of grace; but he cannot forget the year of his life in which his mind was expanded to its proper form and dimensions."

76 16. **rapid progress.** In his journal Gibbon records the work of this year as follows: "December 1755. — In finishing this year, I must remark how favorable it was to my studies. In the space of eight

months, from the beginning of April, I learnt the principles of drawing; made myself complete master of the French and Latin languages, with which I was very superficially acquainted before, and wrote and translated a great deal in both; read Cicero's *Epistles ad Familiares*, his *Brutus*, all his *Orations*, his *Dialogues de Amicitiâ*, and *De Senectute;* Terence, twice; and Pliny's *Epistles*. In French, Giannone's *History of Naples*, and l'Abbé Bannier's *Mythology*, and M. de Boehat's *Mémoires sur la Suisse*, and wrote a very ample relation of my tour. I likewise began to study Greek, and went through the grammar. I began to make very large collections of what I read. But what I esteem most of all, from the perusal and meditation of De Crousaz's *Logic*, I not only understood the principles of that science, but formed my mind to a habit of thinking and reasoning I had no idea of before."

76 17. **an excellent method.** See a similar method pursued by Franklin in acquiring an English style; his own account is in his *Autobiography*, *Works* (Bigelow), I, 47.

76 20. **Vertot.** René Aubert de Vertot d'Aubeuf (1655–1735), a celebrated French historian often praised for his style.

77 4. **Dr. Middleton's History.** For an account of Middleton see note on 59 25. The work referred to is the *History of the Life of Marcus Tullius Cicero* (1741) which was long regarded as a model of style.

77 7. **Olivet.** Joseph Thoulier d'Olivet (1682–1768) was the editor, among other works, of a complete edition of Cicero (1740–1742) which excelled in correctness of text and editorial learning, as well as in beauty of typography.

77 8. **Ernesti.** Johann August Ernesti (1707–1781) was one of the ablest German philologists and theologians of the last century. He annotated many classical works, among others Cicero (1737–1739).

77 11. **Ross . . . Verburgius.** John Ross (d. 1792), Bishop of Exeter, edited Cicero's *Familiar Letters* in 1749. Isaac Verburg, or Verburgius (b. 1685), a famous Dutch classical scholar, published his edition of Cicero's *Works* in 1724. In Gibbon the name of the latter is written Verbruggius.

77 19. **Roman orator.** In Memoir C Gibbon adds, "I tasted the beauties of language, I breathed the spirit of freedom, and I imbibed from his precepts and examples the public and private sense of a man."

77 29. **plan of reviewing.** As to this Gibbon has the following entry in his journal: "Jan. 1756.—I determined to read over the Latin authors in order; and read this year, Virgil, Sallust, Livy, Velleius

Paterculus, Valerius Maximus, Tacitus, Suetonius, Quintus Curtius, Justin, Florus, Plautus, Terence, and Lucretius. I also read and meditated Locke, *Upon the Understanding*."

78 10. **Torrentius, Dacier, etc.** The names are here interesting principally as showing the scholarly method of the young Gibbon. He was but twenty-one when completing this extensive and careful reading, most of it done with little assistance from his tutor.

78 16. **a dissertation.** This may be found in Gibbon's *Miscellaneous Works*, IV, 446. The passage describes the Nile as rising in India. Various more or less violent emendations had been proposed, but Gibbon points out with unquestionable accuracy that the passage needs no emendation, since it conforms to the ancient knowledge of geography as shown by many other works.

78 30. **Vos exemplaria.** Horace, *Ars Poetica*, 268–269.

79 29. **my father had been desirous.** It is evident from one of Pavilliard's letters that Gibbon's father had insisted on his son's taking up mathematics. Pavilliard adds that "the taste which he [Gibbon the younger] had for *belles lettres* led him to apprehend that algebra would impede his favorite pursuit."

80 1. **Marquis de l'Hôpital.** Guillaume François Antoine l'Hôpital (1661–1704), Marquis de Saint-Mesnil and Count d'Eutremont, was a famous mathematician, whose *Traite Analytique des Sections Coniques* was long the best text-book on the subject.

80 18. **Grotius, Puffendorf.** Hugo Grotius, or Huig van Groot (1583–1645), was one of the greatest Dutch scholars and publicists of the seventeenth century. Samuel Puffendorf (1631–1694) a German publicist and historian, whose most important work is *De Jure Naturæ et Gentium*, to which reference is no doubt made.

80 24. **Barbeyrac.** Jean Barbeyrac (1674–1744) was professor of law at Lausanne and Groningen. He is best known for the preface and notes to his translation of Puffendorf's great work mentioned above; he also translated the *De Jure Belli et Pacis* of Grotius.

80 27. **Montesquieu.** Charles Louis de Secondat, Baron de Montesquieu (1689–1785), is best known for his justly famous *L'Esprit des Lois* (1749).

81 4. **Philosophic Dictionary.** The reference is probably to the *Dictionnaire Philosophique* of Voltaire, though it may possibly be to the *Historical and Critical Dictionary* of Bayle, for its time a master work of curious and interesting information.

81 12. **Provincial Letters.** This masterpiece, properly called *Lettres Écrites par Louis de Montalte à un Provincial de ses Amis*, is a

famous satire upon the casuistry of the Jesuits, written in 1656 by the great philosopher, man of letters, mathematician, and physicist, Blaise Pascal (1623–1662).

81 17. **Abbé de la Bletterie.** Jean Philippe René de la Bletterie (1696–1772), a French physician and man of letters, wrote the *Vie de l'Empereur Julius* in 1735.

81 20. **Giannone.** Pietro Giannone (1676–1748), one of the greatest Italian historians, published his *History of Naples* in 1723 after twenty years of labor. To Gibbon's use of this work in the later volumes of the *Decline and Fall* is largely due the appreciation of Giannone among English scholars.

81 31. **that what is twice read.** The quotation is from the *Idler*, No. 74, in praise of memory. Johnson was answering the objection that "nothing is certainly remembered but what is transcribed," and with true Johnsonian fondness for the antithesis contends that "The act of writing itself distracts the thoughts, and what is read twice is commonly better remembered than what is transcribed."

82 2. **tour of Switzerland.** A letter from Gibbon to Miss Porten, (*Letters*, I, 5) will give some idea of this tour and of his other interests in Lausanne. It was written Sept. 20, 1755, and part of it reads as follows:

". . . Now for myself. As my father has given me leave to make a journey round Switzerland, we set out to-morrow. Buy a map of Switzerland, it will cost you but a shilling, and follow me. I go by Iverdun, Neufchatel, Bienne or Biel, Soleurre or Solothurn, Bale or Basel, Bade, Zurich, Lucerne, and Berne. The voyage will be of about four weeks, so that I hope to find a letter from you waiting for me. As my father had given me leave to learn what I had a mind, I have learned to ride, and learn actually to dance and draw. Besides that, I often give ten or twelve hours a day to my studies. I find a great many agreeable people here, see them sometimes, and can say upon the whole, without vanity, that though I am the Englishman here who spends the least money, I am he who is the most generally liked. I told you that my father had promised to send me into France and Italy. I have thanked him for it; but if he would follow my plan, he won't do it yet a while. I never liked young travelers; they go too raw to make any great remarks, and they lose a time which is (in my opinion) the most precious part of a man's life. My scheme would be, to spend this winter at Lausanne: for though it is a very good place to acquire the air of good company and the French tongue, we have no good professors. To spend (I say) the winter at Lausanne; go into England to see my friends a couple of months, and after that, finish my studies, either at Cambridge (for after what has passed one cannot think of Oxford), or at an university in Holland. If you liked the scheme, could you not propose it to my father by Metcalf, or somebody who has a certain credit over him? I forgot to ask you whether, in case my father writes to tell me of his marriage, would you advise me to compliment my mother-in-law? I think so. My health is so very regular, that I have nothing to say about it.

I have been the whole day writing you this letter; the preparations for our voyage gave me a thousand interruptions. Besides that, I was obliged to write in English. This last reason will seem a paradox, but I assure you the French is much more familiar to me. I am, &c.

E. GIBBON."

82 5. **fashion of climbing.** Foreign travel and Alpine climbing were not common until after the middle of the eighteenth century. "Where one Englishman traveled in the reigns of the first two Georges, ten now (1772) go on a grand tour. Indeed, to such a pitch is the spirit of traveling come in the kingdom, that there is scarce a citizen of large fortune but takes a flying view of France, Italy, and Germany in a summer excursion." — Lecky, *England in the Eighteenth Century*, III, 179. Gibbon himself says in a letter of October 22, 1784, "The voyage of Switzerland, the Alps, and the glaciers, is become the fashion." — *Letters*, II, 116.

82 28. **Benedictine Abbey of Einsiedeln.** This is in the Canton of Schwyz, eight miles northeast of the city of the same name. The Abbey was founded about the middle of the ninth century, and has been celebrated since that time for its shrine of the Virgin to which 150,000 pilgrims resort annually. Zwingli preached there in 1516–1518. Not far from the town is the house where Paracelsus was born.

83 4. **Zwinglius.** It was when stationed at Einsiedeln (1516–1518) that Huldreich Zwingli (1484–1531) first attracted attention by his denunciation of pilgrimages. From this place he was called to Zurich, where the Swiss reformation may be said to have begun in earnest.

83 19. **substituting otio.** This reading of the passage is now generally adopted.

83 22. **M. Crevier.** Jean Baptiste Louis Crevier (1693–1765) was professor at Beauvais for twenty years, when he was called to Paris. He completed Rollin's *Histoire Romaine*, besides publishing other works. His flattering letter to the young scholar may be found in Gibbon's *Miscellaneous Works*, I, 433.

83 28. **Breitinger.** Johann Jacob Breitinger (1701–1776) was professor of Greek and Hebrew at Zurich. He was also associated with Bodmer in a revival of the older German literature.

84 3. **Matthew Gesner.** Johann Matthew Gesner (1691–1761) was a distinguished classical scholar who became professor of rhetoric at Göttingen on the founding of the University in 1734. He is especially known for the attention which he paid to the explanation and illustra-

tion of the subject-matter of classical authors. Gibbon's slighting remark as to Gesner's enumeration of his titles does not seem to be fully justified by the letter itself, *Miscellaneous Works*, I, 502.

84 12. **M. Allemand.** Nothing seems to be known of this clergyman except what Gibbon tells and the name of the letter mentioned. The latter was *Lettre sur les Assemblées des Religionnaires en Languedoc, écrite à un gentilhomme protestant de cette provènce par M-D-L, F-D-M.* It was printed in France, but with the false imprint of Rotterdam. Bex is not far southeast of Lausanne.

84 33. **Est sacrificulus.** I have not been able to find the source of this quotation.

85 4. **Locke's metaphysics.** Dugald Stewart speaks of Allemand's letters as "containing a criticism on Locke's arguments against innate ideas so very able and judicious that it may be still read with advantage by many logicians of no small note in the learned world." — Quoted by Milman.

85 7. **And found no end.** *Paradise Lost*, ii, 561.

85 19. **the first of kings.** The reference is to Frederick the Great, whom Gibbon again mentions in complimentary terms at 140 32. Voltaire, on his quarrel with his royal patron, had been arrested at Frankfort in May, 1753, and reached Switzerland early in 1754.

85 26. **Virgilium, etc.** The quotation is from Ovid's *Tristia*, iv, 10, 51.

86 8. **A decent theatre.** Voltaire had thought of building a theatre at Lausanne but was deterred by the opposition of the Swiss clergy. For the same reason he later removed to Ferney.

86 20. **Pritchard.** Hannah (Vaughan) Pritchard (1711–1768) was one of the most conspicuous actresses of the revival of the English stage under Garrick. She was famous in many parts and was seen with increasing admiration until the year of her death. See also note on 130 29.

87 15. **Amor, etc.** Virgil, *Georgics*, iii, 244.

88 10. **I saw and loved.** Some brief extracts from Gibbon's journal kept at this time were given by Lord Sheffield: "June. — I saw Mademoiselle Curchod — *Omnia vincit amor, et nos cedamus amori.* August. — I went to Crassy, and stayed two days. Sept. 15. — I went to Geneva. Oct. 15. — I came back to Lausanne, having passed through Crassy. Nov. 1. — I went to visit M. de Watteville at Loin, and saw Mademoiselle Curchod in my way through Rolle. Nov. 17. — I went to Crassy, and stayed there six days." See also the Introduction for a discussion of this interesting episode in the life of the historian.

88 27. **my fate.** In Memoir C Gibbon wrote, "The romantic hopes of youth and passion were crushed on my return by the prejudice or prudence of an English parent. I sighed as a lover; I obeyed as a son; my wound was insensibly healed by time, absence, and the habits of a new life; and my cure was accelerated by a faithful report of the tranquillity and cheerfulness of the lady herself." In Memoir E Gibbon says, "A lover's wishes reluctantly yielded to filial duty; time and absence produced their effect." The 'faithful report' may refer to a letter from Mdlle. Curchod herself; see Introduction. An unpublished letter of Miss Holroyd, daughter of the first editor, says that the famous passage relating to herself was shown to Madame Necker just before her death in May, 1794.

88 29. **friendship and esteem.** Upon the passage in Memoir E Gibbon adds the following note: "See *Œuvres de Rousseau*, tom. xxxiii. p. 88, 89. octavo edition. As an author I shall not appeal from the judgment, or taste, or caprice of Jean Jaques: but that extraordinary man, whom I admire and pity, should have been less precipitate in condemning the moral character and conduct of a stranger." The significant part of Rousseau's letter reads: "You have given me a commission for Mdlle. Curchod of which I shall acquit myself ill, precisely on account of my esteem for her. The coldness of Mr. Gibbon makes me think ill of him. I have again read his book [the *Essay on the Study of Literature*]. It is deformed by the perpetual affectation and pursuit of brilliancy. Mr. Gibbon is no man for me. I cannot think him well adapted to Mdlle. Curchod. A man that does not know her value is unworthy of her; one who knows it and can desert her is a man to be despised. She does not know what she wishes; that man influences her more than her own heart. I should a thousand times rather see him leave her free and poor among us than take her to be rich and miserable in England. In truth, I hope Mr. Gibbon may not come here. I should wish to dissemble but could not; I should wish to do well, and I feel that I should spoil all." For the circumstances under which the letter was written see the Introduction.

89 1. **Duchess of Grafton.** Anne Liddell, daughter of Lord Ravesworth, married the Duke of Grafton in 1756, separated from her husband in 1765, and married Lord Ossory in 1769.

89 14. **Necker.** Jacques Necker (1732–1804), a Genevan by birth, began life in Paris as a bank clerk, but soon became partner in the great banking house of Thelusson and Necker. In 1763 he wooed Mme. de Verméneux, widow of a French officer, but she could not bring herself to marry one who was not of noble birth. At this time,

however, Mme. Verméneux visited Lausanne, met Susanne Curchod, and the next year took her to Paris as her companion. Before the end of the year 1764, Mdlle. Curchod had become Mme. Necker. It was mainly through her encouragement that Necker was led to seek public position. The salon of Mme. Necker had become famous in Paris, and it was doubtless partly through her influence that her husband became director of the treasury in 1776. Necker's political life is well known. The only child of Mme. Necker became the celebrated Madame de Staël.

89 16. **Such as I am.** In Memoir C Gibbon wrote as follows: "Whatsoever have been the fruits of my education, they must be ascribed to the fortunate shipwreck which cast me on the shores of the Leman Lake. I have sometimes applied to my own fate the verses of Pindar, which remind an Olympic champion that his victory was the consequence of his exile, and that at home, like a domestic fowl, his days might have rolled away inactive or inglorious.

. . . ἦτοι καὶ τεά κεν,
Ἐνδομάχας ἅτ' ἀλέκτωρ,
Συγγόνῳ παρ' ἑστίᾳ
Ἀκλεὴς τιμὰ κατεφυλλορόησε . . .
Εἰ μὴ στάσις ἀντιάνειρα
. . . ἄμερσε πάτρας. (*Olymp.* xii.)

Thus, like the crested bird of Mars, at home
Engag'd in foul domestic jars,
And wasted with intestine wars,
Inglorious hadst thou spent thy vig'rous bloom;
Had not sedition's civil broils
Expell'd thee from thy native *Crete*,
And driv'n thee with more glorious toils
Th' *Olympic* crown in *Pisa's* plain to meet.

West's *Pindar*.

If my childish revolt against the religion of my country had not stripped me in time of my academic gown, the five important years, so liberally improved in the studies and conversation of Lausanne, would have been steeped in port and prejudice among the monks of Oxford. Had the fatigue of idleness compelled me to read, the path of learning would not have been enlightened by a ray of philosophic freedom. I should have grown to manhood ignorant of the life and language of Europe, and my knowledge of the world would have been confined to an English cloister. Had I obtained a more easy deliverance from the regions of sloth and pedantry, had I been sent abroad with the indulgence which the favor and fortune of my father might have allowed, I should probably have herded with the young travelers of my nation, and my attainments in language and manners and science would have been such as they usually import from the continent. But my religious error fixed me at Lausanne in a state of banishment and disgrace. The rigid course of discipline and abstinence, to which I was condemned, invigorated the constitution of my mind and body. Poverty and pride estranged me from my countrymen; I was reduced to seek my amusement in myself and my books, and in the society of the natives, who considered me as their fellow-citizen, I insensibly lost the prejudices of an Englishman."

90 30. **Stanislaus.** Stanislow Lezinski (1677–1766), whose career was romantic in the extreme. Sent as ambassador to the court of Charles XII of Sweden, he was elected through the latter's influence to the vacant throne of Poland in 1704. Deposed in 1709 he led a wandering life for some years. In 1733 he returned to Poland and would have been made king but for the influence of Germany and Russia. At the peace of 1736 he was allowed to abdicate and retain for life the title of King of Poland. At the same time he was put in possession of the Duchies of Lorraine and Bar, over which he ruled in contentment till his death.

90 33. **M. de Beaufort.** Louis de Beaufort (d. 1795) wrote, among other historical works, a *Dissertation sur l'Incertitude des Cinq Premiers Siècles de l'Histoire Romaine* (1738), which in some respects paved the way for the great work of Niebuhr.

92 22. **restored to the command.** His debts were so great that they could not be paid without selling part of the estate, and the estate could not be sold, under the laws of entail, without the consent of the eldest son after he became of age.

93 2. **funds.** According to Murray the manuscript reading is 'fund.'

94 3. **trembled before a stern parent.** See page 15, where Gibbon's father's marriage is described.

94 15. **second marriage as an act of displeasure.** That is, Gibbon felt his father had married in order to reduce his son's property at the former's death, a feeling that is naturally encouraged by laws of entail.

94 21. **Ἐχθρά.** Euripides, *Alcestis*, ii, 320–321. In Memoir C Gibbon gives the substance of the passage without quoting the original: "Euripides has observed that a second wife is more cruel than a viper to the children of a former bed."

94 28. **Est mihi.** Virgil, *Eclogues*, iii, 33.

95 25. **Vincentem, etc.** Horace, *Ars Poetica*, 82; quoted again at 165 24.

96 8. **prosperous era of the stage.** The period referred to may be embraced in the theatrical career of Garrick (1741–1776), who revived the Shakespearean drama and made the stage of his time the most brilliant and noteworthy after the Elizabethan age. Garrick also belonged to the Literary Club of which Gibbon was afterwards a member. See Garrick's letter to Gibbon on the reception of the *Decline and Fall*, *Miscellaneous Works*, II, 153.

97 4. **Mr. Mallet.** See note on 69 19. The 'unforgiving enemy' is Johnson. Johnson seems to have disliked Mallet as the editor of Bolingbroke's *Works;* see Boswell's *Life of Johnson* (Hill), I, 268; II, 128.

99 5. **never handled a gun.** A letter in *Notes and Queries*, First Series, IX, 511, in which Gibbon asks pardon of a neighbor for shooting on his property shows that the antithesis is a little strong. Its general truth is clear, however, even from this letter, in which Gibbon says: "I am no sportsman, sir, and was as much tempted this morning by the beauty of the day and the pleasure of the ride, as by the hopes of any sport."

99 8. **reading and meditation.** An old servant of the Gibbons described the young man as "always fond of reading and seldom seen without a book in his hand. He did not cultivate an acquaintance with the young people in his neighborhood, nor even afford his father or mother much of his company. His beloved books riveted his attention, and to books he sacrificed all the amusements of youth." See letter in *Notes and Queries*, Second Series, III, 145.

100 3. **county of Southampton.** More properly at present the county of Hampshire; the older name is no longer used.

100 5. **Lord Bute's influence.** John Stuart, third Earl of Bute (1713–1792), had acquired great influence with George III when Prince of Wales and was made prime minister in the second year of the new reign. Bute was George Third's tool in trying to regain absolute power, and the special influence referred to is thus described by Green, *History of England*, Book IX, chap. I: "George in his turn seized bribery and borough-jobbing as a base of the power he proposed to give to the crown. The royal revenue was employed to buy seats and to buy votes. Day by day the young sovereign scrutinized the voting list of the two houses, and distributed rewards and punishments as members voted according to his will or no. Promotion in the civil

service, preferment in the church, rank in the army, were reserved for 'the king's friends.' Pensions and court places were used to influence debates. Bribery was employed on a scale never known before. Under Bute's ministry an office was opened at the treasury for the purchase of members, and £25,000 are said to have been spent in a single day. Not all of this corruption was due to Bute, but with something of poetic justice Bute received the odium of all, or most of it."

101 2. **Une de ces societés.** The quotation is from Gibbon's *Essai sur l'Étude de la Littérature;* see *Miscellaneous Works*, IV, 19.

101 14. **nullum, etc.** The quotation is from Pliny's *Letters*, III, 5.

101 18. **every Sunday.** In Memoir C Gibbon says, "I deposited in our pew the octavo volumes of Grabe's *Septuagint* and a Greek Testament of a convenient edition; and in the lessons, gospels and epistles, of the morning and evening service, I accompanied the reader in the original text or the most ancient version of the Bible. Nor was the use of this study confined to words alone. During the Psalms at least and the sermon I revolved the sense of the chapters which I had read and heard, and the doubts, alas, or objections that invincibly rushed on my mind were almost always multiplied by the learned expositors whom I consulted on my return home. Of these ecclesiastical meditations few were transcribed and still fewer have been preserved, but I find among my papers a polite and elaborate reply from Dr. Hurd, now Bishop of Worcester, [*Miscellaneous Works*, II, 83] to whom I had addressed, without my name, a critical disquisition on the sixth chapter of the book of Daniel. Since my escape from popery I had humbly acquiesced in the common creed of the Protestant churches, but in the latter end of the year 1759 the famous treatise of Grotius, *De Veritate Religionis Christianæ*, first engaged me in a regular trial ot the evidence of Christianity. By every possible light that reason and history can afford I have repeatedly viewed the important subject; nor was it my fault if I said with Montesquieu, "Je lis pour m'edifier mais cette lecture produit souvent en moi un effet tout contraire," since I am conscious to myself that the love of truth and the spirit of freedom directed my search. The most accurate philosophers and the most orthodox divines will perhaps agree that the belief of miracles and mysteries cannot be supported on the brittle basis, the distant report, of human testimony, and that the faith as well as the virtue of a Christian must be fortified by the inspiration of grace."

101 27. **Greaves, Arbuthnot, etc.** John Greaves (1602–1652), professor of geometry at Gresham College London, and later of astronomy at Oxford. The work which Gibbon consulted was doubtless the *Dis-*

course on the Roman Foot and Denarius (1649). John Arbuthnot (1675?–1735), physician and wit of Queen Anne's time, published among other works *Tables of the Grecian, Roman, and Jewish Measures.* Bishop George Hooper (1640–1727) wrote a *Treatise on Ancient Weights and Measures* (1721) to which reference is here made. James Bernard (1658–1718) was professor of philosophy and mathematics at Leyden. Jean Gaspard Eisenschmid (1656–1712), a celebrated mathematician, also wrote a treatise concerning the weights and measures of the ancients. Johann Friedrich Gronov, or Gronovius (1613–1671), a classical scholar who was professor at Deventer and later at Leyden. He edited Livy and also published *De Sestertiis* to which Gibbon no doubt refers. Louis François Joseph de la Barré (1688–1738) an historical writer and member of the Academy of Inscriptions. Perhaps his *Dictionnaire du Antiquités Grecques et Romaines* is the work which Gibbon consulted. Nicolas Fréret (1688–1749) was one of the most eminent scholars of his time. He wrote on many historical subjects, among them chronology, for which Gibbon here notices him.

101 30. **manuscript remarks.** These are to be found in Gibbon's *Miscellaneous Works*, V, 66.

102 28. **The old reproach.** In the *Rambler* of May 18, 1751, Johnson wrote: "It is observed that our nation, which has produced so many authors eminent for almost every other species of literary excellence, has been hitherto remarkably barren of historical genius; and so far has this defect raised prejudices against us, that some have doubted whether an Englishman can stop at that mediocrity of style, or confine his mind to that even tenor of imagination which narration requires." In his *Proposal for Correcting, Improving, and Ascertaining the English tongue*, Swift had tried to account for the same lack of historical writing on account of the instability of the English language.

102 30. **Robertson.** William Robertson (1721–1793), the eminent Scotch historian, published a *History of Scotland*, perhaps his greatest work, in 1759.

102 31. **Hume.** David Hume (1711–1776), better known as philosopher than as historian, had published the first volume of his *History of England* in 1754, the last in 1762. In Memoir C Gibbon says, "My emulation was kindled by the recent histories of Hume and Robertson, far distant as I was from the presumptuous hope that my name might one day be ranked with those celebrated names."

103 7. **the Essay.** Gibbon's *Essai sur l'Étude de la Littérature* may be found in his *Miscellaneous Works*, IV, 1. It is now interesting mainly as showing the breadth of the young man's conception of litera-

ture, his evident fondness for history, and the extent of his reading at this time.

103 13. **Academy of Inscriptions.** This was an offshoot of the French Academy founded in 1635. The two other royal societies referred to are the French Academy itself, and the Academy of Sciences founded in 1640. There was also, however, an Academy of Fine Arts founded in 1648.

103 16. **Lipsius and Causaubon.** Justus Lipsius (1547–1606), the Latinized form of Joest Lips, was a famous humanist of the Low Countries, especially noted for his knowledge of the Latin historians and of Roman antiquities. His greatest works were editions of Tacitus (1573) and Seneca (1605). Lipsius was the least of a celebrated triumvirate of scholars, of whom the others were Scaliger and Causabon. Isaac Causabon (1559–1614) was professor of Greek at Geneva from 1581 to 1596, at Montpelier after the latter date. In 1604 he became sub-librarian of the Royal Library at Paris, being excluded from a university professorship because he was a Catholic. In 1610 he went to England where he remained till his death. As commentator and critic he edited many classical authors.

103 24. **I began.** The following extracts from Gibbon's journal relate to the composition of the *Essay:* "March 8, 1758.—I began my *Essai sur l'Étude de la Littérature*, and wrote the twenty-three first chapters (excepting the following ones: 11, 12, 13, 18, 19, 20, 21, 22) before I left Switzerland. July 11.—I again took in hand my *Essay*, and in about six weeks finished it, from chapters 23 to 55 (excepting 27, 28, 29, 30, 31, 32, 33 and note to 38) besides a number of chapters from 55 to the end, which are now struck out. Feb. 11, 1759.—I wrote the chapters of my *Essay*, 27, 28, 29, 30, 31, the note to 38, and the first part of the preface. April 23, 1761.—Being at length, by my father's advice, determined to publish my *Essay*, I revised it with great care, made many alterations, struck out a considerable part, and wrote the chapters from 57 to 78, which I was obliged myself to copy out fair. June 10, 1761.—Finding the printing of my book proceeded but slowly, I went up to town, where I found the whole was finished. I gave Becket orders for the presents: twenty for Lausanne; copies for the Duke of Richmond, Marquis of Carnarvon, Lords Waldegrave, Litchfield, Bath, Granville, Bute, Shelburne, Chesterfield, Hardwicke, Lady Hervey, Sir Joseph Yorke, Sir Matthew Featherstone, Messrs. Mallet, Maty, Scott, Wray, Lord Egremont, M. de Bussy, Mademoiselle la Duchesse d'Aiguillon, and M. le Comte de Caylus; great part of these were only my father's or Mallet's acquaintance."

104 4. **French prisoners at Petersfield.** No doubt prisoners taken in the Seven Years War, and at that time stationed near Gibbon's home.

104 10. **Dr. Maty.** Matthew Maty (1718–1776), physician, writer, and librarian of the British Museum, was the son of Paul Maty, a French Protestant refugee, and was the author of numerous works beside the *Journal* referred to. He brought upon himself the dislike of Johnson by criticising the latter's relations to Lord Chesterfield, and the *Dictionary* itself because the lexicographer sometimes allowed his personal opinions to obtrude themselves unnecessarily. One or two letters recently printed for the first time show that Gibbon's relations with Maty were not entirely harmonious; see *Letters*, I, 20, 21.

104 29. **school of Fontenelle.** This probably means no more than that Dr. Maty was a man of ability rather than a genius, that he possessed a pleasing style, and is to be remembered more for the manner than the matter of his works.

105 1. **I reviewed my essay.** This careful revision of his first work should be compared with the similar painstaking rewriting of the first chapters of his *Decline and Fall*; see p. 164.

105 9. **nonumque, etc.** Horace, *Ars Poetica*, 388.

105 10. **Father Sirmond.** Jacques Sirmond (1559–1651), one of the most learned French writers. His first published work was not the edition of Sidonius Apollinaris, as Gibbon says, but the *Opuscules* of Geoffroy (1610). Even at this time, however, Sirmond was fifty years old.

106 16. **My dedication.** The dedication is interesting as showing the change which had taken place in this species of literature since the seventeenth, and early eighteenth, century. Gibbon says at the beginning, "No performance is, in my opinion, more contemptible than a dedication of the common sort, when some man is presented with a book which, if science, he is incapable of understanding, if polite literature, incapable of tasting; and this honor is done him as a reward for virtues which he neither does nor desires to possess."

106 29. **Duke of Richmond, etc.** No special note seems necessary upon these public men of the eighteenth century, who were rather friends of Gibbon's father than of himself, or persons who might assist in getting the appointment which Gibbon desired; see 105 29.

106 34. **Count de Caylus.** Anne Claude Philippe de Tubières, Count de Caylus (1692–1765), was a distinguished man of letters,

artist, and antiquary. The Count compliments Gibbon's *Essay* (see p. 108 and *Miscellaneous Works*, II, 42), but Gibbon failed to find him particularly interesting on his Paris visit; see extract from Gibbon's Journal quoted in *Miscellaneous Works*, I, 163.

107 1. **Duchesse d'Aiguillon.** She seems to have borne no public character in her own right, but was wife of the minister of foreign affairs under Louis XV.

107 10. **journals of France.** In a note to Memoir E Gibbon says, "The copious extracts which were given in the *Journal Étranger* by M. Suard, a judicious critic, must satisfy both the author and the public. I may here observe, that I have never seen in any literary review a tolerable account of my *History*. The manufacture of journals, at least on the continent, is miserably debased." See also the note to 124 34.

108 20. **brevis esse.** Horace, *Ars Poetica*, 25, 26.

108 34. **design of the Georgics.** Gibbon supposes that the Georgics were written to assist in bringing tranquillity to the empire by celebrating the life of the peaceful citizen as opposed to the danger and difficulty in the life of the soldier; see *Miscellaneous Works*, IV, 36, 37. This view, whether first proposed by Gibbon or not, is now generally accepted; see Seller's *Virgil*, chap. v.

109 29. **Bishen . . . Kishen.** The first is probably the Bengal form of the more common Vishnu; the second is a vernacular form for Krishen, or Krishna. On the other hand, the latter appears as Krishen in the poems of Sir William Jones (Chalmers, *English Poets*), and this form was perhaps intended by Gibbon.

109 32. **Upon the whole.** Milman says in a note: "The intelligent modern reader will be inclined to adopt Gibbon's estimate of his early work. Its faults are very clearly indicated; it is a collection of shrewd and acute observations without order or connection. The defense of the early history of Rome and of Newton's chronology are not more than specious; there is ingenuity but little more in the theory of the Georgics; and Gibbon, in his mature judgment, might have smiled at his attributing the thirty years' quiet of the turbulent veterans who composed the military colonies to the pacific influence of Virgil's poetry. No subject has been pursued with greater erudition and variety of opinion by continental scholars than the origin of polytheism. Gibbon's theory was far advanced beyond his age, and might suggest something like an amicable compromise between the symbolists and anti-symbolists of Germany, the respective schools of Creuzer and Voss."

110 2. **Sir Joshua Reynolds.** This greatest English portrait painter of the eighteenth century (1723–1792) was also distinguished for literary taste and judgment, so that he was gladly reckoned as the friend of men of letters. Reynolds suggested the Literary Club (1764) so famous at the time; see note on 164 9. After Goldsmith's death (1774) Gibbon became the special companion of Sir Joshua, attending him to public entertainments and social gatherings.

110 13. **repudiating.** Bentley's use of the expression is explained by the following quotation: "He [Phalaris] is defended by the like practice of other writers who, being Dorians born, repudiated their vernacular idiom." *Works* I, 359.

111 1. **Ciceronianus of Erasmus.** This is "an elegant and stinging satire on the folly of those pedants who, with a blind devotion, refused to use in their compositions any words or phrases not to be found in Cicero."

111 30. **Sir William Temple and Lord Chesterfield.** These are taken as typical examples of more cosmopolitan Englishmen of the seventeenth and eighteenth centuries. Sir William Temple (1628–1699), statesman, diplomatist, and author, resided abroad for many years, both as private citizen and as representative of England. While best known as a diplomatist, his literary works are highly regarded for their style even to this day. Philip Dormer Stanhope, Earl of Chesterfield (1694–1773), is too well known to need special comment. The famous letters to his son were written in French.

111 33. **Lord Bolingbroke.** Henry St. John, Viscount Bolingbroke (1678–1751), who resided on the continent from 1698 to 1700. The praise by Voltaire is found in the dedication to Bolingbroke of the former's tragedy of *Brutus*. Voltaire himself uses words which Horace had first applied to Mæcenas, *Odes* iii, 8, 5.

112 6. **Count Hamilton.** Anthony Hamilton (1646–1720) is reckoned among French classical authors, although born in Ireland as Gibbon says. His family had moved to France on the execution of Charles I, so that he lived in France from his fourth to his fourteenth year, as also from the battle of the Boyne to his death. For the *Memoirs* see note on 3 29.

112 13. **primus ego.** Virgil, *Georgics*, iii, 10, where, however, the last word reads *mecum*. Gibbon often quoted from memory.

113 2. **social life.** The greatest single change made in the *Memoirs* by the first Lord Sheffield is at this place. He here leaves the later and fuller Memoir B for the briefer account in C. The only reason for the change seems to have been that certain persons were mentioned in

a not wholly complimentary way, and certain opinions were expressed which Lord Sheffield did not care to print.

113 24. **The country rings.** Dryden's *Cymon and Iphigenia*, 399–408. In a note to Memoir E Gibbon tells us that he had first recorded this satire of Dryden in an old pocket-book of the time.

115 7. **progress in the year forty-five.** See note on 22 11.

115 8. **invitation of the Hessians and Hanoverians.** In the year 1756 French preparations at Dunkirk and Brest made the English fear an invasion. The nation was without defense — it was said that there were not three regiments fit for service in the country. At length, to the great indignation of Pitt, parliament invited over a large body of Hessian and Hanoverian soldiers who were distributed about the country. This irritated beyond measure the national pride which had long been jealous of the favor shown by the Georges to their Hanoverian possessions.

115 12. **establishment of a militia.** Lecky, *History of England in the Eighteenth Century* II, 533, says: "An act organizing a national militia, which had long been a popular demand and a favorite project of Pitt, had been levied chiefly by the exertions of George Townshend just before the accession of Pitt to power (1757); but it was an extremely ominous sign that it produced the most violent discontent. Notwithstanding the critical condition of affairs, great numbers of the country gentry and farmers resented the duties thrown upon them."

115 13. **Otia qui.** Virgil, *Æneid* vi, 814.

115 18. **constitutional.** The MS. reads constutional, following Gibbon's pronunciation no doubt. See also note on 61 18.

116 28. **Sir Edward Hawke.** Baron Hawke (1705–1781), who had succeeded Admiral Bing in the Mediterranean, gained a signal victory over the French at Belleisle.

117 13. **accession of a British king.** George II was the first of the Hanoverian kings to be regarded by his subjects as an Englishman.

117 18. **They have changed the idol.** I have not succeeded in finding this quotation in any of Burke's published speeches.

118 20. **Winchester.** These and the other places mentioned in the account of Gibbon's military life are in the extreme south of England, between Dorset and Wiltshire on the west and Kent on the east.

118 28. **Major Sturgeon.** A character in *The Mayor of Garratt*, a farce by Samuel Foote, first acted in 1763. Major Sturgeon is represented as a fishmonger of Brentford, and the play is a caricature of the very militia in which Gibbon was serving.

119 31. **new reign.** That of George II who came to the throne in 1760.

120 26. **Lord Bruce.** Thomas Bruce Brudenell (1730–1814) became Baron Bruce of Tottingham in 1747 on the death of his uncle.

120 29. **extremos pudeat.** *Æneid*, v, 196.

121 3. **Effingham.** Thomas Howard, second Earl of Effingham (d. 1763), had succeeded his father in the earldom in 1743. He does not seem to have been known to fame. His wife was the sister of the author of *Vathek*.

121 9. **Colonel Barré.** Isaac Barré (1726–1802), son of a French refugee, was with Wolf at Quebec, and at this time commanded the 106th regiment, raised in 1761. Barré was a member of parliament from 1761 to 1790, and favored the cause of America in her struggle with Britain. He left the army in 1773 and about ten years later had to give up office on account of blindness.

121 13. **stock-purse.** An English military term meaning "money saved out of the expenses of the company or regiment and applied to objects of common interest."

122 20. **complaints of Cicero.** See *Epistles Ad Atticum*, v, 15. The passage is pieced together from various parts of the original letter, not even following the original order.

123 2. **disputes.** Those with the Duke of Bolton referred to on p. 118.

124 2. **Mémoires Militaires.** Karl Gottlieb Guichard (1724–1775), after failing to get a professorship entered the army, first the Dutch service (1747) and last the Prussian during the Seven Years War. Frederick the Great, appreciating his value as a scholar, made him major though with the strange name of Quintus Icilius. The latter was owing to an odd mistake of Frederick. In speaking of Quintus Cæcilius, centurion of the tenth legion at the battle of Pharsalia, Frederick called him Quintus Icilius. Corrected by the author of the *Mémoires Militaires*, the king responded, "So? Well you shall be Quintus Icilius at any rate," and the next day he was entered accordingly, with the promotion to major. See Carlyle's *Frederick the Great*, Book XIX, chap. 1.

124 12. **first seven or eight months.** In his journal Gibbon wrote: "Jan. 11, 1761.—In these seven or eight months of a most disagreeably active life, I have had no studies to set down; indeed, I hardly took a book in my hand the whole time. The first two months at Blandford, I might have done something; but the novelty of the thing, of which for some time I was so fond as to think of going into the

army, our field-days, our dinners abroad, and the drinking and late hours we got into, prevented any serious reflections. From the day we marched from Blandford I had hardly a moment I could call my own, almost continually in motion; if I was fixed for a day, it was in the guard-room, a barrack, or an inn. Our disputes consumed the little time I had left. Every letter, every memorial relative to them fell to my share; and our evening conferences were used to hear all the morning hours strike. At last I got to Dover, and Sir Thomas left us for two months. The charm was over, I was sick of so hateful a service; I was settled in a comparatively quiet situation. Once more I began to taste the pleasure of thinking. Recollecting some thoughts I had formerly had in relation to the system of Paganism, which I intended to make use of in my Essay, I resolved to read Tully *De Natura Deorum*, and finished it in about a month. I lost some time before I could recover my habit of application."

124 25. **Beausobre.** Isaac de Beausobre (1659–1738), a learned French Protestant who was forced to live abroad because of his religion. In 1694 he became chaplain to the king of Prussia and a royal counsellor. He published numerous works, that mentioned by Gibbon being the most famous.

124 34. **Devises.** In his journal Gibbon says of his life here: "Nov. 2, 1761.—I have very little to say for this and the following month. Nothing could be more uniform than the life I led there. The little civility of the neighboring gentlemen gave us no opportunity of dining out; the time of year did not tempt us to any excursions round the country; and at first my indolence, and afterwards a violent cold, prevented my going over to Bath. I believe in the two months I never dined or lay from quarters. I can therefore only set down what I did in the literary way. Designing to recover my Greek, which I had somewhat neglected, I set myself to read Homer, and finished the four first books of the Iliad, with Pope's translation and notes: at the same time, to understand the geography of the Iliad, and particularly the catalogue, I read books 8, 9, 10, 12, 13, and 14 of Strabo, in Casaubon's Latin translation. I likewise read Hume's *History of England* to the reign of Henry the Seventh, just published, ingenious but superficial; and the *Journal des Sçavans* for Aug., Sept., and Oct. 1761, with the *Bibliothèque des Sciences*, etc. from July to Oct. Both these Journals speak very handsomely of my book."

125 4. **literary repose.** One of Gibbon's entries in his journal at this time shows the candor with which he criticised his own character. It reads: "May 8, 1762.—This was my birth-day, on which I entered

into the twenty-sixth year of my age. This gave me occasion to look a little into myself, and consider impartially my good and bad qualities. It appeared to me, upon this inquiry, that my character was virtuous, incapable of a base action, and formed for generous ones; but that it was proud, violent, and disagreeable in society. These qualities I must endeavor to cultivate, extirpate, or restrain, according to their different tendency. Wit I have none. My imagination is rather strong than pleasing. My memory both capacious and retentive. The shining qualities of my understanding are extensiveness and penetration; but I want both quickness and exactness. As to my situation in life, though I may sometimes repine at it, it perhaps is the best adapted to my character. I can command all the conveniences of life, and I can command too that independence, (that first earthly blessing,) which is hardly to be met with in a higher or lower fortune. When I talk of my situation, I must exclude that temporary one, of being in the militia. Though I go through it with spirit and application, it is both unfit for, and unworthy of me."

125 8. **Mr. George Scott.** George Lewis Scott (1708–1780), "one of the most accomplished of all amateur mathematicians who never gave their works to the world" (Brougham), was tutor to Prince George, afterwards George III, and his younger brothers, and later commissioner of excise till his death. His letter to Gibbon may be found in *Miscellaneous Works* II, 44.

125 21. **Ἐν δ' ἄνεμος.** *Iliad* i, 481. Bryant translates:

> "The canvas swelled
> Before the wind, and hoarsely round the keel
> The dark waves murmured as the ship flew on;
> So ran she, cutting through the sea her way."

125 28. **Gale.** Thomas Gale (1636–1702), though an eminent classical scholar, is chiefly remembered as a collector of old works bearing on English history.

126 4. **Dr. Hurd.** Richard Hurd (1720–1808), author of numerous works, controversial and critical. He published an edition of the *Ars Poetica* (*Epistola ad Pisones*) in 1749 and the *Epistola ad Augustum* in 1751. Gibbon had before him the second edition (1757) of the two epistles. See also note to 154 9.

126 6. **thirty close-written pages.** According to Murray Memoir B reads 'fifty' instead of 'thirty.' This must be a mistake, however, since at the close of the paper (*Miscellaneous Works* IV, 113) Gibbon

says, "I reckoned upon six or seven pages; I am now writing the thirtieth."

126 10. **After his oracle Dr. Johnson.** In the *Life of Cowley* Johnson says: "The true genius is a mind of large general powers, accidentally determined to some particular direction." See also *Rambler*, 19.

126 27. **a dissertation.** It may be found in *Miscellaneous Works* III, 206, where it makes fifteen printed pages.

127 7. **Marquis of Montrose.** The others mentioned are too well known to need comment. James Graham, Marquis of Montrose (1612–1650), no doubt attracted Gibbon both as a brilliant soldier and as a vigorous supporter of the Stuarts.

127 18. **Dr. Birch.** Thomas Birch (1705–1766) was the author of many historical and biographical works. The *General Dictionary*, was an edition of Bayle's *Historical and Critical Dictionary* with numerous additions. For this Dr. Birch had also written the article on Bacon, which accounts for the apparently tautological expression 'his copious article in the *General Dictionary* by the same hand.' Birch published the *Miscellaneous Works of Sir Walter Raleigh with his Life* in 1750, and *Memoirs of the reign of Elizabeth illustrated from the papers of Anthony Bacon*, to which reference is made in l. 26.

127 27. **Sir Robert Naunton** (d. 1635) was an English statesman employed on various diplomatic missions, and finally made secretary of state under James I. The book referred to contains much curious information concerning the court of Elizabeth.

127 30. **Sir William Monson** (1569–1643) was a naval officer who distinguished himself in the reigns of Elizabeth and James I.

127 31. **Mr. Oldys.** William Oldys (1696–1761), an antiquary and author of many works, of which the *Life of Raleigh* is the best known.

130 10. **stirps quasi.** Gibbon was apparently quoting from memory as often in such cases. The full sentence is, "Neque nollem, vel Mediceæ stirpis causa, fataliter pæne dixerim natæ ad hæc studia instauranda vel fovenda." —*Justi Lipsi Epistolarum Selectarum Centuria Prima Miscellanea*, Antwerp, 1614.

130 17. **Res alta.** *Æneid* vi, 266.

130 24. **rash engagement.** In his journal Gibbon reviews his military life as follows: "As this was an extraordinary scene of life, in which I was engaged above three years and a half from the date of my commission, and above two years and a half from the time of our embodying, I cannot take my leave of it without some few reflections. When I engaged in it, I was totally ignorant of its nature and conse-

quences. I offered, because my father did, without ever imagining that we should be called out, till it was too late to retreat with honor. Indeed, I believe it happens throughout, that our most important actions have been often determined by chance, caprice, or some very inadequate motive. After our embodying, many things contributed to make me support it with great impatience. Our continual disputes with the duke of Bolton; our unsettled way of life, which hardly allowed me books or leisure for study; and more than all, the disagreeable society in which I was forced to live.

"After mentioning my sufferings, I must say something of what I found agreeable. Now it is over, I can make the separation much better than I could at the time. 1. The unsettled way of life itself had its advantages. The exercise and change of air and of objects amused me, at the same time that it fortified my health. 2. A new field of knowledge and amusement opened itself to me; that of military affairs, which, both in my studies and travels, will give me eyes for a new world of things, which before would have passed unheeded. Indeed, in that respect I can hardly help wishing our battalion had continued another year. We had got a fine set of new men, all our difficulties were over; we were perfectly well clothed and appointed; and, from the progress our recruits had already made, we could promise ourselves that we should be one of the best militia corps by next summer; a circumstance that would have been the more agreeable to me, as I am now established the real acting major of the battalion. But what I value most, is the knowledge it has given me of mankind in general, and of my own country in particular. The general system of our government, the methods of our several offices, the departments and powers of their respective officers, our provincial and municipal administration, the views of our several parties, the characters, connections, and influence of our principal people, have been impressed on my mind, not by vain theory, but by the indelible lessons of action and experience. I have made a number of valuable acquaintance, and am myself much better known, than (with my reserved character) I should have been in ten years, passing regularly my summers at Buriton, and my winters in London. So that the sum of all is, that I am glad the militia has been, and glad that it is no more."

130 29. **Elvira**. Gibbon's journal contains two entries with regard to this play, as follows: "Nov. 26, 1762.—I went with Mallet to breakfast with Garrick; and thence to Drury Lane House, where I assisted at a very private rehearsal, in the Green-room, of a new tragedy of Mallet's, called *Elvira*. As I have since seen it acted, I shall defer

my opinion of it till then; but I cannot help mentioning here the surprising versatility of Mrs. Pritchard's talents, who rehearsed, almost at the same time, the part of a furious queen in the Green-room, and that of a coquette on the stage; and passed several times from one to the other with the utmost ease and happiness.

"Jan. 19, 1763. — My father and I went to the Rose, in the passage of the play-house, where we found Mallet, with about thirty friends. We dined together, and went thence into the pit, where we took our places in a body, ready to silence all opposition. However, we had no occasion to exert ourselves. Notwithstanding the malice of party, Mallet's nation, connections, and indeed imprudence, we heard nothing but applause. I think it was deserved. The plan was taken from de la Motte, but the details and language have great merit. A fine vein of dramatic poetry runs through the piece. The scenes between the father and son awaken almost every sensation of the human breast; and the counsel would have equally moved, but for the inconvenience unavoidable upon all theatres, that of entrusting fine speeches to indifferent actors. The perplexity of the catastrophe is much, and I believe justly, criticised. But another defect made a stronger impression upon me. When a poet ventures upon the dreadful situation of a father who condemns his son to death, there is no medium, the father must either be a monster or a hero. His obligations of justice, of the public good, must be as binding, as apparent, as perhaps those of the first Brutus. The cruel necessity consecrates his actions, and leaves no room for repentance. The thought is shocking, if not carried into action. In the execution of Brutus's sons I am sensible of that fatal necessity. Without such an example, the unsettled liberty of Rome would have perished the instant after its birth. But Alonzo might have pardoned his son for a rash attempt, the cause of which was a private injury, and whose consequences could never have disturbed an established government. He might have pardoned such a crime in any other subject; and as the laws could exact only an equal rigor for a son, a vain appetite for glory, and a mad affectation of heroism, could alone have influenced him to exert an unequal and superior severity."

131 6. **In this first visit.** See two letters regarding it in *Miscellaneous Works* II, 52. About the same time Horace Walpole was revisiting Paris and writing interesting accounts of it; see *Letters of Horace Walpole* IV, 403 ff.

131 27. **sands of Versailles.** In order to provide water for the palace and pleasure grounds of Versailles immense sums had been spent by Louis XIV. An aqueduct was built from the Seine, the water of

the plateau between Versailles and Rambouillet was brought in a vast system of pipes, and an unsuccessful attempt was made to utilize the waters of the Eure. The waters of the Seine were also diverted to Marly-le-Roi where Louis XIV built a castle and laid out pleasure grounds.

131 34. **Inverary to Wilton.** Used to imply the whole extent of the country; a sort of English Dan to Beersheba.

132 1. **Marylebone to Westminster.** These represent the fashionable parts of west London. Gibbon wrote 'Marybone,' following pronunciation.

132 7. **St. Sulpice.** St. Sulpice is one of the richest and most important of the churches on the left bank of the Seine. The corner stone was laid in 1646 but work upon the building ceased in 1678 for lack of funds. The 'late curate' was Languet de Gergy who zealously solicited subscriptions, established a lottery by permission of the king, and thus secured funds for continuing the work.

132 22. **Clarum et.** The quotation is from Lucan's *Pharsalia*, ix, 202.

133 4. **Duke de Nivernois, Lady Hervey.** Louis Jules Mazarini, Duke de Nivernois (1716–1798), was French ambassador at various courts, including that of St. James. He translated from the Latin poets and wrote numerous works. Gibbon describes him in his journal as "a little emaciated figure, but appears to possess a good understanding, taste, and knowledge. He offered me very politely letters for Paris." Lady Hervey was the widow of John, Lord Hervey (1696–1743), a politician and wit of the reign of George II, who appears as 'Narcissus,' 'Sporus,' and 'Lord Fanny' in Pope's *Satires*. Lady Hervey was the beautiful Mary Lepell, maid of honor to Queen Anne.

133 12. **national urbanity.** Gibbon writes in his French journal (May, 1763): "In a capital like Paris it is proper and necessary to have some letters of recommendation to distinguish you from the crowd; but as soon as the ice is broken, your acquaintances multiply and your new friends take a pleasure in introducing you to others still more new, —happy effect of the light and amiable character of the French, who have established in Paris a freedom and ease in society unknown in antiquity, and still unpracticed by other nations. In London a way must be made into people's houses, the doors of which are with difficulty opened. There, people think that they confer a favor by receiving you; here, they think that they confer one on themselves. Thus I know more houses in Paris than in London."

133 17. **Rousseau.** Jean Jacques Rousseau (1712–1778) was forced to leave France at his threatened arrest on the condemnation (June 11, 1762) of his *Émile* by the parliament of Paris. This was the beginning of a wandering life, during which the philosopher resided in Switzerland and England. He returned to France in 1770.

133 20. **Buffon.** George Louis Leclerc, Count de Buffon (1707–1788), was an eminent French naturalist whose fame rests mainly on his *Histoire Naturelle*, the publication of which extended over more than fifty years (1749–1804). Cuvier says of him, "But Buffon has not less the merit of having been the first to point out clearly that the actual condition of the globe is the result of a succession of changes, of which we can find the evidences to-day; but he also first drew the observation of all investigators to the phenomena by which these changes can be unraveled." See also note to 189 24.

133 21. **d'Alembert and Diderot.** Jean le Rond d'Alembert (1717–1783), an eminent mathematician and philosopher. He was united with Denis Diderot (1713–1784), one of the best-known men of letters of the eighteenth century, in the preparation of the great *Encyclopédie* (1751–1772). For this reason their names are usually coupled as here.

133 26. **Count de Caylus, etc.** Most of these men, while not of the first rank to-day, were distinguished in their own time in various ways. All were members of the various French Academies. For Caylus and Bletterie see notes to 106 34 and 81 17. Jean Jacques Barthélemy (1716–1795) is best known for his *Voyage of Young Anacharsis into Greece in the fourth century before the Christian Era*, an attempt to give an account of the government, manners, and customs of the ancient Greeks in the form of a book of travels. Guillaume Thomas François Raynal (1711–1796) was the author of a *History of the Parliament of England.* He lost his property under the tyranny of Robespierre and died in great poverty. François Arnaud (1721–1784) was associated with Suard in editing the *Journal Étranger* and other works. Charles Marie de la Condamine (1701–1774), geographer and mathematician, was the first to explore the Amazon (1743). Charles Pinaud du Clos (1704–1772) was a talented writer of romances, history and travel. Jean Baptiste de Sainte Palaye (1697–1781) was the author of important works on the antiquities of France. Jean Louis de Bougainville (1729–1814), an able admiral and man of learning, is distinguished as the first French circumnavigator of the globe (1766–1768). Jean Capperonier (1716–1775) was the editor of Joinville's *L'Histoire de St. Louis* and of various classical authors. Joseph de Guignes (1721–1800) was a famous orientalist, best known for his *History of the Huns, Mongols,*

Turks and Tartars (1756). Jean Baptiste Antoine Suard (1734–1817) edited the *Journal Étranger*, *Gazette Littéraire de l'Europe*, translated Robertson's *Histories*, and wrote numerous works of less importance. See also note to 183 5.

134 2. **Mesdames Geoffrin and du Bocage.** Marie Theresa Rodet, Madame Geoffrin (1699–1777), was famous for her salon which was frequented by the most celebrated men of the time. Marie Anne le Page, Madame du Bocage (1710–1802), was the author of several poems and member of the academies of Rome, Bologne, Padua, Lyons, and Rouen, besides being a leader in Parisian society.

134 3. **Helvetius.** Claude Adrien Helvetius (1715–1771) is best known for his book *De L'Esprit*, in which the author unsuccessfully attempted to rival the famous *Esprit des Lois* of Montesquieu. In a letter to his stepmother (Feb. 12, 1763) Gibbon says: "Among my acquaintance I cannot help mentioning M. Helvetius, the author of the famous book *De L'Esprit*. I met him at dinner at Mme. Geoffrin's where he took great notice of me, made me a visit next day, and has ever since treated me, not in a polite, but a friendly manner. Besides being a sensible man, an agreeable companion, and the worthiest creature in the world, he has a very pretty wife, a thousand livres a year, and one of the best tables in Paris."

134 4. **Baron d'Holbach.** Paul Thyry, Baron d'Holbach (1713–1789), was born at Hildesheim but was educated and lived in Paris. He allied himself with the *Encyclopédists* and wrote, probably with the aid of Diderot, *Le Système de la Nature*.

134 9. **'Αυτόματοι.** This line is one of the fragments of a lost comedy by Eupolis called *The Golden Age* (Χρυσοῦν Γένος). It is quoted as a proverb by Zenobius (ii, 19), and may be freely translated, "To the feasts of the wicked even the good are glad to go."

134 18. **M. de Foncemagne.** Étienne Laurealt de Foncemagne (1694–1779), an eminent Academician, wrote many excellent dissertations and distinguished himself in a literary quarrel with Voltaire over Richelieu's *Testament Politique*, which the latter thought spurious.

134 21. **the Italians.** Horace Walpole, who was in Paris about this time, wrote, "The Italian comedy, now united with their opéra comique, is their most perfect diversion." —*Letters* (Cunningham) IV, 407.

134 25. **Clairon . . . Dumesnil.** Claire-Josepha Lyrie de la Tude (1723–1803), better known as Mdlle. Clairon, was a famous actress who began to play at the age of thirteen and soon rivaled Mdlle. Dumesnil. She quitted the stage in 1765 and in 1799 published her *Memoirs*. Marie Françoise Marchand (1711–1803), called Mdlle. Dumesnil, was

especially successful in tragic rôles in which she received the praise of Garrick.

134 32. **Madame Bontemps.** Marie Jean de Chatillon (1718–1768) was the wife of Pierre Henri Bontemps, paymaster of the forces in Paris. She was the first to introduce the poet Thomson to a French public, by a translation of the *Seasons* and *Hymn to the Creator* (1759).

136 18. **Lewis of Würtemburg.** Ludwig Eugen (1731–1795), to whom Gibbon refers, withdrew from his retirement to become reigning duke on the death of his brother in 1793. He had been engaged in the armies of France, Prussia, and Austria, and was now living in retirement near Lausanne where he enjoyed the company of Rousseau and Voltaire.

138 19. **Mr. Holroyd.** John Baker Holroyd, first Earl of Sheffield (1735–1821), politician and pamphleteer. For his writings see note to 181 6.

138 34. **Mabillon . . . Montfaucon.** Jean Mabillon (1632–1707), the learned historian of the Benedictine order, whose chief work is the *Acta Sanctorum Ordinis S. Benedicti* (1668–1701). The *De Re Diplomatica* is his most important monograph. Bernard de Montfaucon (1655–1741), scholar and critic. His *Palæographia Græca sive de Ortu et Progressu Literarum Græcarum* is still regarded as a standard work.

139 16. **Nardini, Donatus.** Famiani Nardini (d. 1661), an Italian archæologist, wrote *Roma Antica* (1666), an important study of ancient Rome. In his reference to Donatus, it is not clear whether Gibbon means Ælius Donatus, a grammarian of the fourth century, and author of *Commentaries on Terence*, or Tiberius Claudius Donatus, a later grammarian, who wrote a *Commentary on Virgil*. The former is best known for a Latin grammar, so popular in the middle ages that it has given us the word 'donet,' formerly used in the sense of an elementary treatise on any subject.

139 18. **Grævius.** Georg Græf, or Grævius (1632–1703), one of the greatest classical scholars of his time, is most famous for two important treatises on Roman antiquities, the *Thesaurus Antiquitatum Romanorum* (1694–1699), and the *Thesaurus Antiquitatum et Historiarum Italiæ*, published after his death. He also edited many of the classics.

139 19. **Cluverius.** Philip Cluver, or Cluverius (1580–1623), a German geographer still regarded as an authority. The work to which Gibbon refers was published in 1624, the year after the death of its author.

139 24. **Strabo, etc.** Strabo is known only as a geographer. Pliny the elder incorporated into his *Natural History* a geographical account

of the known world. Pomponius Mela wrote a compendium of geography, the only systematic treatise in Latin outside of Pliny. Numatianus, a native of southern Gaul, composed a Latin poem describing a coasting voyage from Rome to Gaul in 416.

139 26. **Wesseling.** Peter Wesseling (1692–1764) was professor at Dewenter and later at Utrecht. He edited numerous classical works, among them the *Veterum Romanorum Itineraria* (1735), which contains the Itinerary of Antoninus.

139 28. **d'Anville.** Jean Baptiste Bourguignon d'Anville (1697–1782), an eminent geographer and author of many important works. The *Mesures Itinéraires* appeared in 1769. Nicolas Bergier (1567–1625), a celebrated archæologist, who is best known by the work referred to in the text.

139 34. **insulæ.** The Latin name for the great tenement houses of ancient Rome. For the 'learned notes' see *Miscellaneous Works* V, 317.

140 3. **Addison's agreeable dialogues.** These are the *Dialogues on Medals* written in 1702 while Addison was in Germany, but not published until after his death. Gibbon means to imply that the work has little scholarly value.

140 4. **Ezechial Spanheim** (1629–1710), statesman as well as numismatist, was minister of the Elector-Palatine to England, and ambassador of the Elector of Brandenburg to France. Besides the work referred to, he wrote *Letters and Dissertations on Medals*, and other works.

140 8. **Perhaps.** With this sentence Memoir C is taken up, Memoir B ending with the preceding. Lord Sheffield began with the next paragraph, but these two sentences seem to belong unusually well with the last part of Memoir B, and also serve to explain the allusion to Hannibal's passage of the Alps in l. 26.

140 32. **Charles Emanuel.** This is Charles Emanuel III (1701–1773), who succeeded his father in 1730. He was not only a famous general but an excellent administrator, so that the kingdom was remarkably prosperous during his reign.

140 33. **proximus.** The quotation is a reminiscence of the *Æneid* v, 320, where the line reads, *proxumus* [*proximus*] *huic, longo sed proxumus intervallo.*

141 4. **Borromean islands.** A group of four small islands, near the western shore of Lago Maggiore in the north of Italy. In 1671 they were made into pleasure gardens by Vitaliano Borromeo. For a description of the place see Richter's *Titan*.

141 13. **Farnese and Este collections.** These collections, named after famous Italian families instrumental in making them, are at Parma and Modena, respectively.

141 19. **the Tribune.** A room of the celebrated Uffizi Gallery at Florence in which are the most famous statues of antiquity.

141 28. **conversations.** Gibbon here transfers the Italian word *conversazione* into English. Sir Horace Mann (1701–1786), British envoy to Florence, was chiefly engaged in watching the Pretender and his family in Italy. His less important duties were to receive and conciliate English visitors, and see that young English noblemen were properly deferential to the petty states through which they passed. See his correspondence with Horace Walpole.

142 10. **Mr. Byers.** James Byers (1733–1817) lived at Rome for forty years, studying archæology and making collections. He gave lectures for many years on his favorite subjects, doing much to form the taste of his young countrymen.

142 18. **boy king.** This was Ferdinand I (1751–1825), king of the two Sicilies, a son of Charles III of Spain, to whom the throne had been resigned in 1759. Deposed by Napoleon, he regained the throne as king of Naples in 1817.

142 19. **Sir William Hamilton** (1730–1803), a Scotch antiquary, naturalist, and patron of the fine arts, was minister to Naples from 1764 to 1800. He published several works on the eruptions of Vesuvius and the antiquities of Pompeii.

142 31. **paradox of Montesquieu.** Gibbon perhaps refers to a statement in Montesquieu's *Grandeur et Décadence du Romains*, chap. xvii, in which he says that on the establishment of the seat of empire at Constantinople "almost the entire population of Rome proceeded thither, the principal citizens being accompanied by their slaves, — that is to say by nearly all the people; and thus Italy was deprived of its inhabitants." This also appears to explain the question at 143 7.

143 6. **Palladio.** Andrea Palladio (1518–1580), one of the greatest architects of his century, most of whose works are in Vicenza and northern Italy. He also wrote a work on architecture, which has passed through many editions, and has been translated into all European languages.

144 23. **In my Journal.** The passage, which Lord Sheffield inserted at this point in the *Memoirs*, reads as follows: "It was at Rome on the fifteenth of October, 1764, as I sat musing amidst the ruins of the Capitol while the bare-footed friars were singing vespers in the temple

of Jupiter, that the idea of writing the decline and fall of the city first started to my mind."

145 28. **fumum, etc.** Horace, *Odes*, iii, 29, 12. Gibbon quotes it again on page 176.

147 8. **Mr. Godfrey Clark.** This friend had made the tour of Italy with Gibbon. He afterwards became member of parliament for Derbyshire and is often mentioned in Gibbon's letters.

147 12. **Roman Club.** In a note Lord Sheffield tells us that "The members were Lord Mountstuart (now Earl of Bute), Col. Edmonstone, William Weddal, Rev. Mr. Palgrave, Lord Berkley, Godfrey Clark, Holroyd (Lord Sheffield), Major Ridley, Thomas Charles Bigge, Sir William Guize, Sir John Aubrey, Lord Abingdon, Hon. Peregrine Bertie, Rev. Mr. Cleaver, Hon. John Damer, Hon. George Damer (Lord Milton), Sir Thomas Goscoygne, Sir John Hort, E. Gibbon."

149 3. **domestic disorders.** The financial difficulties of Gibbon's father, described at length on page 159.

149 20. **three peasants of the Alps.** Gibbon refers to the tradition that three peasants, Werner Stauffacher, Erny (Arnold) an der Halden, and Walter Fürst, on the night of Nov. 7, 1307, took oath for the three cantons of Schwyz, Unterwalden, and Uri against the Austrian oppressors of their country. Though a league was formed at some time, or at several times, in the early history of Switzerland, the details of the tradition are no longer believed.

149 30. **Manus haec.** Source unknown. It is found in Algernon Sidney's works, though probably not original with him.

150 4. **the German language.** "In Gibbon's youth German was little cultivated beyond its local sphere, nor did he study it; but we are assured that on hearing read the translation of Homer by Voss, the corresponding resonance of some noted passage . . . in the Germanic rendering so struck him that he declared his determination to learn the language. We cannot however find that he ever attempted it." — *Dublin Review*, XXIV, 391 note.

150 7. **Schilling.** Diebold Schilling (d. 1509), wrote a *Chronique de la Ville de Berne* from 1152 to 1484, the last part of which, from 1468 to 1484, relates to the war of the Swiss against the Duke of Burgundy, in which he took part. This latter part, called *Description des Guerres de Bourgogne* (Berne 1743), is especially important.

150 9. **Tschudi.** Giles Tschudi (1505–1572), at great labor, attempted to collect the early records of the Swiss confederation. His work the *Chronicon Helvetiorum* was partly published in 1734–1736. It is chiefly valuable for the use made of original documents.

150 11. **Lauffer . . . Lew.** Jacob Lauffer (1688–1734), wrote a *History of the Swiss* which was published in Germany after his death. Hans Jacob Lew (1689–1768) is best known for his *Universal Swiss Lexicon* (1747–1763) to which Gibbon refers. It is a vast collection of materials for Swiss history in the broadest sense of the term.

150 15. **slender materials.** In a note to Memoir E Gibbon says, "I soon found on a trial that these materials were insufficient. An historian should command the language, the libraries, and the archives of the country of which he presumes to write."

150 20. **my judges.** Either before or after this Gibbon sent his manuscript to Hume who gave a more favorable judgment of the work as shown by the following letter dated Oct. 24, 1767:

"SIR, It is but a few days since M. Deyverdun put your manuscript into my hands, and I have perused it with great pleasure and satisfaction. I have only one objection, derived from the language in which it is written. Why do you compose in French, and carry faggots into the wood, as Horace says with regard to the Romans who wrote in Greek? I grant that you have a like motive to those Romans, and adopt a language much more generally diffused than your native tongue: but have you not remarked the fate of those two ancient languages in following ages? The Latin, though then less celebrated, and confined to more narrow limits, has in some measure outlived the Greek, and is now more generally understood by men of letters. Let the French, therefore, triumph in the present diffusion of their tongue. Our solid and increasing establishments in America, where we need less dread the inundation of barbarians, promise a superior stability and duration to the English language.

Your use of the French tongue has also led you into a style more poetical and figurative, and more highly colored, than our language seems to admit of in historical productions; for such is the practice of French writers, particularly the more recent ones, who illuminate their pictures more than custom will permit us. On the whole, your History, in my opinion, is written with spirit and judgment; and I exhort you very earnestly to continue it. The objections that occurred to me on reading it, were so frivolous, that I shall not trouble you with them, and should, I believe, have a difficulty to recollect them. I am, with great esteem,

SIR, &c.

DAVID HUME."

150 22. **I delivered.** This is not strictly true. Lord Sheffield tells us that Gibbon left the introduction or first book at Sheffield Place. It may be found in *Miscellaneous Works* III, 239–330.

151 34. **Lord Lyttleton.** George, Lord Lyttleton (1709–1773), statesman and man of letters, whose history is no longer considered an authority. The judgment of Gibbon is thus confirmed.

152 25. **Earl of Chesterfield.** Lord Chesterfield became both deaf and blind in his old age and was forced to retire from the world. To this period belongs his famous jest, "Tyrawley and I have been dead these two years, but we don't choose to have it known." Deyverdun afterwards became traveling companion to his son; see l. 30 and note on 175 25.

152 31. **a reply.** This review, *Doutes Historiques sur la Vie et la Regne du Roi Richard III par M. Horace Walpole*, is included in *Miscellaneous Works* III, 331–349, with a note to the effect that it was written by Gibbon in 1768 for the *Mémoires Britanniques*. But this must rather be the reply of Hume referred to, since Gibbon could certainly not have written on the same subject, for the same periodical in the same year. Possibly Hume's article was translated, or revised and written out by Gibbon.

153 6. **sally of love and resentment.** In Memoir E Gibbon says, "The love of Virgil, the hatred of a dictator, and the example of Lowth awakened me to arms." The dictator is of course Warburton (see following notes).

153 14. **Ibant, etc.** *Æneid*, vi, 268. The lines below are from the same book, lines 640–641, and 896.

153 27. **Bishop Warburton.** William Warburton (1698–1779), Bishop of Gloucester and man of letters, was more celebrated for brilliant paradoxes than for any real contributions to human knowledge. In his *Divine Legation of Moses* (1738) he attempted to prove the divine authority of the Mosaic writings against the position of the deists. The latter argued that, if Moses had been inspired, he would have revealed immortality. Warburton, with his fondness for paradox, argued on the contrary that, if Moses were not inspired, he would certainly not have omitted the hope of immortality as a sanction of morality; therefore the writings of Moses must be of divine origin. It is not strange that Gibbon could add the following note on the book: "*The Divine Legation of Moses* is a monument, already crumbling in the dust, of the vigor and weakness of the human mind. If Warburton's new argument proved anything, it would be a demonstration against the legislator, who left his people without the knowledge of a future state. But some episodes of the work, on the Greek philosophy, the hieroglyphics of Egypt, &c., are entitled to the praise of learning, imagination, and discernment."

154 4. **dictator and tyrant.** "It was the conviction of William Warburton, Bishop of Gloucester, that he would hold in the eyes of posterity much the same preëminence and isolated greatness that Samuel Johnson actually maintains. He cultivated the majestic airs of a tyrant in literature; he argued, he denounced, he patronized the orthodox, and he bellowed like a bull at the recalcitrant. He was so completely certain of his own intellectual supremacy, that the modern reader feels almost guilty in being able to feel but scant interest in him and in his writings." — Edmund Gosse in *History of English Literature* (Eighteenth Century) 281.

154 9. **Delicacy of Friendship.** This *Dissertation* as it was called was written in 1755 by Richard Hurd, Bishop of Winchester and disciple of Warburton. It was a bitter attack on the Rev. John Jortin who had himself attacked Warburton. In a note to Memoir E Gibbon says: "Our literary Sylla [Warburton] was encompassed with a guard of flatterers and slaves ready to execute every sentence of proscription which his arrogance had pronounced. The assassination of Jortin by Dr. Hurd, now Bishop of Worcester, is a base and malignant act which cannot be erased by time or expiated by secret penance."

154 16. **pointed and polished epistle.** For a quotation from this letter see 46 26 and note. Of the letter Milman says, "It is a masterpiece of its kind; and if our calmer judgment is offended by the unseemly spectacle of two Christian prelates engaged in this fierce intellectual gladiatorism, the chief blame must fall on the aggressor Warburton."

154 22. **Critical Observations.** For the Essay see *Miscellaneous Works* IV, 467.

155 2. **vetabo.** Horace, *Odes*, iii, 2, 26.

155 5. **discreet silence.** Gibbon adds a note to Memoir E as follows: "The editor [Dr. Parr] of the Warburtonian tracts (p. 192) considers the allegorical interpretation 'as completely refuted in a most clear, elegant, and decisive work of criticism; which could not, indeed, derive authority from the greatest name; but to which the greatest name might with propriety have been affixed.'"

155 8. **Professor Heyne.** Christian Gottlob Heyne (1729–1812), one of the most distinguished philologists of modern times, and the author of numerous critical works. In 1761 he succeeded Gesner in the Göttingen professorship, and retained it until his death. See the characteristic *Life of Heyne* in Carlyle's *Miscellaneous Works.* In a note to Memoir E Gibbon says: "That incomparable scholar who, after so many hundred editions, has enriched the world with the *first*

edition of Virgil, declines the examination of Warburton's hypothesis; '*Otium fecit vir doctus qui eam in singulari libello paulo acrius quam velis perstrinxit*' (*Virgilii Opera* II, 804). He afterwards approves a conjecture '*elegantissimi Britanni, etc.*'"

155 12. **Mr. Hayley.** William Hayley (1745–1820), friend and biographer of Cowper, first came into notice through his poetical *Essays on Painting, History and Epic Poetry*. Those on History were inscribed to Gibbon (see note on 182 24). Hayley's most important work, however, is his *Life of Cowper*.

156 13. **Augustan History.** This is the name of a collection of lives of Roman emperors written by several hands in the reigns of Diocletian and Constantine.

156 20. **Tillemont.** Sébestien le Nain de Tillemont (1637–1698), an eminent church historian, whose *Mémoires pour servir à l'Histoire Ecclésiastique des Premiers Siècles* (1697–1712) is a model of patient scholarship.

156 25. **Muratori.** Ludovico Antonio Muratori (1672–1750), a learned historian and antiquary. The works referred to are the *Annali d'Italia* (1744–1749) and *Antiquitates Italicæ Medii Ævi* (1738–1742), two among many of his important writings.

156 27. **Sigonius, etc.** The first is Carlo Sigonio, or Sigonius (1520–1584), classical scholar, antiquary, and author of many treatises on Roman history and antiquities. Francisco Scipione, Marchese di Maffei (1675–1755), was an archæologist and man of letters whose *Verona Illustrata* is no doubt the book referred to here. Caesar Baronius (1538–1607) wrote *Annales Ecclesiastici*, a most important work for the subject and period. Antoine Pagi (1624–1721), a French chronologist, edited Baronius and tried to correct some of his errors.

156 32. **James Godefroy.** Jacques Godefroy, or Gothofred (1587–1652) was a writer on Roman jurisprudence and is best known for the work referred to, the *Theodosian Code*, on which he labored for thirty years.

157 11. **Dr. Lardner.** This is Nathaniel Lardner (1684–1768), a Presbyterian clergyman who wrote several treatises in defense of Christianity. The one referred to in the text is *A large Collection of Ancient Jewish and Heathen Testimonies to the Truth of the Christian Revelation* (1764–1767).

157 12. **ample dissertation.** This has either not been preserved, or has not been included in the published *Miscellaneous Works* of Gibbon.

157 25. **multum legere.** This is perhaps a reminiscence of Pliny's *Epistles* vii, 9, 15, where the reading is "*aiunt enim multum legendum esse non multa*"; or possibly of Quintilian x, 1, 59: "*multa magis quam multorum lectione formanda mens.*"

157 31. **Essay on the Cyropædia.** This essay is not included in the *Miscellaneous Works* of Gibbon, and if preserved must still be with his manuscripts.

158 23. **Beatus ille.** Horace, *Epodes*, ii. Lord Lytton translates:

> "Blessed is he — remote, as were the mortals
> Of the first age from business and its cares —
> Who ploughs paternal fields with his own oxen;
> Free from the bonds of credit or of debt."

159 19. **remedia.** Tacitus, *Historia* iii, 54, where the passage reads '*remedia potius malorum quam mala differebat.*'

159 28. **Flatus.** The character of Flatus is drawn in chapter xii of the *Serious Call*; but see note on 17 28.

161 30. **Mrs. Gibbon.** The historian was scrupulously careful in selling Buriton, to provide for his step-mother's settlement, so that she could not have the slightest uneasiness regarding the provision for her old age. Indeed his devotion to her is attested by numerous references in his letters.

163 26. **I had now attained.** With this sentence Memoir E begins, Memoir C being completed with the preceding. Memoir E is a brief sketch, to which Gibbon added many notes. The latter were usually incorporated into the text by Lord Sheffield, thus destroying the continuity of Gibbon's narrative. In all cases Gibbon's notes have been placed at the end of the volume in this edition.

164 9. **fashionable clubs.** To this Gibbon adds a note as follows: "From the mixed, though polite, company of Boodles, White's, and Brooks's, I must honorably distinguish a weekly society, which was instituted in the year 1764, and which still continues to flourish, under the title of the Literary Club. (Hawkins's *Life of Johnson*, p. 415. Boswell's *Tour to the Hebrides*, p. 97.) The names of Dr. Johnson, Mr. Burke, Mr. Garrick, Dr. Goldsmith, Sir Joshua Reynolds, Mr. Colman, Sir William Jones, Dr. Percy, Mr. Fox, Mr. Sheridan, Mr. Adam Smith, Mr. Steevens, Mr. Dunning, Sir Joseph Banks, Dr. Warton, and his brother Mr. Thomas Warton, Dr. Burney, &c., form a large and luminous constellation of British stars."

164 11. **a stranger.** Gibbon adds a note: "It would most assuredly be in my power to amuse the reader with a gallery of portraits and a collection of anecdotes. But I have always condemned the practice

of transforming a private memorial into a vehicle of satire or praise." Did he have Boswell in mind when he wrote this?

164 27. **Many experiments.** What a comment upon this painstaking manner of writing the history are the six sketches of his own life, with all of which, as is known, Gibbon himself was dissatisfied.

165 14. **Mr. Eliot.** See notes on 69 26 and 171 2.

165 15. **first cousin.** Gibbon explains in a note that she was "Catherine Elliston, whose mother Catherine Gibbon was my grandfather's second daughter. The education of Lady Eliot, a rich heiress, had been intrusted to the Mallets, and she is thus invited to their hymeneal feast." He then quotes Mallet's *Wedding Day*. For the latter see 33 26 and note. Gibbon adds, of her husband Lord Eliot, "In the year 1784 he was raised to the honor of an English peerage, and their three sons are all members of the House of Commons."

165 16. **Liskeard.** A market town and parliamentary borough in the county of Cornwall, at this time controlled by Mr. Eliot.

165 17. **memorable contest.** Gibbon's views on American affairs can be thoroughly understood and appreciated only from the numerous references in his *Letters;* see general index.

165 24. **Vincentem.** Horace, *Ars Poetica*, 82; already quoted at 95 25.

165 31. **first men of the age.** At this point in the Memoirs all the early editions have the following striking passage: "The cause of government was ably vindicated by Lord North, a statesman of spotless integrity, a consummate master of debate, who could wield with equal dexterity the arms of reason and of ridicule. He was seated on the Treasury bench between his attorney and solicitor general, the two pillars of the law and state, *magis pares quam similes*, and the minister might indulge in a short slumber, whilst he was upholden on either hand by the majestic sense of Thurlow, and the skillful eloquence of Wedderburne. From the adverse side of the house an ardent and powerful opposition was supported, by the lively declamation of Barré, the legal acuteness of Dunning, the profuse and philosophic fancy of Burke, and the argumentative vehemence of Fox, who in the conduct of a party approved himself equal to the conduct of an empire. By such men every operation of peace and war, every principle of justice or policy, every question of authority and freedom, was attacked and defended, and the subject of the momentous contest was the union or separation of Great Britain and America." This passage nowhere occurs in the recent reprint of the manuscript memoirs, and a note from the editor, John Murray, informs me that it is not in the manuscript,

but is pencilled on the side in the hand of Maria Holroyd, daughter of Lord Sheffield, who seems to have prepared the original copy for the press. That the passage must have been written by the historian, no one could for a moment doubt. It certainly does not occur in the *Letters* or *Miscellaneous Works*, and I can only conjecture that it must have been one of the numerous notes which Gibbon added to Memoir E, and that it has disappeared from the manuscripts since they were first published, or has been overlooked in the recent reprint of them.

166 4. **Mr. Elmsley.** Peter Elmsley (1736–1802), bookseller and friend of Gibbon, was a man of wide general knowledge besides having a remarkable acquaintance with the French language and literature. It was at his house, 76 St. James street, corner of Little St. James street, that Gibbon died.

166 5. **Mr. Thomas Cadell.** Thomas Cadell (1742–1802), bookseller and publisher in the Strand, published, in conjunction with Strahan, the works of Johnson, Robertson, and Blackstone, besides Gibbon's *History*.

167 1. **pirates of Dublin.** The copyright laws of the time did not protect authors from the Dublin printers, so that popular books were often pirated; see also 107 23 and 183 9.

167 12. **candor of Dr. Robertson.** In a letter to Mr. Strahan, Robertson praised the *Decline and Fall* in the highest terms, but also expressed his regret as to the last two chapters 'that he has taken such a tone in them as will give great offence.' *Miscellaneous Works* II, 159. No doubt Gibbon had this letter in mind when he wrote.

167 13. **letter from Mr. Hume.** Gibbon appends this note: "That curious and original letter will amuse the reader, and his gratitude should shield my free communication from the reproach of vanity.

'EDINBURGH, 18th March 1776.

DEAR SIR,

As I ran through your volume of history with great avidity and impatience, I cannot forbear discovering somewhat of the same impatience in returning you thanks for your agreeable present, and expressing the satisfaction which the performance has given me. Whether I consider the dignity of your style, the depth of your matter, or the extensiveness of your learning, I must regard the work as equally the object of esteem, and I own that if I had not previously had the happiness of your personal acquaintance, such a performance from an Englishman in our age would have given me some surprise. You may smile at this sentiment, but as it seems to me that your countrymen, for almost a whole generation, have given themselves up to barbarous and absurd faction, and have totally neglected all polite letters, I no longer expected any valuable production ever to come from them. I know it will give you pleasure (as it did me) to find that all the men of letters in this place concur in their admiration of your work, and in their anxious desire of your continuing it.

When I heard of your undertaking (which was some time ago), I own I was a little curious to see how you would extricate yourself from the subject of your two last chapters. I think you have observed a very prudent temperament, but it was impossible to treat the subject so as not to give grounds of suspicion against you, and you may expect that a clamor will arise. This, if anything, will retard your success with the public; for in every other respect your work is calculated to be popular. But among many other marks of decline, the prevalence of superstition in England prognosticates the fall of philosophy and decay of taste, and though nobody be more capable than you to revive them, you will probably find a struggle in your first advances.

I see you entertain a great doubt with regard to the authenticity of the poems of Ossian. You are certainly right in so doing. It is indeed strange that any man of sense could have imagined it possible, that above twenty thousand verses, along with numberless historical facts, could have been preserved by oral tradition during fifty generations, by the rudest perhaps of all the European nations, the most necessitous, the most turbulent, and the most unsettled. Where a supposition is so contrary to common sense, any positive evidence of it ought never to be regarded. Men run with great avidity to give their evidence in favor of what flatters their passions and their national prejudices. You are therefore over and above indulgent to us in speaking of the matter with hesitation.

I must inform you that we all are very anxious to hear that you have fully collected the materials for your second volume, and that you are even considerably advanced in the composition of it. I speak this more in the name of my friends than in my own, as I cannot expect to live so long as to see the publication of it. Your ensuing volume will be more delicate than the preceding, but I trust in your prudence for extricating you from the difficulties, and in all events you have courage to despise the clamor of bigots.

I am with great regard, Dear Sir, your most obedient and most humble servant,

DAVID HUME.'

Some weeks afterwards I had the melancholy pleasure of seeing Mr. Hume in his passage through London, his body feeble, his mind firm. On the twenty-fifth of August of the same year (1776) he died at Edinburgh the death of a philosopher."

167 15. **triumvirate of British historians.** This modesty is characteristic of Gibbon. Yet he is now the only one of the three whose work is still considered an important authority.

167 16. **second excursion to Paris.** The Neckers had visited London in May 1776, and Gibbon had promised to be their guest in Paris within two months (*Letters* I, 282). He did not really make the journey until May 1777, and was back again in London in November of the same year.

167 17. **had visited England.** In a letter to Holroyd (Lord Sheffield) Gibbon writes under date of May 20, 1776: "At present, I am very busy with the Neckers. I live with her, just as I used to do twenty years ago, laugh at her Paris varnish, and oblige her to become a simple reasonable Suissesse. The man who might read English husbands lessons of proper and dutiful behavior, is a sensible good-natured creature."

168 5. **Abbé de Mably** (1709–1785), an historical writer whose most famous work is *Observations sur l'Histoire de France*, while he also wrote among others *De la Manière d'écrire l'Histoire*. This was answered in a *Supplément à la Manière, etc.*, by an unknown critic. On the dispute (l. 5) Gibbon adds the following note: "As I might be partial in my own cause, I shall transcribe the words of an unknown critic (*Supplément de la Manière de l'écrire l'Histoire*, p. 125, etc.), observing only that this dispute had been preceded by another on the English constitution, at the house of the Countess de Froulay, an old Jansenist lady. 'Vous étiez chez M. de Foncemagne, mon cher Théodore, le jour que M. l'Abbé de Mably et M. Gibbon y dinèrent en grande compagnie. La conversation roula presque entièrement sur l'histoire. L'Abbé, étant un profond politique, la tourna sur l'administration quand on fut au dessert; et comme par caractère, par humeur, par l'habitude d'admirer Tite Live, il ne prise que le système républicain, il se mit à vanter l'excellence des républiques; bien persuadé que le savant Anglois l'approuverait en tout, et admireroit la profondeur de génie qui avoit fait deviner tous ces avantages à un François. Mais M. Gibbon, instruit par l'expérience des inconvéniens d'un gouvernement populaire, ne fut point du tout de son avis, et il prit généreusement la défense du gouvernement monarchique. L'Abbé voulut le convaincre par Tite Live, et par quelques argumens tirés de Plutarque

en faveur des Spartiates. M. Gibbon, doué de la mémoire la plus heureuse, et ayant tous les faits présens à la pensée, domina bientôt la conversation; l'Abbé se fâcha, il s'emporta, il dit des choses dures; l'Anglois, conservant le phlegme de son pays, prenoit ses avantages, et pressoit l'Abbé avec d'autant plus de succès que la colère le troublait de plus en plus. La conversation s'échauffait, et M. de Foncemagne la rompit en se levant de table, et en passant dans le salon, où personne ne fut tenté de la renouer.'" On Mably himself Gibbon adds another note as follows: "Of the voluminous writings of the Abbé de Mably (see his *Éloge* by the Abbé Brizard), the *Principes du droit public de l'Europe*, and the first part of the *Observations sur l'Histoire de France*, may be deservedly praised; and even the *Manière d'écrire l'Histoire* contains several useful precepts and judicious remarks. Mably was a lover of virtue and freedom; but his virtue was austere, and his freedom was impatient of an equal. Kings, magistrates, nobles, and successful writers were the objects of his contempt, or hatred, or envy; but his illiberal abuse of Voltaire, Hume, Buffon, the Abbé Reynal, Dr. Robertson, and *tutti quanti* can be injurious only to himself."

168 6. **revenged itself.** Gibbon's note reads: "Est il rien de plus fastidieux (says the polite censor) qu'un M. Guibbon; qui dans son eternelle *Histoire des Empereurs Romains*, suspend à chaque instant son insipide et lente narration, pour vous expliquer la cause de faits que vous allez lire. (*Manière d'écrire l'Histoire*, p. 184. See another passage, p. 280.) Yet I am indebted to the Abbé de Mably for two such advocates as the anonymous French critic (Supplément, p. 125–134) and my friend Mr. Hayley. (Hayley's *Works*, octavo edition, Vol. ii. 261–263)."

168 13. **Dr. Hunter.** William Hunter (1718–1783), a celebrated physician, and the first great teacher of anatomy in England. In 1770 he built a lecture-hall with dissecting rooms, where he delivered lectures until his death.

168 14. **Mr. Higgins.** About this time Dr. Bryan Higgins (1734?–1820) was lecturing on chemistry in London and no doubt is the one here referred to. He published numerous studies in chemistry and physics.

168 30. **always been my practice.** Lord Sheffield says, "It is very true that before he (Gibbon) sat down to write a note or a letter, he completely arranged in his mind what he meant to express. He pursued the same method in respect to other composition, and he occasionally would walk several times about his apartment, before he had rounded a period to his taste. He has pleasantly remarked to me that it

sometimes cost him many a turn before he could throw a sentiment into a form that gratified his own criticism." — *Miscellaneous Works* I, 278.

169 8. **two invidious chapters.** These are the fifteenth and sixteenth, or the last two of the first volume as originally published. They treat the extension of Christianity in the first centuries of our era, and though containing little to which exception would be taken today, raised a storm of controversy when first published.

169 14. **Mr. Davies.** Henry Edwards Davies, or Davis (1756–1784), at the age of twenty-two, attacked Gibbon's first volume in an *Examination of the fifteenth and sixteenth chapters.* While showing some acquaintance with the subject, he merely followed Gibbon's references, in the main without sufficient knowledge for verification. He later became fellow of Balliol College, Oxford.

169 16. **My Vindication.** In a note Gibbon adds: "*A Vindication of some passages in the fifteenth and sixteenth chapters of the History of the Decline and Fall of the Roman Empire*, by the author. London, 1779, in octavo — for I would not print it in quarto, lest it should be bound and preserved with the *History* itself. At the distance of twelve years, I calmly affirm my judgment of Davies, Chelsum, etc. A victory over such antagonists was a sufficient humiliation."

169 21. **Chelsum.** James Chelsum D.D. (1740–1801) published anonymously *Remarks on the two last Chapters of Mr. Gibbon's History of the Decline and Fall, in a Letter to a Friend* (1776). The work was enlarged with the assistance of Dr. Randolph, President of Corpus Christi College, and published with the author's name in 1778. He also wrote a reply to Mr. Gibbon's *Vindication* (1785). Chelsum sent his *Remarks* to Gibbon when it appeared with his name; see the short and vigorous correspondence in *Miscellaneous Works* II, 217.

169 22. **Dr. Watson.** Richard Watson (1737–1816), Bishop of Llandaff, is best known for his *Apology for the Bible* (1796) in answer to Thomas Paine. His *Apology for Christianity, in a series of letters to Edward Gibbon*, appeared in 1776. On its appearance Gibbon wrote him a polite note, declining controversy and desiring his acquaintance; see *Miscellaneous Works* II, 180. Gibbon adds: "Dr. Watson, now Bishop of Llandaff, is a prelate of large mind and liberal spirit. I should be happy to think that his *Apology for Christianity* had contributed, though at my expense, to clear his theological character. He has amply repaid the obligation by the amusement and instruction which I have received from the five volumes of his *Chemical Essays*. It is a great pity that an agreeable and useful science should not yet be reduced to a state of fixity."

169 24. **Dr. Apthorpe.** East Apthorpe (1733–1816), an American who was educated at Cambridge, published in 1778 *Letters on the prevalence of Christianity before the Civil Establishment, with Observations on a late History of the Decline and Fall of the Roman Empire.*

169 26. **Taylor the Arian . . . Milner the Methodist.** Henry Taylor (d. 1785) was rector of Crawley and vicar of Portsmouth. Gibbon's note on him is as follows: "The stupendous title, *Thoughts on the Causes of the Grand Apostacy*, at first agitated my nerves, till I discovered that it was the apostacy of the whole church, since the Council of Nice, from Mr. Taylor's private religion. His book is a thorough mixture of high enthusiasm and low buffoonery, and the millennium is a fundamental article of his creed." Joseph Milner (1744–1797) is best known for a curious *History of the Church of Christ* (1794–1797). He also wrote *Gibbon's Account of Christianity considered* (1781). Of him Gibbon says, "From his grammar-school at Kingston-upon-Hull, Mr. Joseph Milner pronounces an anathema against all rational religion. His faith is a divine taste, a spiritual inspiration; his church is a mystic and invisible body; the natural Christians such as Mr. Locke, who believe and interpret the Scriptures, are, in his judgment, no better than profane infidels."

169 29. **Dr. Priestley.** Joseph Priestley (1733–1804), a nonconformist clergyman and scientific experimenter, best known for his discovery of oxygen. Besides his *Corruptions of Christianity*, referred to by Gibbon, Priestley wrote a *General History of the Christian Church to the Fall of the Western Roman Empire*, and numerous works of controversy or quasi-scientific character. In politics Priestley was a pronounced radical, a friend of America and of the French revolutionists. He finally came to America and died in this country. The correspondence between Priestley and Gibbon may be found in *Miscellaneous Works* II, 265. Gibbon adds the following note: "In his *History of the Corruptions of Christianity*, Dr. Priestley threw down his two gauntlets to Bishop Hurd and Mr. Gibbon. I declined the challenge in a letter, exhorting my opponent to enlighten the world by his philosophical discoveries, and to remember that the merit of his predecessor Servetus is now reduced to a single passage, which indicates the smaller circulation of the blood through the lungs, from and to the heart. (*Astuce de la Structure de Cœur*, Tom. 1, pp. 77–79). Instead of listening to this friendly advice, the dauntless philosopher from Birmingham continued to fire away his double battery against those who believed too little, and those who believed too much. From my replies he has nothing to hope or fear; but his Socinian shield has repeatedly been pierced by

the spear of the mighty Horsley, and his trumpet of sedition may at length awaken the magistrates of a free country."

Sir David Dalrymple. Sir David Dalrymple (1726–1792), afterwards Lord Hailes, a Scotch lawyer and historian, published *An Inquiry into the Second Causes which Mr. Gibbon has assigned for the Rapid Growth of Christianity* (1786). While this answer was free from theological rancor, it seems to merit the criticism of the historian in the following note: "The profession and rank of Sir David Dalrymple (now a Lord of Session) has given a more decent color to his style. But he scrutinized each separate passage of the two chapters with the dry minuteness of a special pleader, and as he was always solicitous to make, he may have succeeded sometimes in finding, a flaw. In his *Annals of Scotland*, he has shown himself a diligent collector and an accurate critic."

Dr. White. Rev. Joseph White (1746–1814) in 1783 delivered the Bampton Lectures, which were soon after published under the title *A View of Christianity and Mahometanism.* The lectures were brilliant and White was rewarded by Lord Chancellor Thurlow with a valuable church position. Unfortunately for his reputation, it was later discovered that he had employed the Rev. Samuel Badcock and Dr. Parr to assist him in preparing the lectures; see *Memoirs of Dr. Parr* by Dr. John Johnstone (1828), pp. 216–290. Gibbon adds in a note, "I have praised, and I still praise, the eloquent sermons which were preached in St. Mary's pulpit at Oxford by Dr. White. If he assaulted me with some degree of illiberal acrimony in such a place and before such an audience, he was obliged to speak the language of the country. I smiled at a passage in one of his private letters to Mr. Badcock, 'The part where we encounter Gibbon must be brilliant and striking.'"

169 31. **discharged his sermon.** Gibbon adds a note as follows: "In a sermon preached before the University of Cambridge, Dr. Edwards complimented a work, 'which can only perish with the language itself,' and esteems the author as a formidable enemy. He is, indeed, astonished that more learning and ingenuity has not been shown in the defense of Israel; that the prelates and dignitaries of the church (alas, good man!) did not vie with each other whose stone should sink the deepest in the forehead of this Goliath." Gibbon also quotes the *Monthly Review* for October 1790, which says: "But the force of truth will oblige us to confess, that in the attacks which have been leveled against our skeptical historian, we can discover but slender traces of profound and exquisite erudition, of solid criticism and accurate investigation; but we are too frequently disgusted by vague and inconclusive

reasoning, by unseasonable banter and senseless witticisms, by imbittered bigotry and enthusiastic jargon, by futile cavils and illiberal invectives. Proud and elated by the weakness of his antagonists, he condescends not to handle the sword of controversy."

169 33. **first volleys.** For a list of the pamphlets written in criticism of the *History*, see Lowndes, *Bibliographer's Manual*, under Gibbon.

170 11. **Mémoire Justificatif.** The paper is published in *Miscellaneous Works* V, 1, where it bears the title *Mémoire Justificatif pour servir de Réponse a l'Expose des Motifs de la Conduite du Roi de France relativement à l'Angleterre*. It was written in 1778 in answer to a French manifesto connected with the aid France had given America in her struggle against England. Lord Sheffield says in his advertisement to the first edition, that the *Mémoire* obtained the highest praise in foreign courts.

170 15. **Beaumarchais.** Pierre Augustin Caron de Beaumarchais (1732–1799), a writer of comedies, and man of great influence in France just before the Revolution. He visited England as a secret agent of the king, became interested in the American colonies, and finally persuaded the French government to assist the Americans, at first privately and then by a public recognition of the new country. Gibbon adds in a note: "See *Œuvres de Beaumarchais* III, 299–355. 'Le style ne seroit pas sans grâces, ni la logique sans justesse,' etc. if the facts were true, which he undertakes to disprove. For these facts my credit is not pledged — I spoke as a lawyer from my brief; but the veracity of Beaumarchais may be estimated from the assertion that France, by the treaty of Paris (1763) was limited to a certain number of ships of war. On the application of the Duke of Choiseul he was obliged to retract this daring falsehood."

170 20. **Mr. Wedderburne.** Alexander Wedderburne (1733–1805) became solicitor-general in 1771. For a complimentary reference see note to 165 31.

170 24. **Lord North.** Frederick North (1732–1792), by courtesy Lord North, the well known minister of George III. In the preface to the fourth volume of the *Decline and Fall* Gibbon gives, under the guise of a dedication, this interesting tribute to his friend: "Were I ambitious of any other patron than the public, I would inscribe this work to a statesman who, in a long, a stormy, and at length an unfortunate administration, had many political opponents almost without a personal enemy; who has retained in his fall from power many faithful and disinterested friends, and who, under the pressure of severe infirmity,

enjoys the lively vigor of his mind and the felicity of his incomparable temper. Lord North will permit me to express the feelings of friendship in the language of truth; but even truth and friendship should be silent if he still dispensed the favors of the crown."

170 29. **perpetual . . . adjournment.** Gibbon adds in a note, "See Mr. Burke's *Speech on the Bill of Reform*, pp. 72–80. I can never forget the delight with which that diffusive and ingenious orator, was heard by all sides of the house, and even by those whose existence he proscribed. The Lords of Trade blushed at their insignificancy, and Mr. Eden's appeal to the 2,500 volumes of our Reports, served only to excite a general laugh. I take this opportunity of certifying the correctness of Mr. Burke's printed speeches, which I have heard and read."

171 2. **most unjustly accused.** In a note Lord Sheffield tries to show that Gibbon had really acted with the government throughout the American war, and this seems justified by the opinions expressed in the historian's letters. Gibbon's own position is best explained by a letter to Mr. Eliot of July 2, 1779 (*Miscellaneous Works* I, 236):

"Dear Sir, Yesterday I received a very interesting communication from my friend the attorney-general, whose kind and honorable behavior towards me I must always remember with the highest gratitude. He informed me that, in consequence of an arrangement, a place at the Board of Trade was reserved for me, and that as soon as I signified my acceptance of it, he was satisfied no farther difficulties would arise. My answer to him was sincere and explicit. I told him that I was far from approving all the past measures of the administration, even some of those in which I myself had silently concurred; that I saw, with the rest of the world, many capital defects in the characters of some of the present ministers, and was sorry that in so alarming a situation of public affairs, the country had not the assistance of several able and honest men who are now in opposition. But that I had not formed with any of those persons in opposition any engagements or connections which could in the least restrain or affect my parliamentary conduct: that I could not discover among them such superior advantages, either of measures or of abilities, as could make me consider it as a duty to attach myself to their cause; and that I clearly understood, from the public and private language of one of their leaders (Charles Fox), that in the actual state of the country, he himself was seriously of opinion that opposition could not tend to any good purpose, and might be productive of much mischief; that, for those reasons, I saw no objections which could prevent me from accepting an office under the present government, and that I was ready to take a step which I found to be consistent both with my interest and my honor.

It must now be decided, whether I may continue to live in England, or whether I must soon withdraw myself into a kind of philosophical exile in Switzerland. My father left his affairs in a state of embarrassment, and even of distress. My attempts to dispose of a part of my landed property have hitherto been disappointed, and are not likely at present to be more successful; and my plan of expence, though moderate in itself, deserves the name of extravagance, since it exceeds my real income. The addition of the salary which is now offered will make my situation perfectly easy; but I hope you will do me the justice to believe that my mind could not be so, unless I were satisfied of the rectitude of my own conduct."

In Nichols's *Illustrations of Literature*, it is said that the following remarks on this occasion were found in an odd volume of Gibbon's *History* owned by Fox. "I received this book from the author. N. B. I heard him declare at Brooks's the day after the Rescript of Spain was notified, that nothing could save this country but six heads (of certain ministers whom he named) upon the table. In fourteen days after this anathema he became a Lord of Trade, and has ever since talked out of the House, as he has voted in it, the advocate and champion of those ministers. Charles Fox." Fox is also said to have written the following lines on the occasion:

"King George in a fright
Lest Gibbon should write
The story of Britain's disgrace,
Thought no means more sure
His pen to secure
Than to give the historian a place.

But his caution is vain,
'T is the curse of his reign
That his projects should never succeed;
Though he wrote not a line
Yet a cause of decline
In our author's example we read."

Notes and Queries, First Series, VIII, 312.

171 24. **mischievous madman.** This was Lord George Gordon (1750–1793), who headed a mob of petitioners against a parliamentary bill for the relief of Roman Catholics. Dreadful riots followed, and fires in many parts of London. It was in Lord George Gordon's behalf that Lord Erskine made one of his most famous speeches.

171 28. **electors of Liskeard.** The borough was of course controlled by Mr. Eliot. The latter had supported the North ministry until the employment of Hessians in the war with America, against which he voted and in consequence of which he resigned his place at the board of trade. As Gibbon did not follow the lead of his patron, he soon lost his seat in parliament.

172 6. **animadversions of the Catholics of Italy.** Gibbon explains in a note: "The piety or prudence of my Italian translator has provided an antidote against the poison of his original. The fifth and seventh volumes are armed with five letters from an anonymous divine to his friends Foothead and Kirk, two English students at Rome, and this meritorious service is commended by Monsignore Stonor, a prelate of the same nation, who discovers much venom in the fluid and nervous style of Gibbon. The critical essay at the end of the third volume was furnished by the Abbate Nicola Spedalieri, whose zeal has gradually swelled to a more solid confutation in two quarto volumes. Shall I be excused for not having read them?"

172 7. **Mr. Travis.** George Travis (1740–1797), archdeacon of Chester, wrote *Letters to Edward Gibbon, Esq., in Defence of the authenticity of the 7th verse of the fifth chapter of the first Epistle of St. John* (1784). The *Letters* were answered by Porson as explained in next note. Of Travis Gibbon says in a note: "The brutal insolence of his challenge can only be excused by the absence of learning, judgment, and humanity, and to that excuse he has the fairest or foulest pretension. Compared with Archdeacon Travis, Chelsum and Davies assume the title of respectable enemies."

172 12. **Porson.** Richard Porson (1759–1808), one of the greatest Greek scholars of modern times, best known for important editions of various classical writers. The *Letters to Archdeacon Travis* appeared in the *Gentleman's Magazine* for 1788–89, and were afterwards reprinted in book form (1790). Porson conclusively proved the spuriousness of the passage, and showed that Gibbon merely followed well known authorities of his time. In spite of this the verse remained in the Bible until the last revision, from which it was wholly omitted. Gibbon's note on Porson reads: "I consider Mr. Porson's answer to Archdeacon Travis as the most acute and accurate piece of criticism which has appeared since the days of Bentley. His strictures are founded in argument, enriched with learning, and enlivened with wit, and his adversary neither deserves nor finds any quarter at his hands. The evidence of the three heavenly witnesses would now be rejected in any court of justice; but prejudice is blind, authority is deaf, and our

vulgar Bibles will ever be polluted by this spurious text; *sedet æternumque sedebit.* The more learned ecclesiastics will indeed have the secret satisfaction of reprobating in the closet what they read in the church."

172 19. **enemies.** In a note Gibbon explains this as follows: "Bishop Newton, (see his *Life* in *Posthumous Works*, vol. I, pp. 173–4, octavo edition) in writing his own life, was at full liberty to declare how much he himself and two eminent brethren were disgusted by Mr. G[ibbon]'s prolixity, tediousness, and affectation. But the old man should not have indulged his zeal in a false and feeble charge against the historian who had faithfully and even cautiously rendered Dr. Burnet's meaning by the alternative of sleep or repose. That philosophic divine supposes that in the period between death and the resurrection human souls exist without a body, endowed with internal consciousness, but destitute of all active or passive connection with the external world. *Secundum communem dictionem Sacræ Scripturæ, mors dicitur somnus, et morientes dicuntur obdormire, quod innuere mihi videtur statum mortis esse statum quietis, silentii, et ἀεργασίας.* (*De Statû Mortuorum*, ch. v. p. 98)."

172 29. **a French translation.** This was undertaken by Le Clerc de Septchenes; see note on 183 5. Gibbon had hoped to secure M. Suard, translator of Robertson, for his *History*, and Gibbon's letter to him is still preserved (*Letters* I, 292).

172 31. **personal reflection.** Gibbon's note in explanation is as follows: "It may not be generally known that Louis XVI. is a great reader, and a reader of English books. On perusing a passage of my *History* which seems to compare him to Arcadius or Honorius, he expressed his resentment to the Prince of B—, from whom the intelligence was conveyed to me. I shall neither disclaim the allusion, nor examine the likeness; but the situation of the late King of France excludes all suspicion of flattery, and I am ready to declare that the concluding observations of my third volume were written before his accession to the throne." The Prince of B. is probably the Prince of Brunswick; see note on 178 24.

175 18. **Lausanne.** Gibbon's first plan seems to have been to retire to Lausanne only until the completion of his *History*; see *Letters* II, 55, in which he speaks of a temporary retreat to a quiet and less expensive scene.

175 25. **several English.** Note the Gallicism for Englishmen. Gibbon tells us that those with whom Deyverdun traveled as companion were "Sir Richard Worsley, Lord Chesterfield, Broderick Lord Midleton, and Mr. Hume, brother of Sir Abraham."

176 11. **fumum** etc. Horace, *Odes* iii, 29, 12; already quoted at 145 28.

177 28. **Possessed of every comfort.** An English traveler, John Owen, who met Gibbon at Lausanne about 1791, thus describes him: "Gibbon is the Grand Monarque of literature at Lausanne. I have seen, conversed and dined with him. There are, I think, three requisites to know something of a man. His conversation is correct and eloquent, his periods are measured, and his manner of delivering them pleasing. He appears rather inditing to an amanuensis than holding a conversation with a stranger. But, though he likes to talk oracularly, he is at his table cheerful, frank, and convivial. His hospitalities are not, however, strictly patriotic; his predilection for the Swiss is notorious; and, as a love of preëminence is not among the least of his failings, he seems to have decided well on the choice of his society." — *Travels of John Owen*, p. 218.

178 21. **long habits of the English.** Gibbon doubtless refers to the English custom of traveling. Of this he says (*Letters* II, 134): "The only disagreeable circumstance [at Lausanne] is the increase of a race of animals with which this country has been long infected, and who are said to come from an island in the Northern Ocean. I am told, but it seems incredible, that upwards of 40,000 English, masters and servants, are absent on the continent; and I am sure we have our full proportion, both in town and country, from the month of June to that of October." See also note on 82 5.

178 22. **Dr. Tissot.** Simon André Tissot (1728–1797), a famous physician of the Pays de Vaud.

178 24. **M. and Mme. Necker.** After resigning the ministry of finance in September 1790, Necker retired to Coppet, an estate which he had previously purchased. Here Gibbon often saw them as he tells us in a note: "I saw them frequently in the summer of 1784, at a country house near Lausanne, where M. Necker composed his *Treatise on the Administration of the Finances*. I have since (in October 1790) visited him in his present residence, the castle and barony of Coppet, near Geneva. Of the merits and measures of that statesman various opinions may be entertained, but all impartial men must agree in their esteem of his integrity and patriotism." See also the correspondence of Gibbon and the Neckers in *Miscellaneous Works* II, 440 ff.

Prince Henry of Prussia (1726–1802) was the youngest brother of Frederick the Great, and a famous general in the Seven Years war. Of him Gibbon says in a note: "In the month of August

1784, Prince Henry of Prussia, in his way to Paris, passed three days at Lausanne. His military conduct has been praised by professional men, his character has been vilified by the wit and malice of a demon (*Mémoires Secrêts de la Cour de Berlin*); but I was flattered by his affability, and entertained by his conversation." The *Mémoires Secrêts* were written by Mirabeau.

178 25. **Mr. Fox.** In a note Gibbon says: "In his tour to Switzerland (September 1788) Mr. Fox gave me two days of free and private society. He seemed to feel, and even to envy the happiness of my situation, while I admired the powers of a superior man, as they are blended in his attractive character with the softness and simplicity of a child. Perhaps no human being was ever more perfectly exempt from the taint of malevolence, vanity, or falsehood."

179 8. **Dr. Prideaux.** Dean Humphrey Prideaux (1648–1724) of Norwich who wrote, besides various political pamphlets connected with the Revolution of 1688, *The Old and New Testament connected in the History of the Jews*, and a *Life of Mahomet*, from the preface of which Gibbon quotes in his note. The latter reads as follows: "It had been the original design of the learned Dean Prideaux to write the history of the ruin of the Eastern Church. In this work it would have been necessary, not only to unravel all those controversies which the Christians made about the hypostatical union, but also to unfold all the niceties and subtle notions which each sect entertained concerning it. The pious historian was apprehensive of exposing that incomprehensible mystery to the cavils and objections of unbelievers, and he durst not, seeing the nature of this book, venture it abroad in so wanton and lewd an age. (See preface to the *Life of Mahomet*, p. xxi)."

179 12. **barbarians of the East.** On this Gibbon says: "I have followed the judicious precept of the Abbé de Mably, (*Manière d'écrire l'Histoire*, p. 110), who advises the historian not to dwell too minutely on the decay of the eastern empire; but to consider the barbarian conquerors as a more worthy subject of his narrative. Fas est et ab hoste doceri."

180 22. **sent to the press.** Gibbon adds a note as follows: "I cannot help recollecting a much more extraordinary fact, which is affirmed of himself by Rétif de la Bretonne, a voluminous and original writer of French novels. He labored, and may still labor, in the humble office of corrector to a printing-house; but this office enabled him to transport an entire volume from his mind to the press, and his work was given to the public without ever having been written with a pen."

180 24. **exclusively my own.** A note in Gibbon's Common-place

Book gives the dates of beginning and finishing the last three volumes of the *History*: "The IVth Volume of the *History of the Decline and Fall of the Roman Empire*, begun March 1st, 1782—ended June 1784. The Vth Volume, begun July 1784—ended May 1st, 1786. The VIth Volume, begun May 18th, 1786—ended June 27th, 1787. These three volumes were sent to press August 15th, 1787, and the whole impression was concluded April following."

181 7. **commercial intercourse with America.** Gibbon adds the following note: "*Observations on the Commerce of the American States*, by John, Lord Sheffield: the sixth edition London, 1784, in octavo. Their sale was diffusive, their effect beneficial; the navigation act, the palladium of Britain, was defended, and perhaps saved, by his pen, and he proves, by the weight of fact and argument, that the mother-country may survive and flourish after the loss of America. My friend has never cultivated the arts of composition, but his materials are copious and correct, and he leaves on his paper the clear impression of an active and vigorous mind."

181 8. **and Ireland.** Gibbon's note is as follows: "*Observations on the Trade, Manufactures, and Present State of Ireland*, by John, Lord Sheffield: the third edition, London, 1784, in octavo. Their useful aim was to guide the industry, to correct the prejudices, and to assuage the passions of a country which seemed to forget that she could only be free and prosperous by a friendly connection with Great Britain. The concluding observations are expressed with so much ease and spirit, that they may be read by those who are the least interested in the subject."

181 31. **august spectacle.** Although Gibbon here takes an impartial view of the impeachment of Hastings, Lord Sheffield tells us that "he considered the persecution of that highly respectable person to have arisen from party views."

182 1. **personal compliment.** The report of this part of Sheridan's speech, as published in the *Morning Chronicle*, June 14, 1788, is as follows: "He said the facts that made up the volume of narrative were unparalleled in atrociousness, and that nothing equal in criminality was to be traced, either in ancient or modern history, in the correct periods of Tacitus, or the luminous page of Gibbon." In the *Table Talk* of Samuel Rogers it is said that "after Sheridan had finished, one of his friends reproached him with flattering Gibbon. 'Why what did I say of him?' asked Sheridan. 'You called him the luminous author.' 'Luminous! Oh, I meant vo-luminous.'"

182 2. **British nation.** To this Gibbon appends a note: "From

this display of genius, which blazed four successive days, I shall stoop to a very mechanical circumstance. As I was waiting in the managers' box, I had the curiosity to inquire of the short-hand writer, how many words a steady and rapid orator might pronounce in an hour. From 7000 to 7500 was his answer. The medium of 7200 will afford 120 words a minute, and two words in each second. But this computation will only apply to the English language."

182 11. **Assises de Jérusalem.** The *Assises et Usages du Royaume de Jérusalem* is the work of Jean d'Ibelin (d. 1270).

182 12. **De Bello, etc.** Paulo Ramusio, or Ramusius (1532–1600), translated into Latin, with many additions, Villehardouin's *History of the Conquest of Constantinople.* The work was printed in 1609 and never reprinted, so that this accounts for Gibbon's not being able to use it before. In his manuscript Gibbon abbreviated the title to De Bello C. Pano., and this has regularly appeared in all editions, including that of Murray, in the incorrect and meaningless form C. Paro., without note or explanation.

182 24. **compliment from Mr. Hayley.** For Hayley see note on 155 12. The lines were as follows (see *Occasional Stanzas* in Hayley's *Works*):

"GENII of ENGLAND and of ROME!
In mutual triumph here assume
The honors each may claim!
This social scene with smiles survey!
And consecrate the festive day
To Friendship and to Fame!

Enough, by Desolation's tide,
With anguish, and indignant pride,
Has ROME bewail'd her fate;
And mourn'd that Time, in Havoc's hour,
Defac'd each monument, of power
To speak her truly great.

O'er maim'd POLYBIUS, just and sage,
O'er LIVY'S mutilated page,
How deep was her regret!
Touch'd by this Queen, in ruin grand,
See! Glory, by an English hand,
Now pays a mighty debt:

Lo! sacred to the ROMAN Name,
And rais'd, like ROME's immortal Fame,
By Genius and by Toil,

The splendid Work is crown'd to-day,
On which Oblivion ne'er shall prey,
Nor Envy make her spoil!

ENGLAND, exult! and view not now,
With jealous eye each nation's brow,
Where Hist'ry's palm has spread!
In every path of liberal art,
Thy Sons to prime distinction start,
And no superior dread.

Science for Thee a NEWTON rais'd;
For thy renown a SHAKESPEARE blaz'd,
Lord of the drama's sphere!
In different fields to equal praise
See History now thy GIBBON raise
To shine without a peer!

Eager to honor living worth,
And bless to-day the double birth,
That proudest joy may claim,
Let artless Truth this homage pay,
And consecrate the festive day
To Friendship and to Fame!"

To this Gibbon adds the note: "Before Mr. Hayley inscribed with my name his *Epistles on History*, I was not acquainted with that amiable man and elegant poet. He afterwards thanked me in verse for my second and third volumes, and in the summer of 1781 the Roman eagle (a proud title) accepted the invitation of the English sparrow, who chirped in the groves of Eartham near Chichester." The following lines from Hayley's *Works* will explain the note:

"SONNET *to* EDWARD GIBBON, esq.

On the Publication of his Second and Third Volumes, 1781.

WITH proud delight th' imperial founder gaz'd
On the new beauty of his second Rome,
When on his eager eye rich temples blaz'd,
And his fair city rose in youthful bloom;
A pride more noble may thy heart assume,
O GIBBON! gazing on thy growing work,
In which, constructed for a happier doom,
No hasty marks of vain ambition lurk:
Thou may'st deride both Time's destructive sway,
And baser Envy's beauty-mangling dirk;

Thy gorgeous fabric, plann'd with wise delay,
  Shall baffle foes more savage than the Turk;
As ages multiply, its fame shall rise,
And earth must perish ere its splendor dies."

HAYLEY'S *Works*, 8vo. ed. I. 162.

"*A* CARD *of* INVITATION *to* Mr. GIBBON, *at Brighthelmstone*, 1781.

  AN English sparrow, pert and free,
Who chirps beneath his native tree,
Hearing the Roman eagle's near,
And feeling more respect than fear,
Thus, with united love and awe,
Invites him to his shed of straw.
  Tho' he is but a twittering sparrow,
The field he hops in rather narrow,
When nobler plumes attract his view,
He ever pays them homage due,
He looks with reverential wonder
On him whose talons bear the thunder;
Nor could the Jackdaws e'er inveigle
His voice to vilify the eagle,
Tho' issuing from the holy tow'rs,
In which they build their warmest bow'rs,
Their sovereign's haunt they slyly search,
In hopes to catch him on his perch,
(For Pindar says, beside his God
The thunder-bearing bird will nod,)
Then, peeping round his still retreat,
They pick from underneath his feet
Some moulted feather he lets fall,
And swear he cannot fly at all. ——
  Lord of the sky! whose pounce can tear
These croakers, that infest the air,
Trust him! the sparrow loves to sing
The praise of thy imperial wing!
He thinks thou'lt deem him, on his word,
An honest, though familar bird;
And hopes thou soon wilt condescend
To look upon thy little friend;
That he may boast around his grove,
A visit from the bird of Jove."

HAYLEY'S *Works*, I. 189.

183 1. **censors of morals.** Gibbon explains in a note as follows: "I never could understand the clamor that has been raised against the

indecency of my three last volumes. 1. An equal degree of freedom in the former part, especially in the first volume, had passed without reproach. 2. I am justified in painting the manners of the times. The vices of Theodora form an essential feature in the reign and character of Justinian, and the most naked tale in my history is told by the Rev. Joseph Warton, an instructor of youth (*Essay on the Genius and Writings of Pope*, pp. 322–324). 3. My English text is chaste, and all licentious passages are left in the obscurity of a learned language.

"Le Latin dans ses mots brave l'honnêteté,"

says the correct Boileau, in a country and idiom more scrupulous than our own."

183 3. **at home.** Gibbon adds the following note: "I am less flattered by Mr. Porson's high encomium on the style and spirit of my *History*, than I am satisfied with his honorable testimony to my attention, diligence, and accuracy — those humble virtues, which religious zeal has most audaciously denied. The sweetness of his praise is tempered by a reasonable mixture of acid (see his preface pp. xxviii–xxxii)." The acid of Porson's criticism is in the following passage from the preface of his *Letters to Travis*: "Though his style is generally correct and elegant, he sometimes draws out the thread of his verbosity finer than the staple of his argument. In endeavoring to avoid vulgar terms he frequently dignifies trifles, and clothes common thoughts in a splendid dress that would be rich enough for the noblest ideas. . . Sometimes in his anxiety to vary his phrase, he becomes obscure; and, instead of calling his personages by their names, he defines them by their birth, alliance, office, or other circumstances of their history. . . Sometimes epithets are added which the tenor of the sentence renders unnecessary."

and abroad. Gibbon has the following explanation: "As the book may not be common in England, I shall transcribe my own character from the *Bibliotheca Historica* of Meuselius, a learned and laborious German (vol. iv. p't. 1, pp. 342–344):

'Summis ævi nostri historicis Gibbonus sine dubio adnumerandus est. Inter Capitolii ruinas stans primum hujus operis scribendi consilium cepit. Florentissimos vitæ annos colligendo et laborando eidem impendit. Enatum inde monumentum ære perennius, licet passim appareant sinistre dicta, minus perfecta, veritati non satis consentanea. Videmus quidem ubique fere studium scrutandi veritatemque scribendi maximum: tamen sine Tillemontio duce ubi scilicet hujus historia finitur sæpius noster titubat atque hallucinatur. Quod vel maxime fit, ubi de rebus Ecclesiasticis vel de juris prudentia Romana (tom. iv.) tradit, et in aliis locis. Attamen nævi hujus generis haud impediunt quo minus operis summam et οἰκονομίαν præclare dispositam, delectum rerum sapientissimum, argutum quoque interdum, dictionemque seu stylum historico æque ac philosopho dignissimum, et vix a quoque alio Anglo, Humio ac Robertsono haud exceptis, prærepto (*præreptum?*), vehementer laudemus, atque sæculo nostro de hujusmodi historia gratulemur . . . Gibbonus adversarios cum in tum extra patriam nactus est, quia propagationem religionis Christianæ, non, ut vulgo fieri solet, aut more theologorum, sed ut historicum et philosophum decet, exposuerat.'"

183 5. **translations.** Gibbon's note is as follows: "The first volume had been feebly, though faithfully translated into French by M. Le Clerc de Septchenes, a young gentleman of a studious character and liberal fortune. After his decease the work was continued by two manufacturers of Paris, MM. Desmeuniers and Cantwell; but the former is now an active member in the national assembly, and the undertaking languishes in the hands of his associate. The superior merit of the interpreter, or his language, inclines me to prefer the Italian version; but I wish that it were in my power to read the German, which is praised by the best judges."

183 13. **Basil in Switzerland.** Gibbon says in a note: "Of their fourteen octavo volumes the two last include the whole body of the notes. The public importunity had forced me to remove them from the end of the volume to the bottom of the page, but I have often repented of my compliance."

183 16. **the Delaware and the Ganges.** That is America and India. At this time Philadelphia was the great publishing center of the one, Calcutta of the other.

183 17. **gloried in the name of Englishman.** The passage is as follows: "I shall soon revisit the banks of the lake of Lausanne, a country which I have known and loved from my early youth. Under a mild government, amidst a beauteous landscape, in a life of leisure and independence, and among a people of easy and elegant manners, I have enjoyed, and may again hope to enjoy, the varied pleasures of retirement and society. But I shall ever glory in the name and character of an Englishman. I am proud of my birth in a free and enlightened country, and the approbation of that country is the best and most honorable reward of my labors."

183 34. **Tunbridge.** Presumably Tunbridge Wells, a famous watering place of the eighteenth century.

184 2. **Swiss friend.** M. Wilhelm de Severy, one of a family at Lausanne to which Gibbon was much attached; see reference at 185 11.

184 32. **demon of property.** Gibbon adds a note as follows: "Yet I had often revolved the judicious lines in which Pope answers the objections of his long-sighted friend:

> 'Pity to build without or child or wife;
> Why, you'll enjoy it only all your life:'
> 'Well, if the use be mine, does it concern one,
> Whether the name belong to Pope or Vernon?'"

The quotation is from *Imitations of Horace*, second satire of second book, 163–166. The circumstances were almost exactly the same in the two cases. At the death of Mrs. Vernon, who owned Twickenham, Pope was offered the property, much as Gibbon was offered that of Deyverdun. The first two lines in Pope are supposed to be spoken by Swift, in urging his friend to buy the property; the last two are part of Pope's answer.

185 19. **disorders in France.** Gibbon's letters show with what keen interest the historian watched the progress of affairs during the national upheaval. Of his opinions Lord Sheffield says (*Miscellaneous Works* I, 328): "Mr. Gibbon at first, like many others, seemed pleased with the prospect of reform of inveterate abuses; but he very soon discovered the mischief which was intended, the imbecility with which concessions were made, and the ruin which must arise from the want of resolution or conduct in the administration of France."

185 22. **dissolution of the kingdom.** Gibbon adds a note: "I beg leave to subscribe my assent to Mr. Burke's creed on the Revolution of France. I admire his eloquence, I approve his politics, I adore his chivalry, and I can almost excuse his reverence for church establishments. I have sometimes thought of writing a dialogue of the dead, in which Lucian, Erasmus, and Voltaire should mutually acknowledge the danger of exposing an old superstition to the contempt of the blind and fanatic multitude."

186 8. **the French disease.** Owing to the great strictness with which Berne ruled the Vaud, the principles of the French Revolution found ready acceptance there. The Helvetian Club, founded in Paris in 1790, assisted in spreading the new ideas in the western part of the confederation. Revolt after revolt occurred until Napoleon stepped in to manage affairs in 1797.

186 13. **aristocracy of Berne.** Berne had become one of the most remarkable oligarchies of modern times, the privileged class numbering

only sixty-nine families in 1785. The common people had made various attempts to overthrow the aristocracy, but it was not until after the French Revolution that the oligarchic government ceased, and Berne became part of the Helvetic Republic set up in March 1798.

186 16. **of taxes.** Gibbon adds a note as follows: "The revenue of Berne (except some small duties) is derived from church lands, tithes, feudal rights, and interest of money. The republic has nearly 500,000 pounds sterling in the English funds, and the amount of their treasure is unknown to the citizens themselves."

186 31. **fiftieth year.** Gibbon says, "See Buffon, *Supplement à l'Histoire Naturelle*, tom. VII, p. 158–164. Of a given number of new-born infants, one half, by the fault of nature or man, is extinguished before the age of puberty and reason, — a melancholy calculation!"

187 4. **Hic murus.** Horace, *Epistles* i, i, 59–60.

188 9. **Miss Hester Gibbon.** She had died in 1790 at the age of eighty-six. See note on 16 30.

188 11. **Mrs. Gibbon.** Mrs. Gibbon, however, outlived the historian, dying in February, 1796. So little did Gibbon expect that he would not outlive his step-mother, that he did not even mention her in his will.

188 15. **relieve me.** This was changed in the first published edition to read, "My friend Lord Sheffield has kindly relieved me etc.," the alteration being made by the first editor. It is not improbable that the change accorded well with the fact, but of course no such liberty should have been taken by an editor.

188 24. **I am disgusted.** To this Gibbon adds in a note: "M. d'Alembert relates, that as he was walking in the gardens of Sans Souci with the King of Prussia, Frederic said to him, 'Do you see that old woman, a poor weeder, asleep on that sunny bank? she is probably a more happy being than either of us.' The king and the philosopher may speak for themselves; for my part I do not envy the old woman."

189 12. **grandchildren.** Gibbon adds in a note: "In the first of ancient or modern romances (*Tom Jones*), this proud sentiment, this feast of fancy, is enjoyed by the genius of Fielding. — 'Foretell me that some future maid, whose grandmother is yet unborn, etc.'; but the whole passage deserves to be read." The passage reads as follows: "Come, bright love of fame, &c. fill my ravished fancy with the hopes of charming ages yet to come. Foretell me that some tender maid, whose grandmother is yet unborn, hereafter, when, under the fictitious name of Sophia, she reads the real worth which once existed in my Charlotte, shall from her sympathetic breast send forth the heaving

sigh. Do thou teach me not only to foresee but to enjoy, nay even to feed on future praise. Comfort me by the solemn assurance, that, when the little parlor in which I sit at this moment shall be reduced to a worse furnished box, I shall be read with honor by those who never knew nor saw me, and whom I shall neither know nor see." Book xiii, ch. 1.

189 23. **about fifteen years.** Gibbon adds this note: "From our disregard of the possibility of death within the four and twenty hours, Buffon concludes, that a chance, which falls below or rises above ten thousand to one, will never affect the hopes or fears of a reasonable man. The fact is true, but our courage is the effect of thoughtlessness, rather than of reflection. If a public lottery were drawn for the choice of an immediate victim, and if our name were inscribed on one of the ten thousand tickets, should we be perfectly easy?" Even in his last illness Gibbon comforted himself with the hope of ten, twelve, perhaps twenty years, and talked thus on the day before his death; see *Miscellaneous Works* I, 422, and Introduction.

190 3. **solid basis.** Gibbon refers to Buffon (p. 413), and adds: "In private conversation, that great and amiable man added the weight of his own experience; and this autumnal felicity might be exemplified in the lives of Voltaire, Hume, and many other men of letters."

190 27. **above the clouds.** Gibbon's last note to the *Memoirs* is on this passage, as follows: "This celestial hope is confined to a small number of the elect, and we must deduct (1) all the mere philosophers, who can only speculate about the immortality of the soul; (2) all the earthly Christians who repeat without thought or feeling the words of their catechism; (3) all the gloomy fanatics who are more strongly affected by the fear of hell than by the hopes of heaven. 'Strait is the way and narrow is the gate, and few there be who find it.'"